PATTERNS OF POLITICAL INSTABILITY

PATTERNS OF POLITICAL INSTABILITY

David Sanders

Lecturer in Government
University of Essex

St. Martin's Press   New York

Library of Congress Cataloging in Publication Data

Sanders, David, 1950-
  Patterns of political instability.

  Includes bibliographical references and index.
  1. Government, Resistance to.   2. Allegiance.
3. Authority.   4. Comparative government.   I. Title.
JC328.3.S25 1980   323.6'5'01   79-21422
ISBN 0-312-59808-4

For Linda and Ben

Contents

List of Figures   ix

List of Tables   xi

Introduction   xiii

1   The Analysis of Political Stability and Instability: An
    Overview of Approaches and Findings   1

2   Inconsistencies and Inadequacies in Previous Analyses of
    Political Instability   22

3   Problems of Defining Political Instability   49

4   A Definition and Operationalisation of Political Instability   65

5   Interrelationships between the Dimensions of Political
    Instability   93

6   Potential Exogenous Correlates of Political Instability:
    Some Theoretical Considerations   119

7   Exogenous Influences upon Political Instability: Bivariate
    Levels of Correlation   150

8   Four Predictive Models of Political Instability   169

9   Conclusions and Prospects   197

    Appendices   211

    Notes   225

    Index   241

List of Figures

1.1 Schematic representation of the main themes in the current literature relating to stability/instability   4

2.1 Gurr's revised causal model of the determinants of magnitude of civil strife   34

2.2 Types of data and types of theoretical inference   44

2.3 Implicit model used by Lipset in order to establish the relationship between urbanisation and stability   45

2.4 Implicit model used by the Feierabends in order to establish the relationship between urbanisation and instability   46

3.1 Six dimensions of political instability   59

4.1 Different elements in the Blondel and Easton definitions of regime   69

4.2 Coordinates of hypothetical coups variable against time   75

4.3 Coordinates from Fig. 4.2, t_1 to t_{10} only   76

4.4 Coordinates of hypothetical x_t plotted against time   79

5.1 Predicted interrelationships: (a) syndrome; (b) safety valve; (c) Hibbs   96

5.2 Hypothetical occurrences/non-occurrences of two variables, X and Y, over a period of thirty months   100

5.3 Non-recursive estimates of (a) reciprocal linkages between each pair of instability dimensions, and (b) between instability dimensions: significant relationships only   108

5.4 Rank ordering of instability dimensions   114

6.1 Diagrammatic representation of the crisis theorists' concept of development   122

6.2 Diagrammatic representation of the 'curvilinearity hypothesis'   135

8.1 Hypothetical relationship between Y and X showing differential slopes for different groups of cases   173

8.2 Intercept shift model for the regression of Y on X 174

8.3 Multiple slope shift model for the regression of Y on X 175

ix

8.4   Slope shift model for Y on X, Latin American countries
only   176
9.1   Dimensions and indicators of political instability   199
A2.1 Quasi-interval scale underlying 'changes in party
system' scores   216

List of Tables

1.1 Main themes – examples of definitions, dimensions, causes, universe of countries, findings   6–7

1.2 Theoretical propositions with claimed empirical support, and empirical findings, concerning the sources of political instability   16–17

1.3 Hibbs' empirical findings by dimension   20

2.1 Rotated factor matrix of domestic conflict measures   24–5

3.1 Suggested indicators of changes and challenges   62

4.1 Proposed indicators of four dimensions of political instability   68

5.1 Bivariate correlations (Pearson r) between dimensions of instability, at three levels of temporal aggregation   98

5.2 Six-monthly time-series data derived from Fig. 5.2   101

5.3 Significant lagged relationships derived from annual data   111

5.4 Summary of findings derived from annual time-series data   113

6.1 Dimensions and indicators of economic development: (a) as a stasis, and (b) as a process   123–4

6.2 Alternative definitions of political development   126

6.3 Proposed indicators of political development   127

6.4 Hypotheses concerning the possible influences upon the level of political instability, by dimension   140–1

6.5 Summary of the dimensions and indices used for each of the potential exogenous correlates of the level of political instability   142

7.1 Summary of global levels of bivariate correlation ($N = 103$)   151

7.2 Patterns of bivariate correlations in Europe/North America ($N = 30$)   156

7.3 Patterns of bivariate correlations in Middle East/North Africa ($N = 12$)   158

7.4 Patterns of bivariate correlations in Latin America ($N = 20$)   160

7.5   Patterns of bivariate correlation in Sub-Saharan
      Africa ($N = 23$)   161
7.6   Patterns of bivariate correlations in the Far East
      ($N = 22$)   163
7.7   Summary of the number of times each hypothesis
      correctly predicts the observed correlation in Tables
      7.1–7.6   166
7.8   Number of times each instability dimension is cor-
      rectly predicted by H_1 to H_{12} in Tables 7.1–7.6   167
8.1   Predictive model of peaceful challenge instability   178
8.2   Predictive model of violent challenge instability   179
8.3   Predictive model of governmental change instability   182
8.4   Predictive model of regime change instability   184
9.1   Summary of final predictive models of each dimen-
      sion of instability   207
A2.1 The number of dimensions through which a polity
      moves when it experiences a change in regime type   215
A2.2 Scoring system for changes in party system variable   216

Introduction

As far as I am aware, no one has ever tried to argue that the only stable political systems in existence are those which are entirely static. Indeed, most political scientists seem to agree that political stability does not preclude the possibility of quite considerable social and political change. Rather, they recognise that stability consists in the relative absence of certain types of 'destabilising' political events, whether these events take the form of changes in the structure of authority, whether they involve changes in government, or whether they are constituted by peaceful, or even violent, challenges either to the incumbent political authorities or to the structure of political authority itself.

The present study examines two principal sets of questions. The first are primarily definitional: what precisely is meant by the terms 'political stability' and 'instability'? In what circumstances can a particular political system be characterised as unstable? The second set are more directly empirical: what are the major sources of cross-national variations in the incidence of political instability? What factors, if any, might be considered to exert a causal influence upon the levels of stability and instability which different political systems experience? Why, in short, are some political systems more unstable than others?

In attempting to resolve these questions, an eclectic, comparative approach is adopted and the various issues involved are examined at both the theoretical and the empirical level. Chapter 1 consists of a review of previous theoretical and empirical analyses of political instability, and provides a summary of the main empirical findings which have been reported concerning the principal causal influences upon it. Five major approaches are examined: Lipset's analysis of the sources of 'democratic stability'; the investigation by Eckstein *et al.* of 'internal war'; the factor analytic approach of the 'dimensional school'; the 'psychologically oriented' 'causal' studies of Gurr and the Feierabends; and finally the (somewhat amorphously grouped) 'non-psychologically oriented' causal approaches of, among others, Huntington, Snyder and Tilly, and Olsen and Hibbs.

Chapter 2 examines the inconsistencies and contradictions which are evident in the various empirical findings which have been reported in previous analyses. It also provides a detailed discussion of some of the most important methodological weaknesses of these earlier studies. The general conclusion presented is that not as much is known about the sources of stability and instability as might be suggested by the wealth of research papers which have been published over the last fifteen years or so.

Chapter 3 returns to theoretical matters and focuses upon the problems of *defining* political instability. It is argued, first, that stability/instability needs to be regarded as a continuous, interval level phenomenon, and secondly that considerable *temporal* precision is required if it is to be adequately defined. It is also argued that there are four main *types or dimensions* of instability: *regime change*, *governmental change*, *violent challenge* (to either government or regime) and *peaceful challenge* (again, to either government or regime). In addition, Chapter 3 raises the problem of the 'frequency fallacy', the extraordinary assumption made in all previous quantitative research that similar political events, although they take place in *different* countries, have a similar (or identical) destabilising impact upon the respective political systems in which they occur. It is argued that this assumption is almost invariably unwarranted.

Chapter 4 presents a new theoretical definition of political instability which avoids the frequency fallacy and also provides a statistical methodology which allows its operationalisation for any given system and for any given instability dimension. The 'destabilising' impact of any particular political event, x, is determined by the extent to which that event constitutes an 'abnormal' *deviation* from the previous pattern of xs which is evident within that system in the previous time period. This definition of instability, therefore, does *not* assume that all occurrences of 'destabilising' political events constitute equivalent levels of instability regardless of the *context* (the country and the time period) in which they occur. Rather, it attempts directly to *use* that context in order to *modify* the assessment of the 'destabilising' impact of any given event. In this sense, it is a self-avowedly relativist, *system-specific* definition as opposed to a *general* one. It is a definition which does not seek to establish a *single* rule for determining the level of instability (which can be applied wholesale to *all* political systems regardless of their different cultural traditions and historical experiences), but instead recognises that what is a normal part of the process of political interaction will vary both from system to system, and (even within one particular system) from time period to time period. In so far as a specific political event *is* a part of the normal process of political interaction of a given system, it is not necessarily considered to contribute to the instability of that system: it is only in so far as a particular event is 'abnormal' in the context of the system in which it occurs (that is to say, in so far as it constitutes a deviation from the previous system pattern) that it denotes instability.

Using this definition of instability, Chapter 5 explores the pattern of interrelationship between the four types of instability which were identified in Chapter 4. The data are all derived either from the *World Handbook II* data collection or from Blondel's Time Series Data, and cover the period 1948–67. The analysis is conducted on three levels: monthly time series, annual time series and a twenty-year (1948–67) cross-section. For a variety of reasons, the results of the annual time series analysis are considered to be the most conclusive, and it is on the basis of these results that the principal theoretical inferences are drawn as to the nature of the relationships between the different types of political instability. The statistical models reported in this chapter reflect the mixed research strategy which is employed through the subsequent empirical analysis. On the one hand (following the tradition of, among others, Gurr, Hibbs and Blondel),[1] the theoretical propositions examined are subjected to *global* empirical testing; on the other (following the 'most similar systems' strategy advocated by Przeworski and Teune),[2] considerable attention is also paid to any *regional* variations which the data might exhibit.

In Chapter 6 a series of hypotheses are developed which seek to specify the most important causal influences upon political instability. The theoretical relevance of five sets of 'exogenous' variables is examined: *development* (both political and economic), *dependency*, *governmental coercion*, *structured division* (ethnic and religious cleavage), and *structured inequality*. In Chapter 7, each of these hypotheses is tested on a bivariate basis. The global levels of correlation are reported and an analysis of the (considerable) *regional variations* in these levels of correlation is also undertaken. (Five regional groupings are examined: Europe/North America, Middle East/North Africa, Sub-Saharan Africa, Far East and Latin America.) The empirical findings reported emphasise the extreme complexity of the patterns of interrelationship between the various dimensions of instability and their exogenous correlates.

In Chapter 8 an attempt is made to reduce this complexity to rather more theoretically manageable proportions, by the use of a series of multiple regression models which seek to identify the most important influences upon each dimension of instability. The four predictive models which are reported constitute the most coherent explanation of 'why some political systems are more unstable than others' which can be offered on the basis of the empirical analysis undertaken in this study. As the comparatively low levels of statistical explanation achieved in those predictive models indicate, however, this explanation is by no means entirely satisfactory. It is for this reason that in the final part of Chapter 9, which is largely a restatement of the main arguments and findings, a limited number of additional exogenous variables (not included within this analysis principally for reasons of data availability) are identified which may provide fruitful avenues for further research.

Finally, it would seem useful to provide a brief statement of my 'epistemological position'. The final conclusions of this investigation are not posited in any sense as a 'theory' of political instability, but rather as a series of four eclectic probabilistic predictive models. Althusserians, given their belief in the notion of 'theoretical science', would doubtless condemn this entire exercise as 'empiricist' and dismiss it immediately, as for them understanding can only be developed within the context of theory and not in terms of 'outside (observable) objects': theories should be confronted not with observations but with other theories. I do not take this view, but rather share Popper's belief in the paramountcy of the principle of falsifiability: unless a theory, an explanation of some recurrent observable phenomenon, can generate *testable predictions* which prove to be reasonably accurate empirically, then the analytic value of that theory must be strongly questioned. It is for this reason that in Chapters 7 and 8 we attempt to operationalise a number of theories which purport to identify the main determinants of political instability. What emerges quite clearly from the *empirical* analysis which is undertaken in that context, however, is that *considered in isolation* none of these theories (and they include both Marxist and non-Marxist theories) provides even a marginally adequate explanation of the cross-national incidence of political instability. None the less, in these circumstances we do not simply discard all of these theories, but rather follow the principles of the 'retroductive' account of scientific explanation and attempt to retain those *parts* of the theories which are of consistent explanatory value, and to reorganise them into probabilistic predictive models. In short, it is argued that we can only *start* to explain why political instability occurs by drawing on a variety of different (and largely unrelated) theoretical propositions. Even then, however, the task is by no means an easy one: given the somewhat negative results of our data analysis we do not in any sense claim to provide a definitive explanation of the cross-national incidence of political instability. Circumstances dictate that our objectives must be rather more limited: the 'causal' part of this analysis simply attempts to specify which groups of exogenous variables appear to exert a significant influence upon the level of instability, and which, by implication, do not.

As with any study of this sort the intellectual debts which are owed are many. However, I am particularly grateful to Valentine Herman for his constant and entertaining advice, to Ian Budge and to Frank Castles for their detailed comments upon the draft manuscript, and to Jim Alt, David Robertson and Ken Macdonald for their valuable assistance on methodological matters. The statistical analysis for this study was undertaken on the PDP1Ø, University of Essex.[3] The computing would have been impossible without the help of Eric Tanenbaum, Eric Roughley and Rick Blake; the typing needed the expertise and patience of Joanne Brunt. The final responsibility, inevitably, rests with myself.

1 The Analysis of Political Stability and Instability: An Overview of Approaches and Findings

Walter Bagehot's explanation for the long term stability of the British political system was elegant but simple: because of the deep-seated deference which the British working class accorded to its rulers, movements opposed to the established regime could never muster sufficient popular support to effect either a rapid or a radical change in the existing constitutional system.[1] In the post-war period, refinements in the techniques of comparative analysis have meant that political scientists have been less preoccupied with attempting to explain the stability or instability of individual political systems and instead, they have tended increasingly to adopt a broader, more generalised perspective on the problem of stability, seeking to identify processes and mechanisms which operate independently of national boundaries. Moreover, in the last fifteen years or so a number of quantitive comparative studies have been published which, superficially at least, would indicate that significant theoretical and empirical advances have been made in our knowledge of the genesis of stability and instability.

There is at least one school of thought, of course, which condemns these attempts at quantification as 'mindless empiricism' and which accordingly dismisses the findings reported by quantitative researchers without further consideration. While this 'dismissal by fiat' of a number of important and suggestive empirical analyses is in itself clearly unacceptable, a degree of healthy scepticism is nonetheless in order. As the present study will attempt to show, with regard to the analysis of political instability,

1

many of the 'advances' made since the behavioural revolution are more apparent than real: in some respects our empirically based explanations of the cross-national incidence of stability and instability are less than satisfactory. What we will argue, however, is that this situation is not so much the result of faulty theorising (though insufficient attention has been paid to the *definition* of stability/instability) as the consequence of the unconvincing nature of much of the evidence adduced in support of theoretical propositions. In a sense, this book attempts to demonstrate how little is known in terms of hard evidence about the general mechanisms which produce stability or instability in political systems. In the Popperian tradition, it is as much concerned with hypothesis rejection as with corroboration.

Before we proceed further, however, a caveat is necessary concerning the scope of the twin concepts of stability and instability. Although we return to these matters in Chapters 3 and 4, it should be pointed out at this stage that many of the studies which we examine are concerned primarily with cross-national patterns of *political violence*, an emphasis which results from the fact that many scholars seem to regard political violence and instability as synonymous – either by implication[2] or by direct reference.[3] This is not to say, however, that violence is the only manifestation of political instability: several writers associate instability either entirely or in part with the *coup d'état*,[4] with regime change[5] or even with the frequency of changes in government.[6] Although it will be argued later that stability and instability require a rather more complex conceptualisation than can be obtained by a straightforward 'frequency' examination of the kinds of phenomena investigated by previous writers, for the moment we will accept the current view adopted by most contemporary researchers, and assume that political violence, *coups d'état* and changes in regime or government can all be regarded in some sense as indicators of instability.

The general strengths and limitations of contemporary behavioural analyses of stability and instability, however, are best introduced by a brief review, firstly, of the main theoretical themes which are evident within the existing literature, and secondly, of the major empirical findings reported by contemporary scholars. The main theoretical themes can in fact be classified under six general headings:

(i)   the empirical analysis of the determinants of democratic stability;
(ii) internal war: the delimitation of a new subject area;
(iii) the dimensional schoool: the attempt to identify the major types or dimensions of 'domestic conflict behaviour';
(iv) psychologically oriented causal explanations of the sources of 'domestic conflict behaviour';
(v)   micro-oriented refutations of the psychological approach;
(vi) non-psychologically oriented causal explanations of the sources of 'domestic conflict behaviour'.

The six themes and the relationships between them are presented schematically in Figure 1.1. The definition and correlates of instability cited in a representative study from each grouping (together with the time period and universe of countries covered) are summarised in Table 1.1.

LIPSET: THE EMPIRICAL ANALYSIS OF DEMOCRATIC STABILITY

Seymour Lipset's seminal work, *Political Man*,[7] represents the first attempt to undertake a systematic, cross-national, empirical investigation of political stability, and for this reason alone his study is extremely important. Lipset's research design, however, was not concerned with analysing the sources of stability across all political systems. Rather, he was primarily interested in the origins of *democratic* stability in Europe and North America; in its socio-economic correlates; and in the mechanisms through which political institutions are preserved.[8]

Perhaps the most significant feature of Lipset's analysis, however, is his decision to view stability and instability as discrete, alternative states. His definition of stable democracies, as those systems which have experienced

uninterrupted continuation of political democracy since World War I, and the absence over the past 25 years . . . (it will be recalled that *Political Man* appeared in 1959) . . . of a major political movement opposed to the democratic rules of the game.[9]

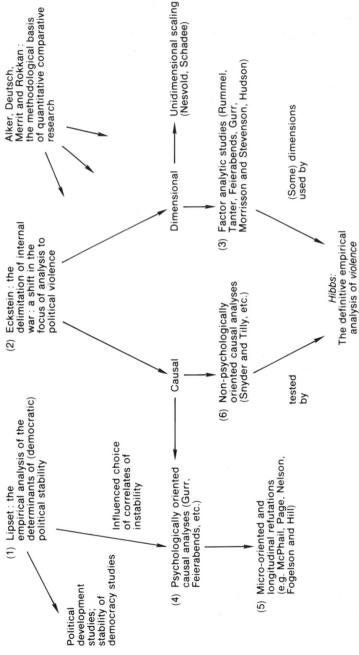

FIGURE 1.1   Schematic representation of the main themes in the current literature relating to stability/instability

implies that polities are either completely stable or completely unstable. It consequently disavows the possibility that stability and instability can be conceptualised as relative, continuous phenomena. While this dichotomous definition can be defended on the grounds that it corresponds to the prevailing *static* approach to comparative politics which dominated social science thinking during the 1950s and early 1960s – Lipset's notion of stability, for example, is conceptually very close to the Eastonian notion of 'system persistence', the only alternative to which is complete system breakdown[10] – it seems more useful analytically to regard stability and instability not as the two branches of a dichotomy but as the two ends of an indeterminate continuum. As we shall argue in a later chapter, a political system can only be characterised with any accuracy as being 'more' or 'less' stable, either in (cross-sectional) comparison with *other* systems *or* in comparison with itself during a different time period.

But even disregarding the fact that Lipset wrongly regarded stability and instability as a dichotomy, his analysis (not through any fault of his own) has left a legacy of theoretical confusion, in the sense that it has been used as a starting point for the investigation of at least three related, but nonetheless distinct, areas of analysis. Lipset's work has been employed by some writers in order to establish why some political systems are more *democratic* than others;[11] by others as the basis for their analyses of *political development;*[12] and by yet others in their investigations of *political instability and political violence.*[13] Moreover, Lipset's own focus – the stability of democracy – has itself continued as a distinct area of analysis in the works of, amongst others, Dahl, Lijphart and Budge.[14]

This springboard effect of Lipset's analysis is certainly to be commended – good analysis should stimulate further research – but the apparent inability to provide any theoretical basis for differentiating between stability, democracy and development undoubtedly has been partly responsible for some of the strange and conflicting findings concerning the role of various socio-economic variables as correlates of stability and development which we investigate in Chapter 2. The point is, that while 'degree of democracy', 'level of political development' and 'stability' may well be *empirically* related (liberal democratic countries also tend to be both stable and politically developed), on the one hand these tendencies are by no means invariant, and on the other, the

TABLE 1.1   Main themes – examples of definitions,

	Universe	Type of stability/ instability examined	Causes/correlates
(1) Lipset – democratic stability	Europe, North America, Latin America: Dictatorships and democracies	Regime change	(1) Wealth (2) Industrialisation (3) Education (4) Urbanisation
(2) Eckstein – internal war	All countries	Violence: Internal war	(1) Balance between conflict-generating and conflict-controlling features of polity (2) 'Strain' (3) Fragmentation of tension management structures
(3) Dimensional	Rummel: 84 nations	Violence	n/a
	Schadee: 136 nations	Violence	n/a
(4) Psychological causal	The Feierabends: 85 nations	Violence	Frustration, coercion, socio-economic change, modernity
	Gurr: 112 nations	Violence	Relative deprivation, legitimacy facilitation, institutionalisation, coercive potential
(5) Micro-oriented refutations	Paige: 247 New Haven blacks	Riots	Rational desire to register protest
(6) Non-psychological causal	Snyder and Tilley: France	Violence	Repression, struggle for power
	Hibbs: 108 nations	Violence Coups	Numerous – see Table 1.3

dimensions, causes, universe of countries, findings

Time period	Stability/instability as focus? If so, how stability/instability defined?	Findings
Cross-sectional 1914–59	Stability of democracy: 'uninterrupted continuation of political democracy since World War I . . .'	All causes verified
Unspecified	Internal war = violent conflict which affects exercise or structure of authority (Janos) Internal war = attempts to change (using violence or the threat of it) policies, rulers or organisations (Eckstein)	None empirical
Cross-sectional 1958–63	n/a	Three main dimensions to conflict behaviour: internal war, turmoil, conspiracy
Cross-sectional 1948–68	n/a	Only one dimension: violent/less violent
1948–62: mainly cross-sectional, but *some* time series	(i) Frequencies of violence (ii) Deviations from a trend	Hypotheses confirmed
1948–65: cross-sectional	Violence (frequencies)	Hypotheses confirmed
Cross-sectional late 1960s	n/a	Motivation for rioting unrelated to frustration/deprivation
1830–1960 time series	Violence	Hypotheses find preliminary confirmation: deprivation thesis invalid
1948–68 cross-sectional	Violence	Various: but deprivation thesis irrelevant

concepts of democracy, development and stability are quite distinct *analytically*. Democracy consists in the existence of high levels of inclusiveness (participation) and public contestation (institutionalised opposition);[15] *development* consists in the achievement of relatively high levels of 'equality', 'differentiation' and 'capacity';[16] and *stability* (as we will attempt to show in Chapter 4) consists in the absence of changes in, and challenges to, the incumbent government and/or regime. Even if the particular definitions of democracy, development and stability which are offered above are rejected, it is none the less clear that the three concepts are fundamentally independent and need to be regarded as such, both in the context of theoretical speculation, and in terms of empirical research. For the moment, therefore, we shall ignore questions of democracy and development (though we return to them in later chapters) and restrict our discussion exclusively to the analysis of stability and instability.

ECKSTEIN AND *INTERNAL WAR*

While Lipset's analysis was essentially concerned with the sources of *democratic* stability, Eckstein's seminal anthology, *Internal War*,[17] reflects the shift in the focus of comparative political enquiry towards the search for paradigms which seek to identify and analyse the problems which are faced by *all* political systems, regardless of their normative structure. The specific aim of Eckstein's work was to propose a theoretical delimitation of a new subject area of political analysis, internal war – 'violent conflict which affects the exercise or structure of authority'[18] – and much of the study is concerned with preliminary attempts to identify its theoretical dimensions and general causes.

The essential limitation of *Internal War*, however, is that the highly abstract nature of much of the analysis makes it extremely difficult to extract *testable* propositions from any of the constituent papers. Feldman, for example, suggests that a society's 'revolutionary potential' – that is, its potential for internal war – is a function of 'strain' and of 'the fragility of tension management devices'.[19] These proposals may well be quite valid, but their measurement, and even their definition, are extremely problematic.

Apart from suggesting that strain is something which characterises all social systems to varying degrees and which 'generates social conflict and provokes change', Feldman offers few, if any, guidelines as to its actual nature, beyond the suggestion that it is characterised by the occurrence of certain violent or quasi-violent events. Yet if this characterisation is all that is constituted by strain, then it would appear to differ very little from the much simpler and more easily observable notion of political violence or turmoil. To suggest that political violence (or internal war) is a *function* of strain, therefore, seems to be a purely definitional and largely redundant proposition, since there is no clear theoretical or operational distinction between violence and strain.

A similar problem arises with the term 'fragility of tension management devices'. If we were to attempt to measure and operationalise this abstraction, in order to examine its predictive power in explaining cross-national patterns of internal war, we could perhaps infer that in systems where the legitimacy of government institutions is high, and where the need for governmental coercion in order to prevent civil disobedience is low, 'tension management devices' will be relatively 'non-fragile', and accordingly effect our operationalisation using the surrogate concepts of 'legitimacy' and 'absence of coercion'. But if such an inference were indeed correct, it would perhaps make sense to consider the concepts of *legitimacy* and the *relative necessity of coercion* as explanatory factors in the genesis of internal war, rather than to undertake an investigation of the role of such an elusive concept as the fragility of tension management devices. While I would not claim that the foregoing remarks in any sense constitute a comprehensive critique of the Eckstein anthology, the examples cited do demonstrate one of its principal limitations in the context of possible empirical research: that it fails to provide any concrete, testable empirical generalisations which might assist in the identification of the causes of internal war.

The fundamental importance of Eckstein's analysis is that together with the more explicitly methodological contributions of a number of scholars, it laid down the guidelines for much of the quantitative research into 'domestic conflict behaviour' which took place throughout the 1960s and 1970s.[20] The two main branches of this later research sought to provide answers to Eckstein's two chief research questions: (1) what are the major types or *dimensions* of internal war or domestic conflict behaviour?; and (2) what are its major *determinants*?

THE DIMENSIONAL SCHOOL: WHAT ARE THE DIMENSIONS OF *INTERNAL WAR*?

During the 1960s a number of cross-national aggregate data-sets were collected under the auspices of various research institutes.[21] The data collected fell into three broad categories: (1) *political events* – for example, assassinations, elections, demonstrations, acts of governmental coercion, outbreaks of guerrilla warfare, and *coups d'états*; (2) *socio-economic characteristics of nation states* – for example, levels of urbanisation, communication development, GNP per capita and industrialisation; and (3) *structural characteristics of regimes* – for example, military/civilian status, level of inequality, degree of ethnic cleavage and type of normative structure.

In order to isolate the major dimensions of internal war/domestic conflict behaviour, a number of analyses (using the 'political event' data mentioned above as their basic raw material) employed what, at first sight, appears to be an eminently suitable (inductive) data analytic tool, *factor analysis*. Since this particular technique is capable of identifying clusters of variables which are highly intercorrelated with each other, and thereby of establishing the major *mathematical dimensions* which are evident within a given data-set, it was assumed that if a data-set was assembled which described a wide range of domestic conflict behaviours, then a factor analysis of that data-set could be undertaken in order to establish the major *empirical dimensions* of these conflict behaviours.

We will return in detail to some of the more important problems associated with the use of factor analysis in aggregate research in Chapter 2. It is sufficient at this stage, however, to point out that the contradictory findings of the various factor analytic studies have perhaps done more to confuse our understanding of the theoretical dimensions of internal war or domestic conflict behaviour or political violence, than to clarify it.

The analyses of Rummel and Tanter,[22] for example, found evidence of the existence of *three* major *factors* or dimensions of domestic conflict behaviour. These were labelled: (1) *internal war* (organised and widespread, *mass* political violence which involves guerrilla warfare, assassinations and deaths from political violence); (2) *turmoil* (unorganised and widespread *mass* political behaviour which does not necessarily involve violence, and which includes strikes, demonstrations and riots); and (3) *conspiracy* (organised *élite* behaviour which includes *coups*, attempted *coups* and acts of governmental repression).

Entirely different factors, however, have been reported in other analyses. Feierabend and Feierabend,[23] for example, found nine factors (mass participation/turmoil, palace revolution/revolt, power struggle/revolt, riot, elections, demonstration, imprisonment, civil war and guerrilla warfare) whereas Hoole[24] identified *five* (demonstrations, guerrilla warfare, riots, strikes and change of office holder). Hibbs,[25] on the other hand, found evidence of only *two* factors – *internal war* (composed of guerrilla warfare, assassinations and deaths from political violence) and *collective protest* (in which Hoole's three dimensions of riots, strikes and demonstrations were subsumed under a *single* factor). Finally, Morrison and Stevenson,[26] in their analysis of Black African states, found evidence of *four* major dimensions of internal conflict behaviour: *élite instability* (which corresponds broadly to Rummel's 'conspiracy'), *mass instability* (which corresponds in part to Rummel's 'internal war'), *turmoil* (identical to Rummel's 'turmoil') and (a new dimension) *communal or ethnic violence*.

Whatever other weaknesses are associated with the factor analytic approach (and in fact we examine these in detail in the next chapter), it is clear that the wealth of contradiction which we have just described must cast considerable doubt upon the adequacy of the empirical findings which the advocates of that approach have reported.

PSYCHOLOGICALLY ORIENTED CAUSAL APPROACHES

While the authors who espoused the factor analytic approach were concerned with attempting to answer Eckstein's first research question – 'What are the major dimensions of domestic conflict behaviour?' – many of the writers who have sought to answer his *second* research question – 'What are the major *causes* of such behaviour?' – have adopted a quasi-psychological theoretical stance. Drawing from Dollard's deprivation-frustration-aggression thesis,[27] a number of theorists have argued that domestic conflict behaviours need to be regarded not as rational political strategies but as the aggressive response to either deprivation or frustration or both.[28]

The most influential of these analyses have almost certainly been those of Gurr and of Feierabend and Feierabend. Gurr, for example, views all violent political behaviours as the consequence of 'relative deprivation', which itself is defined to exist whenever there is a 'gap' between 'value expectations' (what individuals think that they *ought* to obtain from the political system in terms of status, wealth, liberty and justice) and 'perceived value capabilities' (what individuals believe that they *will actually* obtain from the system). The Feierabends, on the other hand, using a very similar concept, contend that *societal frustration* (the ratio of 'want formation' to 'want satisfaction') is the fundamental source of all destabilising and violent political behaviour. Using *indirect* indicators, both Gurr and the Feierabends effect cross-national operationalisations of their respective psychological constructs and also attempt to specify and evaluate the extent to which the effects of these constructs upon the level of domestic conflict behaviours are mediated and supplemented by other socio-economic and political variables. The Feierabends' analysis leads them to conclude that while governmental coercion, a high rate of socio-economic change, and a lack of 'modernity' are all important factors in the genesis of political instability, the most important and immediate source of violence, or instability, is in fact 'societal frustration'. Similarly, Gurr concludes that while 'regime coercive potential', institutionalisation, legitimacy and 'social-structural facilitation'[29] all have a significant impact upon the level of instability, the single most important factor is 'relative deprivation'.

A comparable thesis (though this is not one that its author has attempted to subject to quantitative empirical test)[30] is advanced by Huntington, who argues that the origins of political instability lie in a three-stage process which he refers to as the 'gap hypothesis'.[31] Huntington suggests that the *gap* between (1) the extent to which the process of social mobilisation (exogenous social change) generates new aspirations and expectations among the mass public of a given political system, and (2) the extent to which the level of economic development provides the political authorities with sufficient economic and political resources to satisfy those aspirations and expectations, determines the level of 'social frustration' within that system. This line of reasoning is directly analogous both to the Feierabends' belief that the ratio of want formation to want satisfaction defines the level of 'societal frustration', and to Gurr's contention that the gap between 'value expectations' and 'perceived value capabilities' defines the level of 'relative deprivation'. Moreover, in the same way that the Feierabends and Gurr also specify a number of other exogenous influences upon the level of violence and instability, Huntington argues that the effects of social frustration are mediated by the effects of 'mobility opportunities', 'political participation' and 'institutionalisation'.[32]

Although the apparent empirical support which the Gurr and Feierabend analyses provide for the idea that violence and instability are the consequence (at least in part) of deprivation and frustration can in fact be strongly challenged on *methodological* grounds, we will delay making any such criticisms until the next chapter. None the less, it is necessary at this juncture briefly to review a number of empirical analyses which, given the absence of *direct* measures of the cross-national incidence of such elusive phenomena as 'societal frustration' or 'relative deprivation', have sought to evaluate the utility of the deprivation-frustration-aggression thesis not by the cross-national analysis of political aggregates but instead by the detailed examination of survey data.

MICRO-ORIENTED REFUTATIONS OF THE
DEPRIVATION-FRUSTRATION-AGGRESSION THESIS

Four studies have in fact attempted to put the conclusions of Gurr and the Feierabends to the test at the individual rather than at the system level.[33] The basic presupposition of these studies is that if deprivation and frustration are the fundamental cause of violent political behaviour then it is to be expected that the participants in violent political events will tend to be (or tend to perceive themselves as being) either more relatively deprived and/or more frustrated than (socially and economically comparable) *non*-participants. These four studies, however, found that this expectation was simply not fulfilled. Paige, for example, in his study of 247 blacks who took part in the riots in New Haven, New Jersey, in 1968, concludes that: 'Rioting appears to be a disorganised form of political protest rather than an act of personal frustration ... as has been suggested in some past research.'[34] Similarly, Sears and McConahay, in their analysis of the Watts race riots of August 1965 found that the motivation for rioting was unrelated to any feelings of frustration or deprivation on the part of the respondents, but rather that rioting 'served as the functional equivalent of more conventional grievance redress mechanisms which blacks perceived as ineffective'.[35]

In short, therefore, the micro-oriented investigations of the deprivation-frustration-aggression thesis suggest quite simply that (whatever else is responsible) participation in violent political activities is *not* the consequence of 'relative deprivation' or 'frustration'.

NON-PSYCHOLOGICALLY ORIENTED CAUSAL APPROACHES

While this grouping of analyses is perhaps somewhat amorphous, since it embraces a large number of studies which provide a wide range of theoretical propositions and empirical generalisations, the unifying feature is that, although they seek to identify the determinants of political violence and instability (either in one particular system, or across all systems), they either reject or completely ignore the deprivation-frustration-aggression thesis.

The causal determinants of stability and instability which are in fact proposed in the various studies are of course numerous, diverse, and indeed frequently mutually contradictory. Moreover, the problem of summarising the various propositions is compounded by the fact that they refer to different *aspects* or *types* of stability/instability: some of the studies fail to provide a precise theoretical or operational definition of instability and refer only to instability 'in general';[36] some refer only to 'political violence' or 'internal war';[37] some only to 'regime instability' or *'coups d'état'*;[38] and others only to 'governmental' stability or instability.[39] To clarify this, Table 1.2 reports the various independent variables which have, at some stage, been cited as having either a direct or an indirect influence upon each of these four 'types' of instability.[40]

As Table 1.2 indicates, the propositions relating to the determinants of instability range from Madian's argument that excessive *social stability* (because it results in the fact that the grievances of deprived sectors of the population remain unsatisfied) leads to *political instability*,[41] to Passos' not dissimilar claim that, in Latin America at least, a 'closed social structure' (in which opportunities for vertical social mobility are low) is likely to increase the probability of instability;[42] from Weinert's suggestion that political violence is fundamentally associated with 'transfers of power at the national level' and that it gains increasing intensity when non-*élites* are 'strongly opposed to the secular modernising policies' of the leaders,[43] to the contentions of Horowitz and of Miller that the single most important source of political instability is a low level of 'regime legitimacy'.[44] The Marxist position, to which we return in Chapter 6, is represented by Cockcroft *et al.*, who cite trade and capital dependency as an important source of instability.[45]

Perhaps the most significant feature of Table 1.2, however, concerns the role of 'corruption', 'expansion of political communication networks', 'increases in urbanisation' and 'high rate of economic growth'. It will be noted that each of these four variables is in effect cited as a source of *both stability* and *instability*. With regard to the role of economic change, for example, Flanigan and Fogelman argue that a high rate of economic growth is likely to *reduce* the probability of political violence and instability, whereas Olsen has argued that rapid economic change (whether it takes the form of either an 'upswing' or a 'downswing') produces severe social instability, which in turn leads to conflict and a high potential for political violence.[46] Similarly, while the Feierabends contend that increases in political communications networks in turn increase the probability of political instability, Lerner, and Cnudde and McCrone, claim to find evidence that the expansion of such networks *reduces* the probability of instability.[47] We do not intend at this stage of our analysis to comment upon the inconsistencies which Table 1.2 describes: in Chapter 2, we will attempt to explain why different empirical analyses have obtained apparent empirical support for such contradictory propositions by reference to a methodological problem which we will term the 'similar conditions fallacy'; and in Chapters 7 and 8 we will examine the empirical adequacy of those propositions by reference to the measures of instability which we develop in Chapters 3 and 4.[57]

In some respects, the three most significant studies described in Table 1.2 are those of Flanigan and Fogelman, Snyder and Tilly, and Hibbs.[58] Flanigan and Fogelman's investigation resolved at

TABLE 1.2   Theoretical propositions with claimed empirical support,

General instability	Political violence
(No precise definition of instability provided as no specific type of instability identified)	(Includes riots, guerrilla warfare, assassinations, deaths from violence, strikes, demonstrations)

General Instability varies *positively* with:

1. Increases in urbanisation (the Feierabends)
2. Overpopulation productivity ratio (Staycos & Arias)[48]
3. Social stability (Madian)
4. Weakness of 'social and political enforcement mechanisms' (Nye)
5. Increases in the extent of political communication networks (the Feierabends)
6. Level of trade and capital dependency (Chilcote and Edelstein,[49] Cockcroft *et al.*, Kling[50])

General instability varies *negatively* with:

1. The level of regime legitimacy (Horowitz, Nye, Gurr)
2. Increases in urbanisation (Lipset, Lerner)
3. Development of strong and stable political institutions and institutionalisation (Huntington, Hibbs)
4. Extent of opportunities for social and economic mobility (Huntington)
5. Level of economic development (Huntington, Passos)
6. Expansion of political communication networks (Deutsch, Lerner, Cnudde and McCrone)
7. Sense of national community (Nye)
8. Level of literacy (Lipset)
9. Extent of élite concensus over regime norms (Budge, Field)
10. Level of institutionalisation (Huntington)

The probability of political violence is *increased* by:

1. Administrative corruption (Gluckman,[51] Crozier[52])
2. Apathy (Davies[53])
3. Frustration/relative deprivation
4. Occurrence of take-off phase of industrialisation (Flanigan and Fogelman)
5. Governmental coercion/coercive potential (Snyder and Tilly, Nesvold,[54] Gurr, the Feierabends)
6. Governmental crises or transfers of power (Snyder and Tilly, Weinhert)
7. High rate of economic growth (Olsen, Hurwitz)
8. Multipartism (Hurwitz)
9. High level of ethno-linguistic fractionalisation (Hurwitz)
10. Religious homogeneity (Hurwitz)
11. High level of 'elite instability' (Bwy)
12. High level of 'non-violent repression' (Bwy)
13. High level of land inequality (Russett[55])
14. High level of 'social-structural facilitation' (Gurr)

The probability of political violence is *reduced* by:

1. Concensus (Davies)
2. Corruption (Nye)
3. High rate of economic growth (Flanigan and Fogelman)
4. Low rate of economic growth
5. High level of regime legitimacy (Gurr)
6. High level of institutionalisation (Gurr)
7. High level of 'democratic attainment' (Hurwitz)
8. High level of economic development (Hurwitz)
9. High level of 'personal satisfaction' (Bwy)

and empirical findings, concerning the sources of political instability

Regime instability (coups d'état)	Governmental instability

The probability of a *coup d'état* is *increased* by:

1. Corruption (Gluckman)
2. (In Latin America) the occurrence of elections (Fossum)
3. Past history of coups (Putnam)
4. Relatively high defence expenditure (Putnam)
5. Large and 'sophisticated' military sector (Janowitz)
6. High level of trade dependency (O'Kane[56])
7. Severe proletarian challenge to middle class hegemony (Cockcroft *et al.*, Edelstein)
8. High rate of social mobilisation (Huntington)

Governmental instability (in Western democracies) varies *positively* with:

1. Governmental fractionalisation (Taylor and Herman)
2. Parliamentary fractionalisation (Taylor and Herman)
3. The occurrence of 'turmoil' (Africa only) (Morrisson and Stevenson)
4. The percentage size of anti-system parties (Sanders and Herman)
5. The incidence of protest demonstrations (Sanders and Herman)
6. The incidence of acts of governmental repression (Sanders and Herman)

The probability of a *coup d'état* is *reduced* by:

1. High rate of social mobilisation (Putnam)
2. High level of institutionalisation (Huntington)

Governmental instability (in Western democracies) varies *negatively* with:

1. The fractionalisation of pro-system parties (Taylor and Herman)
2. The fractionalisation of opposition parties (Taylor and Herman)
3. The incidence of strikes (Sanders and Herman)

The variables identified here are not intended as statements of the full complexity of the theoretical positions of the cited authors but simply as summary indications of the major independent variables which they identify. All the studies not referenced here are cited elsewhere in this chapter.

least a part of the rather confused polemic concerning the relationship between political violence and economic development. While many analyses have concluded that higher *levels* of economic development tend to be associated with lower levels of violence and instability (see for example the studies of Lipset, and Feierabend and Feierabend, cited previously), as we saw earlier there has been a considerable amount of disagreement as to the role of *changes* in the level of economic development in the genesis of political violence and instability. By examining some sixty-eight countries (divided into four major groups on the basis of their current levels of economic development) over a period of 150 years in all, Flanigan and Fogelman found that the magnitude of violence *decreases* as the *rate* of economic development *increases*, an observation which strongly questions the validity of Olsen's argument that violence should increase as the rate of change in economic development increases. Flanigan and Fogelman also argued that the fact that there was a peak in the level of violence in the last decade before the agricultural labour force fell below 40 per cent has important implications for the role of industrialisation as a determinant of political instability: the strains and tensions generated by economic change would appear to be greatest during the critical 'take-off' period, and it is during this period, historically, that high levels of political violence are most likely to occur.

Snyder and Tilly's longitudinal analysis of France over the period 1830 to 1960 is important because it supplements the micro-oriented analyses to which we referred in a previous section of this chapter and provides (at the *aggregate* level) a harsh refutation of the deprivation-frustration-aggression thesis by setting up a series of least squares models which relate levels of political violence to various measures of economic deprivation (a food price index, a cost of manufactured goods index, and an index of industrial production). The various deprivation measures, either lagged or unlagged, failed to have any significant impact upon the level of violence. Having dispensed with the deprivation-frustration thesis, however, Snyder and Tilly draw the comparatively trivial conclusion that the two most important correlates of political violence are 'governmental repression' and 'the non-violent struggle for power' (which is operationalised by a dummy variable where 1 = occurrence of an electron and 0 = non-occurrence). Nonetheless, Snyder and Tilly's argument that it seems plausible that *political* violence should be the consequence of other *political* phenomena such as these is an important and attractive one:

> It is only because of the presence of theories emphasising hardship, relative deprivation and other individual states only tangentially related to politics . . . (that we have) . . . to justify the introduction of political struggles into the analysis at all . . . According to our argument collective violence rises, other things being equal, with the extent of non-violent struggles for power.[59]

The most definitive analysis of instability which has been undertaken, however, is Hibbs' 108 nation study of mass political violence and *coups d'état*. Drawing on a wide range of theoretical propositions, a series of 'single equation hypotheses' and 'partial theories' are operationalised and tested, and those relationships which furnish significant parameter estimates are organised into a single multi-equation block recursive model. Hibbs' substantive findings are summarised in Table 1.3.

While the methodological precision of Hibbs' investigation cannot be faulted, and while some extremely valuable conclusions are drawn concerning the sequential interrelationships between 'collective protest', 'internal war', *coups d'état* and 'negative sanctions' (acts of governmental coercion), the analysis is rather short on theoretical interpretation. Indeed, Hibbs' analysis is more a loose collection of verified empirical generalisations than a theory: complex mathematical estimation does not buy theoretical sophistication. Nonetheless, in Hibbs' defence, it could be argued firstly, that a 'loose collection' of verified propositions perhaps provides a better explanation of a given phenomenon than any number of unified but uncorroborated theories, and secondly, that the very diverse nature of his empirical findings in fact make coherent 'theorising' extremely difficult.

The value of Hibbs' work, however, lies (firstly) in the numerous propositions which his analysis indicates are *invalid*. Hibbs shows, for example, that internal war is unrelated to the level of economic development (which, of course, contradicts the findings of several previous analyses), the rate of economic growth and the occurrence of *coups d'etat*; and that collective protest, for example, is unrelated to the level of institutionalisation, the relative extent of communist party representation and the incidence of *coups d'état*. Secondly, Hibbs' analysis is also important because of the relatively

TABLE 1.3   Hibbs' empirical findings by dimension

Coups
  (i)   are not directly related to protest
 (ii)   are partly due to internal war
(iii)   vary negatively with institutionalisation
 (iv)   vary positively with interventions and history
  (v)   vary positively with defence expenditure/total expenditure

Violence (general)
   (i)   is not related to level of economic development directly
  (ii)   is unrelated to rate of population growth
 (iii)   is unrelated to defence spending
  (iv)   is unrelated to level of mass social welfare
   (v)   varies positively with repression (short run)
  (vi)   is less in communist systems
 (vii)   is reduced by institutionalisation, and is therefore *indirectly* related
          to economic development

Protest
   (i)   is not directly related to coups
  (ii)   is unrelated to level of institutionalisation
 (iii)   is unrelated to previous history of protest
  (iv)   is not due to leftist representation
   (v)   is reduced by higher GNP per capita (affluence)
  (vi)   varies positively with size of collective protest
 (vii)   varies positively with social mobilisation

Internal War
   (i)   is unrelated to institutionalisation
  (ii)   is affected marginally by past history of internal war
 (iii)   is not reduced by high economic growth
  (iv)   is not influenced by *coups* directly
   (v)   varies positively with ethno-linguistic fractionalisation
  (vi)   is not reduced by a higher level of economic development
 (vii)   varies positively with repression

high level of statistical explanation which his mathematical models achieve. (The r^2 values for Hibbs' final models range from 0.502 for *coups* to 0.681 for internal war.) The main source of vindication for the *psychologically* oriented theories of Gurr and the Feierabends was the relatively high r^2 magnitudes which *their* models provide. What Hibbs' analysis demonstrates is that similar levels of statistical explanation *can* be obtained in quantitative analysis without the need to resort to the very imperfect measurement of psychological constructs such as systemic frustration or relative deprivation which (as we will see in Chapter

2) require that somewhat questionable assertions are made in order to link theoretical concepts to operational indicators. It is in this sense particularly that Hibbs' work is of great significance in the analysis of political instability.

In this chapter, then, we have reviewed a number of approaches to the analysis of political stability and instability and have attempted to show how these different approaches are related to one another. With the exception of our discussion of Lipset and Eckstein, the 'founding fathers' of contemporary empirical research into instability, we have tried as far as possible to avoid making *direct* criticisms of any of the various approaches and have attempted instead simply to describe the theoretical and empirical orientations which each approach adopts and the major empirical findings which the authors involved have reported. We have established, moreover, that a large number of propositions – some of them mutually contradictory – appear to have obtained some degree of empirical support. In the next chapter we will undertake a systematic critique of the more recent approaches and attempt to specify the extent to which current research findings have provided a satisfactory explanation of the origins of political instability.

2 Inconsistencies and Inadequacies in Previous Analyses of Political Instability

As we intimated in Chapter 1, our intention in this chapter is to identify some of the more important limitations and weaknesses which are evident in previous analyses of political instability. We have already hinted at some of these problems. The contributors to Eckstein's *Internal War* anthology, for example, tend to present their ideas at such an abstract level that it is very difficult to visualise how the theoretical propositions which they develop might be operationalised and tested. Lipset's investigation, since its theoretical (though not its empirical) focus is the stability of Western liberal democracies, is perhaps too restricted in its approach to be of value in the identification of the *general* sources of instability.

Given that we return to the issues raised by Eckstein and Lipset in later chapters, we will confine our discussion in this chapter to an examination of the limitations, first, of the factor analytic approach of the *'dimensional school'*, secondly, of the *psychologically oriented causal approach* of Gurr and the Feierabends, and thirdly, of the *non-psychologically oriented approaches*; all of which were reviewed in Chapter 1. As we will see, the main thrust of our critique is a methodological one, concerned principally with challenging the underlying assumptions of these various analyses. We will conclude this chapter by attempting to show how contradictory theoretical propositions can appear to derive empirical support from a given body of data. This exercise should go at least part of the way towards explaining the conflicting role which previous quantitative research has attributed to a number of socio-economic variables as sources of both stability and instability.

THE DIMENSIONAL SCHOOL: WEAKNESSES AND LIMITATIONS

Perhaps the major weakness of the (dimensional) factor analytic approach which we briefly described in Chapter 1 is the inconsistent findings which the exponents of that approach have provided. As we saw, there is very little agreement among the various studies, firstly, as to how many significant 'dimensions' of 'domestic conflict behaviour' there are, and secondly, as to which groups of these conflict behaviours tend to cluster together. Quite apart from these contradictory findings, however, several additional problems arise from the use of factor analysis in cross-national research.

Firstly, factor analysis will always provide 'a solution': some mathematical dimensions, however weak, will almost invariably appear in the data. It is consequently the researcher's task to assess the strength and relevance of these dimensions upon the basis of (1) the factor loadings which each variable scores on each factor, and (2) the 'percentage of common variance' which each factor explains.

A cursory scanning of any of the factor analytic solutions which were outlined in Chapter 1, however, indicates the rather arbitrary way in which variables are characterised as loading 'high' on a particular factor: the cut-off points for 'significantly high' loadings differ among the various analyses,[1] and frequently when one or two important variables load above the specified cut-off point on *more* than one factor, the variable is attributed to one of these factors not on the basis of any mathematical criterion, but simply because such a manoeuvre is necessary if consistency is to be achieved in the theoretical interpretation. Feierabend and Feierabend's analysis, for example, is a particularly bad offender in this regard. Table 2.1 reports their 'rotated factor matrix of domestic conflict measures', and indicates the existence of a number of highly ambiguous factor loadings within their factor solution. Their 'terrorism and sabotage' variable (variable 25), for example, loads highly ($r = 0.62$) on their '*mass* participation – turmoil' factor, and yet almost by definition terrorist activities are invariably the preserve of a relatively small, tightly-knit conspiratorial group. Moreover, the 'terrorism and sabotage' variable *fails* to load significantly ($r = 0.38$) on the 'guerrilla warfare' factor, and yet again (by definition), it would seem more

TABLE 2.1 Rotated factor matrix of domestic conflict measures

Variables	Factors*								
	Mass participation – turmoil	Palace revolution – revolt	Power struggle – purge	Riot	Election	Demon- stration	Imprison- ment	Civil war	Guerrilla warfare
1. Elections	29	-2	9	-18	70*	-10	-17	-5	-23
2. Vacation of office	38	8	74*	-14	20	-11	-15	-25	9
3. Significant change of laws	38	41	41	-1	31	15	-16	-23	-11
4. Acquisition of office	29	6	75*	-19	15	-4	-25	-19	22
5. Crisis with a non-governmental organisation	40	13	12	-21	4	-9	62*	7	-23
6. Organisation of opposition party	8	10	-2	2	56*	36	19	-39	-10
7. Repressive action against specific groups	46	61	27	1	-3	16	12	4	12
8. Micro strikes	67*	0	-15	-26	-16	5	12	3	23
9. General strikes	73*	13	4	-42	9	-6	3	8	-18
10. Macro strikes	43	-22	-11	-35	15	-17	-33	-12	-19
11. Micro demonstrations	61*	19	-2	2	20	59*	10	3	2
12. Macro demonstrations	73*	-1	0	26	6	19	18	-21	3
13. Micro riots	46	11	-6	68*	27	-3	-3	-15	11
14. Macro riots	69*	28	-4	33	20	2	4	-8	-5
15. Severe macro riots	64*	-3	-4	53*	11	-19	-2	-20	14
16. Arrests of significant persons	9	64	54*	7	-14	-6	23	-10	-1
17. Imprisonment of significant persons	-14	12	49	17	-5	16	38	-33	-22

18. Arrests a few insignificant persons	42	9	5	−8	7	75*	7	7	21
19. Mass arrests of insignificant persons	52*	33	14	54*	−12	−2	−1	5	1
20. Imprisonment of insignificant persons	26	−8	9	8	−12	34	64*	−3	−14
21. Assassination	17	40	23	6	24	23	−7	−10	56*
22. Martial law	11	71*	3	3	15	9	−27	−6	−8
23. Execution of significant persons	−8	1	54*	31	−26	14	−4	31	5
24. Execution of insignificant persons	1	−10	63*	32	−7	12	−2	47	−2
25. Terrorism and sabotage	62*	28	12	−21	13	−1	10	7	38
26. Guerrilla warfare	4	42	7	−19	19	−35	25	21	55*
27. Civil war	−14	25	31	14	45	8	−8	60*	2
28. Coups d'état	3	69*	7	1	−2	12	−40	7	−32
29. Revolts	6	75*	−1	11	7	−1	−10	32	16
30. Exile	−9	40	0	3	−36	32	−19	−13	4
Percentage of common variance	23.37	16.30	13.20	9.67	8.33	8.00	7.99	6.76	6.40 = 100.0
Percentage of total variance	23.33	11.11	7.52	6.77	5.89	5.32	4.18	3.82	3.62 = 71.46

*Asterisks indicate loadings > 0.50. Decimals omitted from loadings.
Source: I. Feierabend and R. Feierabend, 'Systemic Conditions of Political Aggression: An Application of Frustration-Aggression Theory', in I. Feierabend, R. Feierabend and T. Gurr, *Anger, Violence and Politics* (Englewood Cliffs N.J.: Prentice-Hall, 1972).

sensible to assume that such activities are in fact *indicators* of guerrilla warfare, not *unrelated* to it as the Feierabends conclude.

A similar degree of ambiguity exists with regard to two of the variables which load highly on the *'palace revolution – revolt'* factor: 'repressive action against specific groups' (variable 7) and 'arrests of significant persons' (variable 16). While it is *possible* to visualise why these two variables might be definitionally related to the 'palace revolution – revolt' dimension (a 'palace revolution' may well involve some 'repressive action against specific groups' and 'the arrest of significant persons'), it seems far *more* plausible to expect that such variables would be related to Feierabend and Feierabend's *third* factor, *'power struggle – purge'*, since the idea of a governmental 'purge' is rather more obviously associated with both 'repressive action' and 'arrests of significant persons'. A final example of the inconsistency which characterises the Feierabends' factor solution is the loading of $r = 0.62$ which their 'crisis within a non-governmental organisation' variable (variable 5) achieves on their 'imprisonment' factor, a relationship which the Feierabends leave unexplained and which (to me, at least) remains largely inexplicable.

There are, then, considerable ambiguities in the patterns of interrelationship between, on the one hand, the underlying 'factors' and, on the other hand, the factor loadings which the various dimensional analyses identify. A second problem involved in the use of factor analysis, however, concerns the actual nature of the factors themselves. Consider, for example, Hibbs' *internal war* factor, a dimension of 'mass political violence' which corresponds closely to Gurr's and to Rummel's *Internal War*. On the basis of the fact that 'assassinations', 'guerrilla attacks' and 'deaths from political violence' load highly on this factor, these three analysts follow conventional factor analysis procedures and argue that the factor itself represents some 'underlying' or 'latent' aspect or dimension of political behaviour. Purely because factor analysis enables the discovery of the major mathematical dimensions of a given data-set or inputted correlation matrix, these analysts seem to assume that the mathematical dimensions so uncovered directly represent some unobservable, but nonetheless real, dimensions of political behaviour. In a particular instance this may well be true, but an uncritical acceptance of factor analysis results in a sense ignores the nature of the factor analytic solution itself, and consequently can lead to rather obscure and possibly spurious theoretical interpretations.

The extent to which several vectors or variables (for example, assassinations, guerrilla attacks and deaths) cluster together on some mathematical dimension (for example, 'internal war') merely indicates that the three types of behaviour represented by the three vectors tend to co-occur across the sample of countries investigated. To suggest that the variance in these vectors can be explained by some underlying latent factor may be perfectly satisfactory mathematically: the analysis becomes rather more subjective when the mathematical dimensions of a particular correlation matrix are inferred to represent real dimensions of political behaviour. While all of the factor analytic studies to which we have referred in this and in the previous chapter make this kind of inference, none of them appears to recognise that such a step has been taken. Yet, if mathematical dimensions are to be regarded as representing 'real' dimensions, considerable theoretical justification needs to be offered, particularly when different analyses identify different mathematical dimensions.

The most important theoretical consideration which the factor analytic approach ignores – and this constitutes one of the most serious inadequacies of the technique – is the distinction between, on the one hand, an empirical correlation which denotes that the two variables involved are part of the same underlying phenomenon or 'dimension' (in other words, the variables are *definitionally* related), and on the other hand, an empirical correlation which denotes that the two variables are *causally* related. One of the most important contributions of the logical positivist school of philosophy to scientific epistemology was the distinction which it made between *definitional* (or in other words, *tautological*) and *causal* (or in other words, *empirical*) propositions:[2] the factor analysts *assume* that *all* the bivariate correlations which form the basis of their factor solutions represent *definitional* relationships. This assumption seems to me to be highly questionable. Given that on *a priori* grounds it is just as likely (for example) that assassinations and guerrilla attacks have a *causal* effect upon deaths from political violence (how do the factor analysts think political deaths occur?) as it is that assassinations, deaths and attacks are part of the *same* underlying phenomenon, it is surely incumbent upon the factor analysts, if their conclusions are to be held in any regard whatsoever, to demonstrate that the bivariate correlations which they examine do in fact represent definitional relationships.[3]

In the *absence* of any theoretical justification being provided by the factor analysts in support of the assumption that the correlations which they examine are definitional and not causal ones, the clarificatory value of the various factor analyses which have been conducted rests very precariously upon the comparatively high levels of statistical explanation which the studies claim to have obtained. A recent empirical study by Schadee,[4] however, challenges even the statistical basis of these investigations. Schadee found that when the political event variables which were factor analysed by Rummell, the Feierabends, Hibbs *et al.* were scaled on a *single* (more violent–less violent) dimension, a comparable level of statistical explanation to that achieved in the *factor* solutions could in fact be obtained.

The result of Schadee's analysis, the conflicting findings reported by the various factor analytic studies, the questionable inference that the mathematical dimensions of a correlation matrix can be equated with the real latent sources of 'domestic conflict behaviour', and the unjustified assumption that all the correlations analysed in the various factor solutions represent *definitional* relationships, all point to the conclusion that *factor analysis is a fundamentally inappropriate statistical technique for the purposes of identifying the major theoretical dimensions of political instability or 'domestic conflict' behaviour or internal war.* Indeed, they suggest that perhaps the most fruitful way of attempting to answer Eckstein's original research question (what are the major dimensions or types of 'internal war' or for our purposes, of 'political instability'?) is to search for dimensions which can be justified on *theoretical* grounds: this is in fact precisely what we attempt to do in Chapter 4.

PSYCHOLOGICALLY ORIENTED CAUSAL APPROACHES: WEAKNESSES AND LIMITATIONS

It will be recalled from Chapter 1 that the writers of the 'psychologically oriented school' view political violence and instability principally as the aggressive response either to 'societal frustration' (the gap between 'want formation' and 'want satisfaction')[5] or to the fundamentally similar concept of 'relative deprivation' (the gap between 'value expectations' and 'perceived value capabilities').[6] There is, of course, a danger in this kind of approach that the explanation becomes true by definition: in the

Feierabends' or in Gurr's terms, it is possible to pursue the fundamentally tautological argument that wherever political violence or instability occurs, some degree of systemic frustration or relative deprivation must have existed. Aware of this danger of tautology (although as we will see later, not completely avoiding it), both Gurr and the Feierabends attempt to *test* the explanatory power of their respective psychological constructs by effecting cross-national quantitative operationalisations of their respective theoretical propositions, for which both claim to find considerable empirical support.

There are, nonetheless, several important problems associated with the 'psychological' approach to the analysis of political violence and instability. The first of these problems is that by equating political violence with aggression, and by regarding violence as the direct, *unreasoned* and virtually automatic consequence of frustration and/or deprivation, the proponents of this approach heavily *underestimate* the possibility that participation in acts of political violence could be the product of calculated rational decisions on the part of (for example, ideologically motivated) insurgents. While Gurr (for example) admits that 'angry men may resort to public protest and violence on the basis of their estimation that it will improve their circumstances',[7] this is not a theme which he pursues with any vigour, because in his opinion '. . . (rational or) . . . utilitarian motives often are contingent upon and secondary to the "non-rational" motivation to act violently out of anger . . .'[8]

Riker, Markus and Tanter, and Oberschall,[9] however, have all argued quite forcefully that violence-oriented behaviour can in many circumstances be the result of a considered assessment of the likely costs and benefits of a particular form of action; and of course this assertion is entirely consistent with Sears and McConahay's conclusion (to which we referred in Chapter 1) that political violence (or at least, rioting) serves as 'the functional equivalent of more conventional grievance redress mechanisms . . . (which are perceived by the rioters) . . . as ineffective.'[10]

A second and related weakness of the frustration-deprivation thesis is that it fails to explain why the violent response to discontent (which in terms of the Feierabends' argument, for example, is generated entirely by social and economic processes) should be focussed upon the *political* system. Quite simply, the psychologically-oriented approach largely fails to explain why (especially economically generated) discontent should be *politicised.*[11] The questions which are not answered, or indeed asked, are: 'Why should discontent which is generated primarily in the social and economic systems not find violent expression in action directed against the social and economic systems?'; 'Why doesn't socially and economically generated discontent lead to *criminal* violence as opposed to *political* violence?'; 'Why shouldn't an individual who is "frustrated" or "relatively deprived" because of his social and/or economic situation go home and beat his wife or children, or commit common assault, or steal from his employer, or vandalise machinery at his workplace?'; 'What is it that leads men to vent their frustration or deprivation upon the *political* system?'.

These are perhaps obvious questions, but they nonetheless pose important problems which the frustration-deprivation theorists fail to resolve. Intuitively, it would seem that the most plausible explanation for socially and economically generated frustration being directed against the *political* system lies in suggesting that insurgents realise that it is through effecting certain outputs from the political system (which they assume will be the consequence of their violent political action) that they will be able to remedy the structural imbalances in the social and economic systems which (they presumably believe) produced their deprivation and discontent. Such a realisation, however, implies that some sort of *rational choice* has been made, yet it is precisely this rational choice aspect of behaviour which, as we have just noted, is seriously underestimated or even ignored by the frustration-aggression theorists. The essential point, then, is that if we are to explain why discontent or frustration or deprivation is *politicised*, we need to employ the notion of *political rationality* as a fundamental part of our analysis, and yet the frustration-deprivation theorists implicitly deny the utility of such a notion since, following Dollard, they argue that aggression (political violence) is the direct and unreasoned consequence of frustration-deprivation. As we suggested before, therefore, since the frustration-deprivation analysis is unable to explain why discontent is politicised, such an internal inadequacy in the thesis inevitably casts doubt upon the explanatory power of the psychologically oriented approach to political violence and instability.

An additional problem associated with this approach concerns the *units of analysis* which are employed by Gurr and the Feierabends and the relationship of these units of analysis to what has been termed the 'ecological fallacy'. This fallacy was first documented by Robinson, who demonstrated that spurious causal inferences can be drawn from empirical observations if the units of *observation* and the units of *inference* operate at different 'ecological levels'.[12] In the particular study which Robinson criticised, the *units of observation* — the data – were collected and analysed at the level of the *constituency*, but the *inferences* drawn were made at the level of the *individual*. Robinson demonstrated that when the same variables were collected and analysed at the *individual* level, the empirical relationship (and consequently the inferences which could be drawn from that relationship) was substantially weakened. While Gurr and the Feierabends do not make the precise mistake which Robinson warns against – both their data and their causal inferences operate at the level of the national political aggregate – there *is* a discrepancy between (1) the (*individual*) level at which their *theory* is posited and justified[13] and (2) the (*aggregate*) level at which their data is analysed and their causal inferences drawn.

The *implications* of this discrepancy can be seen by reference to the 'micro-oriented refutations' of the frustration-deprivation thesis which we described in Chapter 1. The fact that the frustration thesis achieves so little support at the individual level – despite the apparent support which it achieves at the aggregate level – perhaps suggests that the operational definitions of 'societal frustration' and 'relative deprivation' which the Feierabends and Gurr respectively employ, simply do *not* measure the aggregate of individual frustrations and/or deprivations to the extent that these authors claim. Since frustration and relative deprivation are essentially phenomena which occur at the level of the individual, and since Gurr and the Feierabends do not have access to data relating to individuals, this failure of measurement is perhaps not surprising. What it suggests, however, is that theories which are developed at the level of the individual are *inappropriately tested* when they are operationalised at the level of the national political aggregate. In short, it would seem to be the case that Gurr and the Feierabends *do* commit the ecological fallacy in their respective analyses, and that the veracity of their conclusions suffers accordingly.

Concepts and indicators in the psychological approach

This criticism acquires even greater significance when the final major weakness of the frustration-deprivation analyses is considered: the problem of the *disparity* between the theoretical concepts which are employed by the deprivation-frustration theorists and the operational referents which they use in order to measure them.[14] This is, of course, a continuing problem in all comparative political research, but it is nonetheless particularly acute in the context of the empirical analyses conducted by the advocates of the psychologically oriented approach. As we suggested earlier, it is clearly impossible, given the present constraints of data availability, to collect information (based on cross-national attitudinal surveys) which *directly* measures concepts such as frustration or relative deprivation. In consequence, Gurr and the Feierabends resort to the *indirect* measurement of these phenomena by reference to various aggregate level socio-economic and political characteristics. For the Feierabends, for example,

> The frustration index . . . is . . . a ratio. A country's combined score on . . . six satisfaction indices (GNP, calorie intake, telephones, physicians, newspapers and radios . . . (all per capita) . . .) was divided by either the country's . . . literacy or . . . urbanisation score, whichever was higher.[15]

Whatever else this index measures ('wealth controlled for literacy'?), it is an empirical question as to whether it captures the extent to which 'frustration' exists within any given system. Even superficially, since the indices employed say nothing of the *distribution* of 'caloric intake', 'physicians' and so on, it seems most unlikely that they provide adequate measures of any of the concepts which are specified: indeed the overall inadequacy of the operationalisation speaks for itself.

Gurr's attempt to operationalise the concept of relative deprivation is rather more sophisticated, but equally suspect. Gurr employs six measures of *persisting deprivation* 'economic discrimination', 'political discrimination', 'potential separatism', 'dependence on private foreign capital', 'religious cleavages' and 'lack of educational opportunity') and six measures of *short-term deprivation* ('short-term trends in trade value', 'inflation', changes in 'GNP growth rates', 'adverse economic conditions', 'new restrictions on political participation and representation', and 'new value-depriving policies of governments'.[16]

Clearly, the various measures which Gurr cites cover a wide range of phenomena and all of them seem intuitively to be related to his notion of relative deprivation. What is *not* clear from Gurr's analysis however, is the precise *way* in which those measures are related to relative deprivation. Gurr claims that the twelve measures cited above provide 'a set of cross-nationally comparable indices of conditions that *by inference cause* pervasive and intense types of deprivation'.[17] In other words, Gurr makes deliberate use of a tautology by *defining* his twelve indices to be *causes* of 'relative deprivation'. It is again, however, an *empirical* question as to whether there is in fact a causal relationship between these indices and the actual extent of 'relative deprivation', and since Gurr himself does not have the data necessary to *test* for these relationships, we only have his *assertion* (or in terms of the above quotation, his 'inference') to support the contention that 'relative deprivation', or 'RD', is indeed caused by the twelve variables which he cites.

This assertion, however, raises two important and highly problematic questions. The first question concerns the comparative status of, on the one hand, 'variables which *cause* RD' (the twelve indices of 'short term' and 'persisting' deprivation which we specified above), and on the other, 'variables which mediate and supplement the impact of RD upon civil strife' (the four additional variables specified in Figure 2.1: legitimacy, coercive potential, social-structural facilitation and institutionalisation). Why, it must be asked, does Gurr include political and economic discrimination, potential separatism, capital dependence, religious cleavage and lack of educational opportunity as indicators (or 'asserted/inferred' causes) of 'persisting deprivation', and yet *fail* (in his 'revised causal model of civil strife' – see Figure 2.1) to include 'legitimacy' and 'coercive potential' as indicators of such deprivation? Can it not be 'inferred' that a government or regime either with a low level of 'legitimacy' or with a high level of 'coercive potential' is *also* likely to arouse feelings of 'relative deprivation' among the population of a given political system since both of these conditions are likely to depress perceived value capabilities'?

Given that such inferences *can* be made, a fundamental weakness of Gurr's analysis becomes apparent: *it provides no systematic theoretical or statistical basis for differentiating between those systemic characteristics which can be 'inferred' to 'cause' relative deprivation, and those which cannot.* Gurr's analysis does not identify the theoretical or empirical boundary beyond which it is *not* possible to infer that a particular systemic characteristic

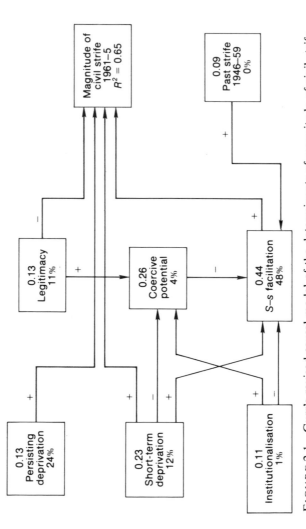

FIGURE 2.1 Gurr's revised causal model of the determinants of magnitude of civil strife

Source: T. Gurr, 'A Causal Model of Civil Strife', in Feierabend *et al.*, *Anger, Violence and Politics* (Englewood Cliffs, N.J.: Prentice-Hall, 1972) p. 208.

causes RD. His method of differentiation is based entirely on his own assertion, and as such the utility of his analysis is highly contentious. While the principle of 'assertion' *can* perform a useful function in comparative political enquiry (notably, if the assertion in question calls for data which is not currently available, or if it entails a proposition whose validity is agreed upon by other analysts), *Gurr's* use of it in differentiating between what can and what cannot be inferred to cause RD, means that *almost any variable* which future research might demonstrate to have a strong influence upon 'civil strife' or 'political violence' *can* be 'inferred' (by Gurr) to do so only because that variable first 'causes' RD. What this in turn implies, of course, is that despite his attempts – in the form of his statistical models – to avoid accusations of a tautological explanation of violent political behaviour, Gurr's analysis in fact remains wide open to such criticisms.

The second problem associated with the 'inferences' which Gurr makes in relation to the 'causes' of RD is that Gurr's quantitative analysis in a sense provides no more empirical support for the proposition that 'relative deprivation causes civil strife' than it does for a number of other hypotheses. In the same way that Gurr 'infers' that discrimination, capital dependence and so on 'cause' relative deprivation, which in turn produces civil strife, it can also be 'inferred' that high levels of discrimination, and capital dependence increase, for example, the 'system potential for mobilisation by revolutionary ideologies'. (This phrase is my own, but I can think of several more, some of them extremely silly, which could be substituted in its place.) I do not intend to pursue the possible theoretical and empirical relevance of this notion of 'potential for mobilisation', firstly, because I do not have access to the data which would be necessary to test its explanatory power cross-nationally, and secondly, because I am aware of the danger of tautologically attributing all manifestations of political violence or civil strife to the incidence of 'potential mobilisation by revolutionary ideologies'. I am convinced that Gurr would have been well advised to have treated the concept of relative deprivation in a similar manner.

WEAKNESSES AND LIMITATIONS OF THE NON-PSYCHOLOGICAL CAUSAL APPROACHES

Although in the preceding section we examined the limitations of the frustration-deprivation thesis in considerable detail, we do *not* intend to investigate the inadequacies of the *non*-psychological approaches to political violence and instability in quite such a comprehensive manner because the findings derived from this latter approach (as we saw in Chapter 1) are so numerous and so varied. Rather, in this section we will confine our discussion to a review of the most important *general* weaknesses which are evident within the non-psychological analyses.

The first inadequacy of many of these investigations again concerns the problem of possible 'disparity' between concepts and indicators. A good example of 'disparity' in this context concerns Deutsch's notion of 'social mobilisation', a concept which has been used in many subsequent empirical and theoretical analyses.[18]

Deutsch's *conceptual definition* of social mobilisation is that it is '. . . the process by which major clusters of old social, economic and psychological commitments are eroded or broken and people become available for new patterns of socialisation and recruitment'.[19] The *operationalisation* of this definition, however, consists in aggregating various measures of *socio-economic change* – for example, changes in urbanisation, changes in education levels, and changes in the extent of communications networks. Now, of course, it *may* be the case that these indicators do provide a perfectly satisfactory means of measuring the extent to which '. . . major clusters . . . of commitments are eroded or broken', but equally, this is essentially an *empirical question* which remains untested given the absence of cross-national survey data which might enable the *direct* measurement of 'commitment' breakdown. Clearly, if the potential gap between concepts and indicators is to be firmly and convincingly closed, then either considerable research effort needs to be devoted to cross-national surveys which might enable such 'empirical questions' to be 'empirically' evaluated, or else concepts need to be redefined in such a manner that they correspond rather more closely to currently available indicators. Given the limited resources which were available for this particular study, in the later part of the present analysis we in fact pursue this second alternative. While this expedient *may* entail some loss of theoretical sophistication (and I am not convinced that this follows inevitably), I would argue that such a loss is both necessary and desirable if the empirical findings which are reported in later chapters are to provide a systematic or reliable basis for predicting cross-national patterns of political instability.

The justification for this apparently atheoretic – and to some, heretical – position is simple. As long as quantitative analysts continue to make questionable assumptions about the relationship between concepts and indicators, we shall continue to be uncertain as to how far a particular empirical finding provides support for a particular theoretical proposition. In the present situation we are faced with two alternatives. Either we continue to undertake analysis at a high level of abstraction and remain fundamentally uncertain as to whether the empirical analysis we undertake 'really' tests the theoretical propositions which have been advanced, or we cease to claim that fairly rudimentary empirical results constitute support for sophisticated theoretical propositions. It is my strong opinion that, given the present state of quantitative comparative politics, political scientists would perhaps be better advised to adopt the second strategy, and recognise that at present we can effectively test only comparatively rudimentary theoretical propositions. At least in these circumstances the boundary between those generalisations which do enjoy empirical support and those which do not might be more clearly delineated.

The second major set of problems associated with the non-psychological approach to political violence and instability concerns the *unreliability of the statistical findings* which some of these studies report. The first source of this unreliability is related to the fact that several of the investigations cited in Chapter 1 conduct their quantitative analysis upon extremely small statistical samples. The Schneiders, for example, investigate only twenty countries in their attempt to operationalise Huntington's notion of institutionalisation, and Hurwitz, in his attempt to identify the sources of democratic stability, also examines only twenty.[20]

Now of course, the use of a small sample is not of itself necessarily problematic. However, when such a usage is combined (as it is in the Schneiders' and in Hurwitz's analyses) with (1) a lack of attention to the problem of multicollinearity, (2) a complete unawareness of the importance of parameter *significance*,[21] and (3) the need to use *corrected R^2* instead of R^2 in small sample situations,[22] then the results obtained from performing fairly sophisticated multidimensional statistical operations upon so small a sample must be treated with extreme suspicion. In consequence, the Schneiders' conclusion that 95 per cent of the variance in their index of political violence is explained by 'institutionalisation', 'social mobilisation' and 'economic development' and Hurwitz's conclusion that 63 per cent of the variance of democratic stability is explained by 'multipartism', 'religious homogeneity', 'level of economic development', 'democratic attainment', 'rate of economic change', and 'ethnic-linguistic homogeneity', cannot realistically be interpreted as contributing very much to our understanding of the genesis of political instability. If empirical 'findings' are to be of any value whatsoever, particularly if powerful statistical techniques such as multiple regression are to be employed, than adequate attention *must* be paid to parameter significance, the danger of multicollinearity, and sample size.

A second source of statistical unreliability in the non-psychological studies stems from the use of time series data and the fact that in most instances insufficient allowance is made for the special problems which the use of those data entails. (Time series analyses of instability have been undertaken in four of the studies cited in Chapter 1.)[23] While it is perfectly normal practice to analyse time series data using multiple regression (or indeed any other sort of correlative) techniques, as Hibbs has shown, serially correlated error (which is a characteristic feature of time series regression and correlation models) can in fact grossly distort any statistical findings which are obtained from empirical observations, and can consequently lead to spurious theoretical inferences.[24]

None of the four studies referred to above, however, pays the slightest attention to the possible problems of serial correlation. Snyder and Tilly's study of 'collective violence' in France 1830–1960, for example, although quite adequate (1) in its use of indicators, (2) in its concern with statistical significance, and (3) in terms of the size of the sample which is investigated, undertakes no systematic investigation of the error terms from the various regression equations which are run. It can only be assumed, therefore, that serially correlated error may have played a confounding role in their statistical analysis, and in consequence the theoretical value of their empirical findings must be questioned.

While I make no pretence to have *demonstrated* that all previous (non-psychological) quantitative analyses of political violence and instability either (1) suffer from the concept/indicator disparity or (2) provide statistically unreliable findings, I would, nonetheless, argue that most of these analyses *are*, to varying degrees, subject to either or both of these criticisms. The only analysis which recognises these two problems, and systematically attempts to avoid them, is Hibbs' investigation of *Mass Political Violence*,[25] the principal findings of which are reported in Table 1.3 in Chapter 1. I do not intend to examine the strengths and limitations of Hibbs' analysis in detail here, however, since I have investigated the adequacy of the core propositions of his model in considerable detail elsewhere.[26] It is, nonetheless, worth providing a brief outline of the main thrust of my earlier study: this is partly because Hibbs' work is sufficiently important in its own right to merit rather more detailed attention than the other investigations which we have mentioned, but also because of the implications which the methodological limitations of Hibbs' findings have for our own analysis in later chapters. It should be recognised from the outset, however, that the usual criticisms which can often be made of quantitative comparative analyses (weak R^2s, questionable techniques of parameter estimation, lack of parameter significance, disparity between concepts and indicators) cannot be fairly applied to Hibbs' very thorough investigation. Given the constraints of his data, the R^2s in Hibbs' models are good; care is taken to avoid under-identification, multicollinearity and non-random errors; adequate attention is paid to parameter variance; and concepts are precisely drawn to fit operational indicators.

Hibbs' analysis: potential limitations[27]

Perhaps the most important feature of Hibbs' study is its use of non-recursive causal modelling techniques[28] which permit the simultaneous estimation of *reciprocal* causal linkages. This is an important innovation in the cross-national analysis of violence and instability since it attempts to resolve, instead of sidestepping as most previous research does, the problem of the relationship between correlation and causal inference.

The nub of this problem centres on how a given correlation coefficient[29] between two variables X and Y is to be interpreted. Statistical evidence can never establish causality: it can only be employed in either support or refutation of some proposition which hypothesises a directional causal linkage between two variables. In short, the problem is really one of the direction of causal arrows. Given the existence of a particular correlation, any one of four possible interpretations can be made:

(i) Y is causually influenced by X.

$$[Y \longleftarrow X]$$

(ii) X is causally influenced by Y.

$$[X \longleftarrow\!\!\!\!\!\longrightarrow Y]$$

(iii) X and Y simply co-occur and are both causally dependent upon some third variable(s) Z.

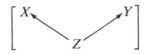

(iv) X and Y are reciprocally related, that is to say, X affects Y and, either simultaneously or with some timelag, Y affects X.

$$[X \rightleftharpoons Y]$$

Clearly, with some types of data or with certain variables the problem of interpretation disappears. The absurdity of concluding from a correlation between age and height that age is causally influenced by height (no matter how good a *predictor* height might be) is readily apparent. In political science, however, and particularly in comparative politics, the direction of causal influence is rarely so obviously inferred: most bivariate correlations can be argued to support any one of the four types of interpretation mentioned above. In consequence, most analyses in fact circumvent the interpretation problem by implicit reference to the hypothetico-deductive paradigm: one of the two variables is, for whatever reason, denoted *dependent* (Y) and the observed correlation is argued to provide supporting evidence for the resultant empirical proposition that $Y = f(X)$. The resort to such a circuitous expedient does not, however, mask the fact that the correlation provides equally good supporting evidence for the proposition that $X = f(Y)$. Purely on the basis of a correlation coefficient, the direction of causality cannot be established: it is only possible to corroborate a proposition which hypothesises that one of the variables is dependent.

There are basically two alternative, rather more respectable, ways of resolving the interpretation problem. One is to obtain time series data in which the time intervals are sufficiently small to enable the analyst to discover if there is any tendency for one variable to precede the other (and, in the context of potentially reciprocal linkages, to compare the relative sizes of the correlations of the two variables at $t - 1$, t and $t + 1$).

The second alternative method of resolution – and this is the one adopted by Hibbs – is to employ non-recursive modelling techniques. By specifying an exactly identified system of simultaneous equations which fulfil the rank and order conditions,[30] it is possible to estimate the relative magnitudes of the linkages $Y = f(X)$ and $X = f(Y)$. The need for identification inevitably prevents the estimation of all potentially reciprocal linkages, since only a limited number of variables can be specified as endogenous. Accordingly, Hibbs is constrained to estimate the reciprocal linkages between only the core variable of his model: sanctions, internal war and collective protest.

Aggregated data

The principal methodological weakness of Hibbs' study, however, are related to his use of temporally aggregated cross-sectional data. (Hibbs' analysis is conducted over two ten-year time intervals, 1948–57 and 1958–67.) The cross-sectional nature of the data does not of itself necessarily pose any severe problems. As Hibbs points out,

> cross-section data tend to measure long run and other effects that are not observable in . . . time series. . . . [Moreover] . . . short duration time series simply cannot pick up the effects of such variables as regime type, levels of institutionalisation, cultural differentiation. . . . These variables . . . do not change much in the short run, and without variance, estimation precision and causal inference are not feasible.[31]

The justification employed here certainly applies to the sort of variables which Hibbs mentions. However, for variables which vary considerably on annual or even monthly basis, such as the political event variables which form the core of Hibbs' model, such as justification ignores the fact that full advantage is not being taken of those data which are available. Nonetheless, since it is impossible to apply any sort of causal modelling techniques to data which is in part time series and in part cross-sectional, Hibbs, with reason, confines his investigation to cross-sectional forms of analysis.

In collapsing a country's monthly or annual scores on a

particular variable into a ten-year aggregate, however, it is possible to generate somewhat perverse causal inferences from any given set of statistical findings. Consider a situation in which one variable consistently occurs two or three months after the occurrence of another variable. That is to say, if the data were in monthly time series form, the two variables would only appear to be related if the necessary lags were incorporated into the relevant models. With data which has been aggregated over a ten-year period, the two variables will still appear to be related, but the lagged effect is clearly impossible to identify, and consequently there is a considerable danger than the 'wrong' variable (if it suits the analyst's theoretical argument) may be identified as dependent. Equally clearly, such an incorrect identification of the direction of the relationship will undoubtedly lead to unsubstantiated, if not faulty, theoretical conclusions; particularly when it is considered that the ten-year aggregate correlation will certainly be as high as, if not higher than, the lagged monthly correlation.

The fundamental potential weakness of Hibbs' methodology, then, is to be found at the interface of his modelling and his data: the time aggregates over which the analysis is conducted are too large, and in consequence insufficient allowance is made for the possibility that the occurrences of the dependent variables may actually *precede* the occurrences of the independent variables. In short, Hibbs' findings may rest on the existence of $t + n$ correlations. Clearly, time series analysis offers an alternative method of identifying the general direction of non-reciprocally related linkages and of disentangling the effects of reciprocal causation, without the danger of the malinterpretation of hidden $t + n$ correlations.

It was precisely such a detailed time series analysis which the present writer undertook in the study cited previously. The most important conclusion suggested by that analysis was that Hibbs' conclusions concerning the interrelationships between the *political event variables* of sanctions, internal war, collective protest and coups simply did not stand up to detailed time series analysis. More specifically, *it was found that the estimation of interrelationships between such event variables can only provide misleading conclusions when cross-sectional data involving relatively large time aggregates* (in the case of Hibbs' investigation, two ten-year periods) *are used*. Hibbs' analysis, it would appear, not only mis-specifies the probable direction of a number of causal relationships, but also fails to recognise that there are very considerable *regional* variations,[32] in the patterns of interrelationship between the four event variables which form the statistical and theoretical core of his model.

The implications of these conclusions for the empirical analysis which we undertake in later chapters are considerable. They mean firstly that, since the dimensions or types of instability which we define in Chapters 3 and 4 fundamentally involve event variables, and since cross-sectional analyses of event variables can only mislead, when we attempt to examine the interrelationships between the different types of instability, we can only make meaningful estimates of the strength and form of those interrelationships if we use *time series* data. This need to use time series data for *event* variables, however, is complicated by the fact that the data which are necessary for testing hypotheses which relate to the socio-economic and structural correlates of instability are *not* available in suitable time series form. In consequence, the ensuing empirical chapters operate on data at two general levels of temporal aggregation: the interrelationships between the dimensions of instability which we define in the following two chapters are examined using time series data (Chapter 5), and the systemic correlates of each dimension are examined using cross-sectional data (Chapters 7 and 8). The second implication is that *in any empirical investigation of political instability, region needs to be considered as a fundamentally important control variable.* For this reason, all of our subsequent empirical analysis examines both the global and the region-specific patterns of interrelationship (1) between the various dimensions of instability which are specified in the next two chapters, and (2) between instability and the exogenous correlates which we identify in Chapter 6.

Before we move on from our review of the existing literature, however, one more qualification is necessary: we need to offer some explanation for the inconsistent and conflicting findings which we reported in Chapter 1. To be sure, not all the contradictions can be resolved: the role of corruption as a source of both stability and instability, for example, must remain unanalysed in the absence of suitable crossnational data. There is, nonetheless, an important methodological principle at work which offers useful insights into the genesis of a number of these apparent inconsistencies.

A METHODOLOGICAL CAVEAT: CONTRADICTORY
INFERENCES FROM HARMONIOUS EMPIRICAL
UNIFORMITIES

As we saw in the previous chapter, empirical support has been claimed, by different analysts, for a number of contradictory hypotheses, hypotheses which principally concern the role of certain socio-economic variables as correlates of political stability and instability. These variables were identified in Chapter 1, but for the purposes of exposition we will focus here upon the *hypothesised role of urbanisation*. For Lipset, for example, increases in the level of *urbanisation* are likely to elicit greater political *stability*; for the Feierabends, on the other hand, such increases are considered to increase the probability of *instability*. How is it that such contradictory conclusions can both receive apparent empirical support?

The resolution to this particular problem in fact lies in recognising that, as Figure 2.2 indicates, there are two different types of data and two different types of causal inference or interpretation. The meaning of the terms 'levels' and 'changes in levels' in Figure 2.2, given the examples cited, are self-evident. An example of a *static* interpretation would be 'countries with high levels of urbanisation also tend to have high levels of political stability'. An example of a dynamic interpretation would be 'increases in the level of urbanisation tend to produce increases in the level of political stability'.

If there were a one-to-one correspondence between types of inference and types of data (for example if it was the case that 'levels' data could only lead to 'static' inferences, and that only 'changes in levels' data could lead to 'dynamic' inferences), the

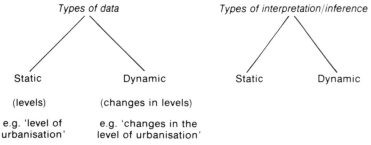

FIGURE 2.2   Types of data and types of theoretical inference

disagreement over the role of urbanisation as a source of stability or instability could easily be resolved. The problem, however, is that there are a large number of analysts whÒ argue that it is in fact possible to draw *dynamic* inferences from (static) 'levels' data.

The basis of this stems from the nature of the estimated coefficient, $\hat{\beta}$, in the linear equation $Y = \hat{\alpha} + \hat{\beta}X + \varepsilon$, where Y and X are two cross-sectional (static) *levels* variables, $\hat{\alpha}$ is the estimated intercept, and ε is a randomly distributed error term. Figure 2.3 describes the implicit model used by Lipset in his analysis of the relationship between urbanisation and political *stability*.

Since $\hat{\beta}$ by definition provides an indication of the estimated change in Y (stability) given a unit change in X (urbanisation), and since $\hat{\beta}$ in Figure 2.3 is positive, Lipset draws a 'dynamic' inference (about *change*) from 'static' data (about *levels*) and predicts that if the level of urbanisation increases in any given country, then that country's level of stability will also increase; in other words, *large increases in urbanisation will produce proportionately large increases in stability*.

If we now consider Figure 2.4, however, which describes the Feierabends' implicit model of the relationship between urbanisation and *in*stability, it can be seen that, using data which is in part dynamic (changes in the level of urbanisation) and in part static (the level of political instability), an entirely different conclusion is suggested.

The *static* inference which is suggested by the Feierabends' analysis is that countries which experience relatively large increases in urbanisation will also tend to experience relatively high levels of *in*stability. (It should be noted that this is essentially a *static*

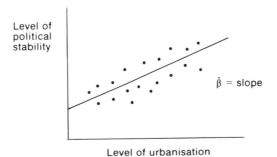

FIGURE 2.3 Implicit model used by Lipset in order to establish the relationship between urbanisation and stability

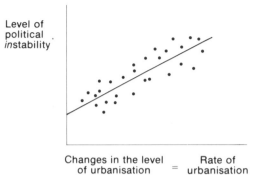

FIGURE 2.4 Implicit model used by the Feierabends in order to establish the relationship between urbanisation and instability

interpretation of Figure 2.4: it does not make use of the concept of $\hat{\beta}$.)[33] *In other words, large increases in urbanisation will produce a proportionately high level of instability.*

We now have two propositions, therefore, both of which claim empirical support.

I Large increases in urbanisation will produce proportionately large increases in stability (dynamic interpretation of static levels data).

II Large increases in urbanisation will produce a proportionately high level of instability (static interpretation of data which is partly static and partly dynamic.)

Now, although these two propositions appear to predict contradictory outcomes, if it is recognised that the dependent variable in proposition I (increases in stability) is slightly different from the dependent variable in proposition II (level of instability) then it can be seen that the empirical observations upon which the two propositions are based are entirely consistent: it is almost certainly the case that countries with low levels of urbanisation (and therefore, given Lipset's findings, with low levels of stability) also tend to experience the highest rate of increase in urbanisation (and therefore, given the Feierabends' findings, tend to have the highest levels of instability). Similarly, countries with high levels of urbanisation (and therefore, with high levels of stability) also tend to experience the lowest rate of increase in urbanisation (and therefore, the lowest levels of instability). In this sense, the initial observations are not inconsistent. Oversimplifying a little, but not to the detriment of the argument,

> there is one group of countries which experiences high stability, a high level of urbanisation and a low rate of urbanisation growth; and another group of countries which experience low stability, a low level of urbanisation and a high rate of urbanisation growth.

Since the original empirical observations are mutually consistent, then, it follows that the apparently inconsistent predictions which propositions I and II engender are essentially the consequence of the different *interpretations* which Lipset and the Feierabends make of their respective findings: Lipset, as we have seen, makes a dynamic inference, while the Feierabends make a static inference. As a result, opposite conclusions are arrived at. The fact that these different interpretations lead to such a confused situation has two important implications. In the first place, it demonstrates the danger of Lipset's practice of drawing dynamic inferences from static data, particularly when those inferences conflict with *static* inferences derived from data which are (at least in part) dynamic. Secondly, it illustrates the need to employ considerable semantic precision when dynamic inferences are drawn from static observations: as we suggested before, a close examination of propositions I and II indicates that the dependent variable in the first proposition is not identical to that in the second.

SUMMARY

In this chapter we have attempted to identify the major weaknesses and limitations which characterise most previous analyses of political instability. The factor analysts of the *dimensional school* were criticised on the grounds that their results are frequently mutually contradictory and that their statistical approach prevents them from differentiating between (1) empirical correlations which are the result of two variables being a part of the same underlying phenomenon, and (2) empirical correlations which are the consequence of two variables being *causally* related. We also attempted to show that the proponents of the *psychologically oriented approach* to the analysis of political violence and instability not only underestimate the 'rational choice' aspect of collective political violence, but also provide explanations of such behaviour which move dangerously close to tautology by virtue of the fact that they fail to define the theoretical or empirical boundaries of those structural phenomena which may be 'inferred' to cause 'systemic frustration' or 'relative deprivation'.

We then turned to the *non-psychologically oriented approaches* to instability, which were criticised largely in terms in the inadequacy of their statistical methodologies – particularly with regard to their lack of attention to parameter significance and their extravagant use of sophisticated statistical techniques in inappropriate circumstances.

Doubt was even cast upon the reliability of some of the findings reported by Hibbs, despite the fact that his analysis consistently avoids the more obvious substantive and methodological errors and omissions which other investigations tend to make. Recent research suggests that an analysis of the interrelationships between political *event* variables which only uses temporally aggregated cross-section data, can produce distorted substantive conclusions which ignore the underlying structure of lag and lead effects, effects which can only be captured through the use of time series analysis. For this reason, in the subsequent analysis of political event variables which we undertake in Chapter 5, we intend to employ time series as well as cross-section data.

Finally, we attempted to explain how 'dynamic' interpretations of 'static' (levels) data can lead to contradictory theoretical conclusions if these dynamic interpretations are contrasted with 'static' interpretations of 'dynamic' (changes in levels) data.

Perhaps the most important observation which can be made, however, is that despite the existence of a considerable body of theoretical and empirical literature aimed at identifying the sources of political instability, the *evidence* which has been amassed in support of the various theoretical propositions is not particularly convincing. This is not to say that the theories themselves are necessarily inadequate but that there are several good reasons for supposing that the empirical findings which have been cited are based on rather questionable assumptions. We will report our own findings – which seek to avoid such assumptions – in later chapters. Initially, however, we return to theoretical matters and address the problems of achieving a satisfactory definition of political instability.

3 Problems of Defining Political Instability

Scientific attempts to 'explain' either a particular phenomenon or a set of phenomena invariably seek to avoid any tautological connection between the dependent and independent variables under analysis. Tautology nonetheless has an indispensable role to play in the process of scientific enquiry in the sense that all definitions are deliberately tautological statements; they involve assigning a specific meaning to a particular concept. Any given definition (a tautology), however, is not amenable to empirical verification or refutation – definitions are starting points for explanations, not explanations in themselves – and consequently the value of that definition is dependent upon its acceptability to the scientific community and the extent to which that community can use it in empirical research. This chapter begins by reviewing a number of meanings which have been assigned to the term 'political instability' and examine their weaknesses and limitations. It then attempts to identify the main elements which, in my opinion, need to be incorporated into a satisfactory definition of political instability. In the next chapter, an alternative definition of instability will be proposed and a general method of operationalising it is outlined.

PREVIOUS DEFINITIONS: CONTINUITY/DISCONTINUITY, FREQUENCY AND UNCERTAINTY

As we saw in Chapter 1, until the mid 1960s, political stability was generally defined in terms of the persistence or *continuity* of certain types of political system: on Lipset's definition, systems which experienced uninterrupted democratic government or uninterrupted totalitarian government over a given number of years were characterised as stable; those which fluctuated between the two were characterised as unstable. This approach found empirical expression in Almond and Verba's 1963 *Civic Culture* study,[1] in which an attempt was made to identify the major attitudinal and normative underpinnings of *democratic* stability. The analysis was nonetheless still based on Lipset's assumption that political systems could be divided into four categories – stable and unstable democracies and stable and unstable non-democracies or dictatorships – and that countries which remained either as democracies or as non-democracies for some minimum time period could be defined as 'stable'. More recently, theorists such as Field and Castles have developed Lipset's continuity/discontinuity notion by defining a stable polity as one which maintains the same broad institutional structure over time.[2]

This emphasis on continuity has been much less pronounced in the analysis conducted by the empirically oriented *frequency school*.[3] Rather, the empiricist approach operates upon the assumption that instability (now a continuous rather than a dichotomous concept) varies in direct proportion to the frequency of occurrence of certain types of political event. For the empiricists, instability is defined in a much wider context than simply in terms of fluctuations between democratic and non-democratic systems of government. During any given time period, the more coups, the more government changes, the more demonstrations, riots, outbreaks of guerrilla warfare and deaths from political violence which a country experiences, the more *unstable* it is considered to be; *stability* consists in the non-occurrence of these various 'destabilising' behaviours or 'events'.

Conventional political science, then, has defined instability primarily in terms of either (1) discontinuity of system, or (2) the frequency of 'unstable' events. A third and rather different approach is that of the political journalist. The 'journalistic' approach does not operate upon the basis of a *formal* definition of instability at all but it nonetheless incorporates two very useful notions which more rigorous political analyses would perhaps do well to take into account. The first of these is an emphasis on relatively short term *political situations*. While the 'discontinuity' and 'frequency' schools examine lengthy time periods of up to several decades, the political journalist's temporal focus is generally restricted to a period of a few days, weeks or, at the most, months. The journalist, in so far as he is interested in political instability at all, is concerned not with dividing countries into 'stable' and 'unstable' groupings (although his approach does not preclude this possibility), but with describing 'the political *situation*' in a particular country at a particular point in time as being more or less 'unstable'. This is not to suggest that political journalists deny the importance of long term political stases or changes, but simply to emphasise the difference between the journalist's and the political scientist's temporal focus.

The journalist's second major contribution is his association of instability with *uncertainty*. While the empiricist can only discuss instability after recording and analysing certain clearly observable types of event, the journalist makes reference to instability on the basis of far less tangible evidence and on the basis, usually, of only one event occurring. In Portugal in March 1974, for example, six weeks or so prior to the army takeover, the BBC correspondent in Lisbon repeatedly described the 'Portuguese political situation' as 'unstable'. Clearly, this was not because the armed forces had actually effected a *coup* – a change had not actually taken place – but because the correspondent himself (along with other political observers) expected that 'something' was going to happen in the next few weeks: he, like everyone else, was uncertain as to what would transpire and when it would occur, but, nonetheless, developments of some sort were anticipated.[4] This expectation of change within the near future, this uncertainty about the course of political events, is the basis of the journalistic notion of instability and we will return to it in more detail later. Despite its extreme intangibility, it is an important aspect of what is conventionally understood by 'political instability' and in consequence it would seem reasonable to argue that some attempt should be made to incorporate at least a part of it into a more rigorous definition of instability.[5]

LIMITATIONS AND WEAKNESSES OF PREVIOUS
DEFINITIONS

The principal deficiency of the political sociologists' 'continuity' definition of stability as the persistence of system – or regime – type, lies in the very typology which is employed as a precursor to deciding whether or not continuity of type exists. It is readily apparent to the most casual observer that the post-colonial era has seen the emergence of many different types of political systems, and, in consequence, to classify systems merely as 'democracies' or 'dictatorships' can only serve to oversimplify the diversity of the contemporary world. This is not to say that typology *per se* is not a necessary prerequisite to meaningful analysis, but that the simple division of all regimes or systems into either democracies or dictatorships is clearly inadequate. A far more satisfactory classification scheme has been proposed by Blondel who argues convincingly that the *norms* of a political system or (as we will see later) of a *regime* should be defined not by reference to a dichotomy (democracy or dictatorship) but by reference to a three-dimensional space.

The coordinates of the space, Blondel suggests, are, firstly, an *oligarchic-democratic axis* (what proportion of the members of the system participate meaningfully in decision making?); secondly, a *radical-conservative axis* (what are the *goals* of the regime: do the policies pursued by the government seek to reinforce or to change the *status quo*?); and thirdly, a *liberal-authoritarian axis* (how does the government attempt to achieve its policy goals – by consent or coercion?). While it is possible in principle for any particular system to be located anywhere within the space defined by these three axes, Blondel argues that *empirically* there are seven major types of political system or regime: 'authoritarian conservative', 'traditional conservative', 'liberal democratic', 'populist right', 'populist centre', 'populist left' and 'radical authoritarian'.[6]

A *change* from one type of regime to another is the consequence of a system undertaking significant movement along one or more of the dimensions of the space. Not all movement, however, is sufficient to produce a change: it is possible for *limited* movements to occur along any or all three axes without a change in regime type resulting. The difference between 'limited' and 'significant' is of course one of degree: unfortunately, at present none of the axes has been sufficiently developed theoretically to permit the quantitative identification of a specific critical point beyond which a change in regime type would inevitably ensue. As we will see later, however, Blondel has in fact made a series of judgemental assessments which enable the identification of critical regime changes for a large sample of nations over the period 1945–70. We will in fact return to the idea of a three-dimensional classification of system or regime type in this and in the next chapter. It is sufficient to note at this juncture that even if we are talking about stability simply as the persistence of system type, it is necessary to adopt a more sophisticated concept of 'system type' than just the 'democracy versus dictatorship' dichotomy.[7]

The second major limitation of the 'continuity' notion of stability or instability is its inability to recognise the possibility that there may be different *types* of instability. As we pointed out in Chapter 1, the continuity definition is insensitive to any form of instability beyond the important but crude idea of change of system type or 'institutional structure'. On Lipset's definition, for example, the UK must be characterised as a stable democracy, and, given his original four-fold classification, such a characterisation is perfectly sound. Essentially, however, such a definition (though it encapsulates an important aspect of what can be understood by stability) is too limited. It denies the possibility that a political system which (on the 'maintenance of institutional structure' criterion) is stable might experience a short *interlude* of comparative instability in the form of some major challenge to the regime. Consider, for example, the British General Strike of 1926. Despite the major challenge to the ruling class which the strike represented, according to the institutional continuity definition, the British political system has been stable throughout (at least) the twentieth century. Indeed, it is almost certainly the case that advocates of the continuity approach would wish to argue that the British political system's ability to weather the storm of the General Strike in fact evidences its basic stability. (It might be observed, of course, that the continuity theorist must concoct some such interpretation of the strike, since on his definition Britain has already been defined as 'stable'.) It seems to me that this interpretation of the strike is fundamentally misleading. During the period of the General Strike there were such enormous strains and divisions in the British body politic that I would want to describe the political situation at the time as 'politically unstable'. That there was no break in institutional continuity does not convince me that the period of the General Strike was a stable one in British politics. Indeed, in my opinion it illustrates the fundamental limitation of the continuity definition – that the question of stability/instability is *not* linked solely to the maintenance of institutional pattern, but rather that it should also include some consideration of the instability associated with *challenges* to governments and to regimes during specific time periods, whether or not the particular institutional pattern persists over time.

In short, the experience of the British General Strike (and one might well derive the same conclusion from the events in Northern Ireland since 1969) highlights two related but nonetheless analytically distinct weaknesses of the continuity definition. Firstly, there are significant forms of behaviour quite apart from system change (in this context, politically motivated strikes and persistent terrorist activity) which are associated with political instability and which the continuity definition is obliged to ignore; and secondly, these different behaviours occur *at discrete points in time*. While I would not wish to describe the UK as an 'unstable democracy' on the basis of the example cited here, what the example demonstrates to me is that *since 1918* (Lipset's date) *the British political system has been more unstable during certain periods than it has during others*.

This may seen a startlingly unoriginal claim, but it bears considerable emphasis precisely because the continuity theorists implicitly deny its validity. We will return later on in the chapter to the consequences which it has for a satisfactory definition of instability.

The empirically oriented studies of the *frequency school* to some extent circumvent the limitations of the continuity approach. As we suggested before, instability is defined by reference to a whole range of behaviours, from strikes and demonstrations through to guerrilla warfare, constitutional changes, and *coups d'état*. As we indicated in Chapter 2, however, a considerable degree of confusion of definition has arisen as a result of the many applications of factor analytic techniques to the various instability indicators; applications which have produced several *contradictory* clusterings of variables. Moreover, since the proponents of the factor analytic approach have claimed that these clusterings represent the underlying dimensions of political instability (if indeed such dimensions exist at all), as we argued in Chapter 2, such a wealth of contradiction alone could be regarded as sufficient justification for disregarding the results of the various factor analyses. More importantly, however (as we also pointed out in Chapter 2) the factor analytic technique fails to distinguish between an empirical correlation which implies that two variables are part of some wider, underlying phenomenon (or dimension), and a correlation which is the result of a *causal* relationship between two analytically distinct variables. In short, the atheoretic sub-categories or dimensions of instability propounded by the frequency school are not only inconsistent; they are also based on a largely unsuitable data-analytic technique which produces operational measures of instability which enjoy a somewhat contentious philosophical pedigree.

The *journalistic* notion of instability as *uncertainty*, given the reporter's purposes, is perfectly adequate: uncertain political situations make good copy. However, a definition of political instability which has any scientific pretensions, that is to say a definition which is capable of repetitive and uniform operationalisation in diverse situations, must necessarily be of a more precise and rigorous nature. The journalistic definition, while it is extremely flexible, is equally impressionistic: the extent to which a correspondent describes any given situation as 'unstable' must inevitably be strongly coloured (1) by his own individual biases, (2) by the network of personal contact upon which he relies for his information, and (3) by the ideological orientation of the media outlet which employs him. Such intangibles do not lend themselves easily to more formal enquiry. Nonetheless, all this is not to suggest that the notion of uncertainty is without utility; rather, that its lack of any *systematic* basis at present precludes its use in academic research.

There are, then, specific criticisms which can be levelled at each of the current definitions of instability: the continuity definition ignores other relevant behaviours; the frequency approach examines these other behaviours but groups them together in a confused and unsatisfactory manner; and the journalistic notion is insufficiently precise. At a more general level, however, all of these definitions are somewhat tainted by what has been variously labelled 'ethnocentrism' or 'culture bias'; the tendency to develop concepts on the basis of one's own cultural experience and to apply them wholesale both to similar and to alien cultures, thereby producing either a distorted or an irrelevant view of the latter.[8] Clearly, this is a criticism which has, on occasion, been rather glibly applied to a large part of the output of Western political sociology, but in this case it is criticism which is fairly well directed.

The frequency approach, for example, rests upon what we shall call the *frequency fallacy*; the assumption that *identical frequencies of a particular event or set of events in different countries denote identical levels of instability*. This in turn implies that *individual events of equal intensities, though they might occur in different countries at different points in time, are equally 'destabilising' for the respective systems in which they occur.* This is unsatisfactory for a number of reasons. Firstly, such a generalised approach fails to take into account the different cultural and structural conditions which exist in different countries: a riot of a given intensity (which involves 10,000 people and does £500,000 damage), is clearly going to have different implications for political stability if it occurs in a country which regularly has riots of equivalent or even greater intensity that if it occurs in a country which has not had a riot for decades. The example provided is undoubtedly extreme, but the principle is of general significance: similar events are of different importance in different countries, because of the different system *contexts* in which they occur. Secondly, the approach assumes that similar events which occur in the same country at different points in time are of equal destabilising significance. Again, the objection to such an assumption is obvious: a riot, say, which occurs towards the end of a series of riots of even greater intensity has different implications for the stability of the system from a similar riot which occurs after a protracted period of civil order.

In short, the frequency notion of instability fails to address a problem which is at the heart of quantitative comparative politics: the question of the cross-national comparability of raw frequency scores. The instability of a political system does *not necessarily* vary in direct proportion to the frequency of (what most political scientists would probably agree are) destabilising events. Rather the destabilising effect of any given event needs to be established by reference to the spatial and temporal context in which it occurs: what constitutes 'instability' in one country or one time period, does not necessarily constitute instability in another.

ELEMENTS OF A SATISFACTORY DEFINITION
OF INSTABILITY

There are, then, considerable limitations to existing definitions of political instability. While it is obvious that some of these do have distinct advantages – the frequency definition enjoys great precision, the journalistic definition, great flexibility, and the discontinuity definition, simplicity – it is now necessary to identify the miniumum features which a satisfactory definition of political instability should encompass; at the same time ensuring that the major weaknesses of these other definitions are avoided.

Clearly, on the basis of the foregoing discussion, an adequate definition must avoid treating stability/instability as a simple dichotomy, but rather should see it as a continuous, relative phenomenon. Stability and instability are relative tendencies, not discrete states. Secondly, it should follow the journalistic notion of instability and recognise that since the level of instability within one country varies over time (and the validity of this proposition seems to be self evident), the time units employed in analysis must be based initially on relatively short term *political situations* of less than two or three months: it is only possible to talk meaningfully about the instability of a given system *at time t*, that is to say, at a particular point in time. (Once the instability of a system has been defined over a series of time points, it is then possible to additively aggregate the various instability scores for that system in order to obtain a composite instability index for some longer time period; but the first step essentially involves examining a series of shorter term 'situations'.)

A third feature of a satisfactory definition is that it should attempt to capture at least a part of the journalistic notion of instability as *uncertainty*. Ideally, this would involve a detailed specification of the cues upon which the political journalist bases his assessment of any given political situation. Unfortunately, not only does the political journalist jealously guard his sources of information (which alone would render such an exercise difficult) but any attempt at systematising those sources would face insurmountable problems arising from the differential degrees of access to information which obtain in different systems; 'Chinawatching' is a very different occupation from British or American political journalism.[9] However, while a general identification of cues is not feasible, as we will see later the notion of uncertainty or unpredictability can in fact be incorporated into a definition of instability to a limited extent.

Perhaps the most important feature of an adequate definition of instability, however, is the acknowledgement of the possibility that there are different *types* of instability. Inevitably, this begs the question of the nature of these different types. As we saw earlier, the proponents of the frequency school recognised this problem and sought a factor analytic solution to it. As we also saw, however, this not only involved the use of an unsuitable statistical technique but also produced a series of contradictory conclusions. Since empirically oriented studies have failed to produce a satisfactory typology, therefore, it seems logical to pursue a more theoretically oriented one.

In order to specify a typology of political instability it is initially necessary to pose the question: instability *of what*? Superficially the answer is engagingly simple: we are ultimately talking about the relative stability or instability of *political systems*. Again, however, a question is begged: what do we mean by 'system'? We could of course follow Easton, the father of systems analysis in political science, and define a system as a number of (non-monolithic) elements interacting with a defined boundary. Defining 'the *political*' as that which is concerned with 'the authoritative allocation of values',[10] we could in turn define an *unstable political situation* as one in which 'the interactions between or within the elements of a political system are *unpredictable* or *uncertain*'. While such a definition would doubtless be faithful to the tradition of the great abstract theorists (one has in mind Parsons and Easton as obvious examples), it would not only be so wide as to potentially include all forms of political behaviour but would also provide few, if any, clear guidelines for operationalisation; and we take it as axiomatic that a 'good' definition *should* provide such guidelines.

Clearly, if we are to use the notion of 'system' at all, we must be able to identify these 'elements' which compose the system. Among the obvious candidates at the level of the national political system we can list political parties, interest groups, the governmental bureaucracy, the government, the legislature, the judiciary, the military, students, primary associations such as kinship or tribal groups, policy outputs, opinion leaders, the attitudes, values and beliefs of the mass public and the communications media. However, it is clearly impractical to attempt to identify a series of conditions under which the behaviour of each of these elements could be described as 'relatively' unstable. It is therefore necessary to group the various elements together in some way in order to make the enterprise more manageable.

Easton in fact proposes three fundamental 'dimensions' of political systems, which subsume all these diverse elements. These are, in his lexicon, the 'objects of support': (1) the *'political authorities'* (the key decision makers who determine and are seen to determine policy during any given time period – the 'government'); (2) the *regime* (the legal and informal rules which govern the resolution of conflicts within the system); and (3) the *political community* ('that aspect of a political system that consists of its members seen as a group of persons bound together by a political division of labour').[11] While we would not argue that Easton is the ultimate source of authority on what constitutes a political system, this three-fold classification of its dimensions provides as sound a basis as any for a discussion of system instability, particularly in view of the relative ease with which the concepts of 'authorities' – or government – and 'regime' can be operationalised. Indeed it is the instability of these three elements of 'government', 'regime' and 'community', which we propose to investigate in some detail in this and in the next chapter.

CHANGES AND CHALLENGES

Having established, then, that our focus is the instability of *governments* (authorities), *regimes* and *political communities*, it is now necessary to identify the behaviour which might be associated with the three types of instability. These behaviours can in fact be divided into two categories – *changes* and *challenges* – yielding the six-fold classification identified in Figure 3.1.

The concept of a *change* in government, regime or community is a relatively simple one, and despite a few ambiguities, the change itself is relatively easy to observe. Given Hurwitz' definition of a

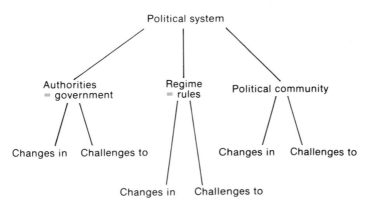

FIGURE 3.1   Six dimensions of political instability

'new' government, for example, as

> an administration which meets any one of the following criteria: (a) post-election formation; (b) change in the Prime Minister; (c) change in the party composition of the cabinet; and (d) an interelection resignation/reformation with the same Prime Minister and Cabinet composition.[12]

the identification of a *change* of *government* (in parliamentary democracies at least) is simple. Similarly, given Taylor and Hudson's more general notion of 'Regular Executive Transfers'[13] changes of government across *all* systems are not impossible to identify.

A change in *regime* can also be identified relatively easily given (say) Blondel's definition of type of regime, by reference to the movement of a system along one or more of the three axes of Blondel's regime space. Moreover, since Blondel has in fact provided annual codings of the regime norms of over 138 countries for the period since 1945, the identification of a change in norms poses no serious problems.

Changes in *political community*, on the other hand, are by their very nature less frequent than changes in either government or regime. As Easton points out, 'communities' change only when geographical boundaries change:

> Authorities typically come and go, regimes or constitutional orders may change. In both cases the (political) community may remain quite stable. If we take Metropolitan France alone as an example, in its community aspects it has experienced little change since the French Revolution aside from minor fluctuations at its geographic boundaries. But this is not equally the case for France's regimes which have undergone innumerable drastic transformations ... (the five Republics) ... Governmental changes ... at the leadership level ... have been too numerous to count easily.
>
> But political communities are capable of changing. This occurs at moments when the membership undergoes some subdivision indicating that whole groups have withdrawn their support from the pre-existing division of political labour. The American Civil War ... illustrates concretely what occurs with the cessation of the input of support.[14]

Change, however, is not the only form of systemic behaviour which constitutes instability: there can also be strong *challenges* to either government regime or community, which are *aimed* at effecting a change, but which may or may not actually achieve one. In a civilian regime, for example, any unsuccessful *coup d'état* represents a challenge to both that government and the regime – that is to say, it is a challenge both to the incumbent political authorities and to the rules which in that system structure the resolution of conflicts. While the failure of the attempted *coup* obviously means that no *change* as such necessarily takes place, it is clear that the system as a whole has experienced some measure of instability; it has experienced both a *governmental* and a *regime challenge*. Indeed, there is a whole range of behaviours which, in different circumstances, constitute challenges to government, regime or community: demonstrations, riots, politically motivated strikes, opposition motions of censure or no-confidence in the government, terrorist activity of various sorts, attempted *coups* and so on. The problem with all these behaviours, however, is that they cannot be easily compartmentalised into government challenge, regime challenge and community challenge categories. A riot, for example, may in some circumstances denote a challenge primarily to the regime (as in the Black South African townships in 1976), and in others (as in Northern Ireland in the early and mid 1970s), it may be concerned with a challenge both to the regime and to the political community as a whole.

Similarly, while a demonstration organised by the TUC against a Conservative government in Britain could well be regarded as a purely governmental challenge, a demonstration organised by the far Left would perhaps be better interpreted as a challenge to the entire liberal democratic regime. In short, similar events may in different contexts represent different types of challenge.

Given that these ambiguities extend to all the event variables which were mentioned previously, it is not possible to establish a general rule for the compartmentalisation of 'challenges' into 'governmental', 'regime' and 'community' boxes. Nonetheless, since challenges cover such a wide range of behaviour, *some* form of categorisation would be of considerable heuristic value. We could of course look to the various factor analyses which were cited earlier for guidance in this matter. As we have repeatedly asserted, however, the technique itself is of doubtful value in that regard, firstly because of its failure to distinguish between empirical relationships which denote causality and those which denote different manifestations of the same underlying phenomenon, and secondly, because it has furnished contradictory conclusions. The most sensible division of challenge behaviours (and I assert this not because it has any real empirical foundation but because to me it seems important) is a division that differentiates between behaviours which eschew the use or the threat of physical violence and those which embrace it. The division which is proposed here is outlined in Table 3.1. While this may still lead to occasional ambiguities (some bloodless *coups* and attempted *coups*, for example, do not, by definition, involve violence; people are occasionally killed or injured at demonstrations), such a division makes the crucial moral and (more important perhaps) motivational distinction between situations in which the perpetrators of a particular challenge behaviour hold the belief that the 'ends justify the means' and those in which they do not. Even if empirical support for the distinction is demanded (and I am firmly of the opinion that from a philosophical point of view, since we are talking about *definitions*, this is neither necessary nor indeed relevant), then the result of Hibbs' (1973) factor analysis can be cited: with the exception of riots (which Hibbs incorporates, along with strikes and demonstrations, into his 'collective protest' dimension), his violence/collective protest distinction corresponds

TABLE 3.1   Suggested indicators of changes and challenges[16]

Regime change	Changes in regime norms
	Changes in type of party system
	Changes in military–civilian status
Government change	Changes in the effective executive
	Cabinet changes
Community change	Successful acts of secession
Violent challenges	Assassinations, acts of guerrilla warfare and political terrorism
	Deaths from political violence
	Riots
	Attempted coups d'état
Peaceful challenges	'Political' strikes or strike threats
	Protest demonstrations
	Opposition motions of censure
	Anti-government speeches by opinion leaders

very closely to the violent challenge/peaceful challenge distinction outlined in Table 3.1.[15]

We are proposing, then, that a good definition of political instability should acknowledge the existence of at least five types of instability: government, regime and community *changes* and violent and peaceful *challenges* to either government regime or community, the three Eastonian 'objects of support'. Such a typology differs considerably both from the Lipset definition, which defines instability principally in terms of regime change, and from the factor analytic typologies of the frequency school, which (although they examine a suitably wide range of behaviour) offer classifications based on an inappropriate technique.

The final necessary feature of a satisfactory definition of instability is that the definition seeks as far as possible to avoid justifiable accusations of ethnocentrism, and yet at the same time is capable of uniform operationalisation across nations and time periods. It will be recalled that previous quantitative analyses of violence and instability were criticised for making the (culture-biased) assumption that a greater frequency of (what we may now call) change and challenge events invariably denoted greater instability. Each event, we argued (whether it involves a change or a challenge), should in fact be set in the temporal and spatial context in which it occurs, before its destabilising impact can be determined. We are suggesting, therefore, that there is a distinction between, on the one hand, the *general definition* of instability which the frequency school employs (the greater the frequency of changes and challenge, the greater the level of instability), and on the other hand, a *system specific definition*, which demands that each destabilising unstable event is set in the *context* of the system in which it occurs; that is to say, there is not necessarily a distinct relationship between frequency and the level of instability. The question as to how such a contextuation would be effected without violating the requirement of uniform operationalisation will be returned to in the next chapter, where a system specific definition of instability is in fact proposed.

SUMMARY

We have suggested, then, that there are three main types of definition of, or ways of describing, political instability: the 'continuity'/discontinuity of system definition of the political sociologists; the 'frequency' definition of the empiricists; and the 'uncertainty' definition of political journalism. Each of these definitions has specific weaknesses which we have outlined, but common to all of them is their failure to provide a satisfactory answer to the accusation of 'culture bias', a bias which in the case of the two 'academic' definitions is largely a function of their implicit rejection of the proposition that the occurrence of the same type of event in two different systems can have differential implications for the stability of those systems. This is not to say however, that previous definitions of instability do not have some useful features. Indeed, in the final part of this chapter we have selected certain features from each of these definitions in an attempt to identify what a satisfactory definition of political instability should encompass and what it should avoid. We argued that, firstly, it should regard stability/instability as a continuous, essentially comparative concept, the terms 'stability' and 'instability' representing the two ends of a continuum rather than a dichotomy; that secondly, an adequate definition should focus, at least initially, upon the stability or instability of relatively short term 'political situations'; that thirdly, it should attempt to make some allowance (even if it is not in the form of identifying a series of specific cues) for the journalistic notion of instability as uncertainty or unpredictability; and that fourthly, it should recognise the existence of different types of instability: in this case, we have argued that the most appropriate typology involves an examination of changes in, and challenges to, government, regime and community. Finally, since the assumption that instability varies in direct proportion to 'frequency' is both ethnocentric and unwarranted, an adequate definition should attempt to assess the destablising impact of any given change or challenge event by reference to the particular conditions of the country and time period in which it occurred.

In the next chapter, we shall still be concerned with the question of how instability can best be identified and measured. In general terms, we will argue that all 'destabilising' events should be seen as deviations from some system specific 'normality', a 'normality' which varies from country to country and from time period to time period. Not surprisingly, the alternative definition of instability which this implies attempts, as far as possible, to incorporate the five characteristics of a satisfactory definition which have just been identified.

4 A Definition and Operationalisation of Political Instability

As we suggested in Chapter 2, one of the most serious problems which empirical analyses of cross-national patterns of political violence and instability face is the question of disparity between theoretical concepts and operational indicators, a disparity which often requires that somewhat tortuous assumptions are made in order that concepts and indicators can be linked together. In this chapter we seek to specify a definition of instability in which the disparity between theoretical and operational constructs is kept at a minimum: our operationalisation is simply a detailed elaboration of the formal principles which our theoretical definition specifies, a situation which would appear to provide the correct relationship between concepts and indicators.

As we will see, the operationalisation which we propose relies on a series of statistical procedures for the identification of the level of instability in any given system at any given time, and we would argue that these *statistical* procedures in fact represent the only way of establishing a *uniform*, non-subjective set of criteria by which the temporal and spatial context of any given 'destabilising' event can be identified. (As we will also see, this context is of vital importance in any descriptive statement about the level of instability associated with a particular event.) What we will argue, therefore, is that the precise level of instability in any given country at time *t* can be best specified by *statistical* means; and in this sense, since it is only our operational definition which will overtly incorporate any statistical notions, it is only our operational definition which defines in precise *quantifiable* terms what we mean by instability in any given context. Nonetheless, the theoretical definition of instability which we propose remains the starting point of our analysis. Indeed, we will begin by positing our formal theoretical definition, turning then to discuss each of its

65

four main elements and their proposed empirical referents in detail.

> The extent to which a political system may be characterised as 'unstable' at any given point in time varies in direct proportion to the extent to which the occurrence or non-occurrence of changes in and challenges to the government, regime or community deviates from the previous system specific 'normal' pattern of regime/government/ community changes or challenges; a pattern which will itself vary over time.

'THE EXTENT TO WHICH A POLITICAL SYSTEM MAY BE CHARACTERISED AS "UNSTABLE" . . .'

Political instability is, or at least should be, an essentially comparative concept: it is a nonsense to characterise any system over any given time period as being either completely stable or completely unstable. The only meaningful descriptive statements about instability which can be made are (1) those which compare the relative degrees of instability of system *A* and system *B* during the same time period (for example, we might say that since 1960 the East German political system has been more stable than the Czechoslovak one); or (2) those which compare the relative stability/instability of the same system at different points in time (for example, governments in the French Fifth Republic have (to date) been more stable than the Fourth Republic); or (3) those which compare the relative stability of different systems at different points in time (for example, the Syrian political system in the 1950s was more unstable than that of the UK in the 1900s).

Even when it is asserted in isolation that a particular system over a given number of months or years was 'highly stable', or 'highly unstable' such a claim implicitly involves one of these three comparisons.

'. . . "UNSTABLE" AT ANY GIVEN POINT IN TIME . . .'

It was suggested in Chapter 3 that any discussion of instability should follow the example of the political journalists and focus upon 'political situations'. In this analysis we propose to effect such a focus by examining monthly time series data drawn primarily from the *World Handbook II* data collection. This choice of the 'month' as a unit of analysis (that is to say, as the duration of our initial 'political situation') is clearly somewhat arbitrary; it was selected as the optimal compromise between theoretical considerations (some 'unstable political situations' may not last longer than a week) and the constraints of practicable data analysis.[1] Nonetheless, such a choice enables us to assess the relative degree of instability of a number of political systems upon a *month to month* basis and therefore also upon the basis, if necessary, of time units of greater duration.

'... VARIES IN DIRECT PROPORTION TO ... THE OCCURRENCE OF CHANGES IN AND CHALLENGES TO THE GOVERNMENT REGIME OR COMMUNITY ...'

The concepts of change and challenge and of government and regime were also discussed in Chapter 3. It is necessary to point out here, however, that, for empirical reasons, although we have included 'community changes' in our formal definition, we do not intend to examine them further. (This is simply because no changes in political community in fact occurred during the period covered by our empirical investigations: had any such changes occurred, this aspect of instability *would* have been included in our analysis.) In consequence, we will confine ourselves to an analysis of, on the one hand, governmental and regime *change*, and on the other, of violent and peaceful *challenge*. In order to define precisely what we mean by '... changes in and challenges to government and regime', however, we must identify the operational indicators of the four dimensions of instability which we propose to use. These are outlined in Table 4.1.

Identifying indicators of regime change

In Chapter 3 we made reference to the concept of *regime* in relation to both Easton and Blondel. We also offered a brief theoretical definition of regime as 'the legal and informal rules (of a political system) which govern or structure the resolution of conflicts' (within that system), a definition which *in principle* covers both Easton's and Blondel's concepts. Moreover, we suggested that

TABLE 4.1   Proposed indicators of four dimensions of political instability

Regime change	Changes in Blondel norms (includes successful coups) Changes in party system Changes in military–civilian status
Government change	Changes in chief executive Executive adjustments (cabinet changes)
Violent challenge	Guerrilla attacks Riots Deaths from political violence Attempted coups (unsuccessful irregular transfers)
Peaceful challenge	Strikes Demonstrations

if Blondel's three-dimensional classification of 'regime norms' was accepted, then the existence of Blondel's time series codings of regime norms for over 138 nation states made operationalisation relatively simple. However, since we originally used *Easton's* concept of regime in order to identify the governmental, regime and community dimensions of political systems, and since the Easton and Blondel definitions differ marginally in their details, it is necessary to make a few slight adjustments to the Blondel codings before we can formulate a satisfactory oprational definition of regime change.

Although the distinction between the two concepts of regime is blurred by an unfortunate semantic confusion, as Figure 4.1 shows, it is in fact relatively straightforward. Blondel, it will be recalled, equates type of regime or 'regime norms' with goals (the radical-conservative axis), means (the liberal-authoritarian axis), and degree of participation (the oligarchic-democratic axis). Easton, on the other hand, equates type of regime with goals, norms (or means) and 'structure of authority'.[2] What Blondel calls 'norms', therefore, includes Easton's goals and Easton's norms. In consequence, although Blondel's concept of norms includes an additional participation dimension (which Easton does *not* mention in this context), it fails to incorporate the notion of 'structure of authority'.

Before we attempt to resolve these inconsistencies, however, it is necessary to point out that while Easton gives quite a lucid description of the 'authority roles'[3] which represent the basic units

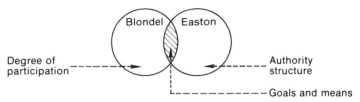

FIGURE 4.1   Different elements in the Blondel and Easton definitions of regime

of 'the authority structure', he is rather unclear as to how the notion of the authority structure itself might be operationalised, beyond observing (in a phrase not overburdened with meaning) that the authority structure is 'the overall way in which authority is organised and used'.[4] Despite this lack of assistance from Easton, we still propose to make some attempt to operationalise the 'structure of authority' aspect of regimes by examining two additional variables: the type of party system and the military civilian status of the regime. These two variables have been chosen, not because they are explicitly identified by either Easton or Blondel as indicators of regime type, but because *changes* in either or both of them seem to provide reasonable indications of changes in 'the overall way in which authority is organised . . .';[5] that is to say, they can be regarded as surrogates for the type of authority structure.

Having identified the various (partially overlapping) elements of the Blondel and Easton definitions of regime, from now on we will formally define a regime as being composed of both Blondel norms (goals, means and degree of participation) and of the type of authority structure. It follows, therefore, that a change in regime type can be produced by either a change in goals, a change in means, a change in the degree of participation or a change in the type of authority structure.

The three indicators of regime change identified in Table 4.1 can now be seen in their operational context: 'changes in Blondel norms' measure changes (or the absence of change) in the goals, means and/or degree of participation which operate within a particular political system; and changes in party system and changes in military-civilian 'status' measure changes in the structure of authority within that political system. Clearly, it is possible for any one, or for any *combination*, of these five types of change to occur at a particular point in time. Equally clearly, when all five types of change do occur simultaneously, the change in regime will be of a greater intensity than when only one occurs.

The precise scoring system which was employed in order to construct the initial regime change index is described in detail in Appendix 2. It is sufficient to point out here that the total regime change score for the ith country in the jth month was defined as a weighted sum of the scores on three Blondel variables:

$$\text{Regime change}_{ij} = (\text{changes in norms} \times 2) + \text{changes in party system} + \text{changes in military status}$$

which produces a theoretical maximum regime change score of 10 for any given country month, and a minimum value of zero.

Identifying indicators of government change, violent challenge and peaceful challenge

While the regime change index poses several rather intricate problems of operationalisation, it is relatively easy to specify indicators of the remaining change and challenge dimensions.

(i) The *World Handbook II* 'regular executive transfers' and 'executive adjustment' variables seem explicitly to measure within regime *governmental changes*. A 'regular executive transfer' is defined as 'a change in the national executive from one leader or ruling group to another, through conventional, legal or customary proceedings'. An executive adjustment, on the other hand, involves 'a modification in the membership of the national executive body that does not signify a transfer of formal power from one leader or ruling group to another . . . (it always involves) . . . movement into or out of office – not just a redistribution of ministerial portfolios'. Clearly, although there are bound to be some ambiguities,[6] these two variables provide a very good indication of what is conventionally understood by governmental change.

(ii) Similarly, it is relatively easy to obtain indicators of *challenge* to the political system, and, given the definitions of the *World Handbook II* variables,[7] the demarcation between violent and non-violent events is generally obvious. As Table 4.1 suggests, therefore, we can regard riots, political attacks, deaths from political violence and unsuccessful irregular transfers (attempted *coups*) as *violent challenges*, and demonstrations and political strikes as *peaceful challenges*.[8]

Of course, it would be convenient if we could argue (1) that because the use of violence transcends the legal procedures for the resolution of conflicts, violent challenges in fact represent challenges to the regime, and (2) that because peaceful challenges operate within legal procedures (generally) they cannot represent challenges to the regime, but only challenges to the government. In short, it would be convenient if we could describe violent challenges as 'regime challenges', and peaceful challenges as 'government challenges'. Such an argument, however, has three serious weaknesses: (1) it assumes that demonstrations and political strikes are legal in all systems, which they are not: when demonstrating (or striking) is legally excluded as a means of influencing decision making, then demonstrations (or strikes) must be regarded as challenges to the regime as well as to the government; (2) it ignores the fact that many violent behaviours are aimed at effecting changes in the political *community* as well as the regime; and (3) it fails to recognise the fact that many peaceful protest behaviours are aimed (by peaceful men unprepared to espouse violence) explicitly at the regime (although this latter point could perhaps be countered by the argument that since peaceful protest does not involve violence, it cannot by definition constitute a real challenge to the regime.) In any event, there are too many ambiguities for us to be able to identify violence with regime challenge and/or protest as government challenge.

Deviations from normality

Having identified the component indicators of our operational measures of changes and challenges, we are now in a position to examine the fourth element of our definition of instability.

'... THE EXTENT TO WHICH THE OCCURRENCE OR
NON-OCCURRENCE OF CHANGES AND CHALLENGES
DEVIATES FROM THE PREVIOUS SYSTEM SPECIFIC
PATTERN OF CHANGES AND CHALLENGES ...'

It is this phrase which marks the most important distinction between this and previous definitions of instability. Thus far we have simply been trying to organise the various behaviours associated with instability on the basis of a more rational framework than those employed in previous studies. The inclusion of the concept of deviations 'from the previous system specific pattern', however, attempts to effect two innovations simultaneously: firstly, it seeks to avoid making the fallacious and ethnocentric assumption that higher frequency (of change or challenge events) necessarily denotes greater instability; and secondly it attempts to take account of the journalistic notion of instability as uncertainty by implying that a change or challenge event only constitutes 'instability' in so far as it is not predictable (or *postdictable*) from the 'previous system specific pattern' of instability. Conversely, of course, this implies that a change or challenge event, if it is entirely predictable on the basis of the 'previous pattern', in fact constitutes relative stability. To reiterate, therefore, we are claiming that this incorporation of 'deviations from the previous system pattern' enables us to circumvent two of the major weaknesses of previous definitions; that they fail to contextualise raw frequency scores on the basis of specific systemic conditions, and that they fail to make any reference to the widely-held (non-academic) view of an unstable political situation as one which is uncertain or unpredictable.

Clearly, however, in order to identify 'deviations . . .' we must first be able to specify precisely what is meant by the '. . . (previous) . . . system specific pattern'. We in fact hinted at this in Chapter 3 when (using the example of riots) we stated axiomatically that similar events (riots) are of differential importance for stability in different countries because of the different system contexts in which they occur. What was being implied in this regard was that each system has a specific riot pattern (where 'pattern' could imply the complete absence of riots) and that the destabilising impact of any given riot needs to be assessed by reference to that riot pattern. The principle, however, is general: any (destabilising) event, x_i, which occurs in country A needs to be assessed by reference to the pattern of x_i which occurred in country A in the previous time period. This statement of general principle, however, again begs the question: What is meant by these 'system specific event patterns' and how can they be identified?

Spatial patterns

The concept of 'system specific patterns' is based upon the assumption that in relation to any given change or challenge event there is, within any particular country, a prevailing or 'normal' pattern of political interaction. The frequency approach to which we referred earlier in fact also makes such an assumption, although the form which that assumption takes, as we will see below, is singularly inappropriate. *The frequency approach assumes that there is a single, universally applicable 'normal' pattern, namely, one in which no destabilising event occurs.* (We will refer to this assumption as 'the norm of non-occurrence'.) In so far as these events *do* occur within a particular system, in so far as events within the system deviate from the norm of non-occurrence, the frequency approach describes that system as relatively unstable. In other words, the approach prescribes that instability exists only in so far as observed reality deviates from the universal 'normal' pattern of non-occurrence.

This principle is most unsatisfactory: it fails, as we suggested earlier when we were criticising the frequency approach in more general terms, to place the events which do occur in their spatial context. It implies (assuming that the unit of analysis is the country year), for example, that the 54 deaths from domestic political violence in Colombia in 1950 denote a higher level of (violent challenge) instability than the 14 political deaths which occurred in Denmark in 1951.[9] Superficially, such a conclusion might seem sensible (more deaths, more instability), but because it fails to take account of the spatial contexts of the events, it is in reality a nonsense. The 54 deaths in Colombia in fact provided a relatively peaceful interlude between two of the most severe onslaughts of what was known as 'The Violence' (1946–52);[10] they represented a period of *relatively* low violence, that is to say, a period of relatively high *stability*. The deaths in Denmark, on the other hand, as an aberration of the first order (these were the only political deaths which occurred in Denmark throughout the period 1948–67), must be associated with a relatively high level of (violent challenge) instability.

What we are suggesting then, is that while the frequency approach's 'norm of non-occurrence' provides a suitable basis for making a descriptive statement about the level of instability associated with the 14 deaths in Denmark, it provides a highly distorted description of the level of instability associated with the 54 Colombian deaths. The norm of non-occurrence implies that the level of instability in the Colombian example was higher than that in the Danish one. By examining the different system contexts of the two death scores, we have shown that the Colombian score, even though it is nominally higher, in fact represents a relatively high level of stability *for the Colombian system*. In order to understand, or in order to make an adequate description of, the level of political instability (associated with political deaths) in Colombia in 1951, it is essential that the raw frequency score is contextualised in terms of the even higher level of political violence (the system specific event pattern) which was prevalent in that country before 1951: to assume a 'normal' pattern of 'no violence' or 'no deaths' (as the frequency approach does) makes no sense at all. Rather, if we are to undertake a comparative analysis of political instability, we must devise measures which disavow the normality of 'non-occurrence', and which instead recognise that identical frequencies can in different spatial contexts mean either greater or lesser degrees of stability or instability for the systems in which they occur. In other words, an approach is needed which acknowledges the utility of the 'normality concept', but which at the same time recognises that what can be considered as 'normal' varies from system to system.

We have supported this argument by reference to deaths from political violence, but the principle applies to all the indicators of political instability which we isolated earlier: events which are a normal part of the pattern of political interaction in some systems cannot be so regarded in others. The *coup d'état* is clearly not a part of the normal political process in most Western systems, but this is not always the case elsewhere. In relation to Peru, for example, Payne has argued strongly that *coups* are 'essential to the functioning of the political system itself', by virtue of the fact that they perform the same function as do elections in constitutional democracies; they promote the circulation of élites.[11] The *coup d'état* in Peru, therefore, is an important aspect of 'normal' Peruvian politics and needs to be evaluated as such; to regard it as an aberration necessarily denoting a high level of instability is to misunderstand the nature of the Peruvian political process. To reiterate yet again, 'normal' patterns of political interaction vary from country to country.

Temporal patterns

It is also the case, however, that even in relation to a specific system *the 'normal pattern' can vary over time*. Consider the *coup* pattern of a hypothetical country *A* (which in fact corresponds closely to Syria during the period 1940–60), which is described in Figure 4.2. For a ten-year period, no *coups* occur, but for the subsequent decade the system experiences a *coup* every two years or so. Analysts of the frequency school would undoubtedly characterise system *A* as exhibiting chronic political instability (one thinks immediately of Huntington's concept of the praeterian society), since the *coup* pattern consistently deviates from the norm of non-occurrence.

A more sensitive characterisation, however, would recognise that while the norm of non-occurrence is appropriate up to t_{10}, during the course of the second decade a fairly regular *coup* sequence has developed. In the second decade, the norm of non-occurrence is so consistently violated that the *coup* could be regarded as a normal part of the political process in system *A*. We have then at least two rather different 'normal patterns' for system *A*: one in which no *coups* occur, and one in which the *coup* is a regular fact of political life. We use the qualification 'at least two patterns' advisedly, however. While it is reasonable to assert that by the time the 4th and 5th coups occur, a relatively stable two-year *coup* cycle has developed, it is obviously not possible to make such an observation in relation to the first coup. That is to say, while the *coups* at t_{16} and t_{18} can be regarded as part of a relatively regular predictable sequence, the idea of a two-year cycle is of no help in predicting the first *coup*.[12] The reason for this is simple: the only information which is relevant to a descriptive statement about the level of instability associated with the 1st *coup* (and what we are debating is the question of what constitutes 'the best' description of any given *coup* or indeed any given event) is that part of Figure 4.2

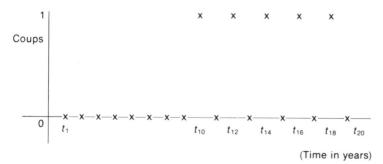

FIGURE 4.2   Coordinates of hypothetical coups variable against time

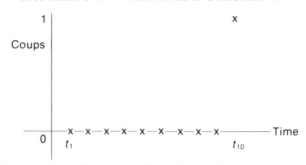

FIGURE 4.3   Coordinates from Figure 4.2, t_1 to t_{10} only

described by Figure 4.3. It follows, of course, that for the 2nd *coup*, the appropriate time period for consideration is t_1 to t_{12}; for the 3rd *coup* t_1 to t_{14}, and so on. Given this changing frame of reference, it is clear that only towards the *end* of the *coup* sequence can we describe 'the *coup*' as being part of the 'normal' political process of country A. Indeed, we would argue that the extent to which the *i*th *coup* is predictable (or *postdictable*) from the previous *coup* pattern (and here we are moving in the direction of the journalistic notion of instability as uncertainty) determines the extent to which that *coup* is a 'normal' part of the political process. And we would also argue that for any given system at any given time, behaviours which are 'normal' (predictable) should not be regarded as constituting political instability: it is only in so far as behaviours *deviate* from what is 'normal' for the system at the particular time point in question that instability exists.

The 'instability scores' for each of the five *coups* in country A, therefore, should vary. The first *coup* should receive a relatively high score, since on the basis of the preceding *coup* pattern (that is to say, no *coups* – in a sense, no pattern), it is entirely unpredictable. The second should receive a similarly high score because it is equally unpredictable. Subsequent *coups*, however, since they are progressively more predictable on the basis of an increasingly apparent two-year cycle, should receive progressively lower instability scores. The fifth *coup*, for example, if it occurred precisely at the predicted time point (i.e. a two-year interval), could in principle have an instability score of zero.

What we have sought to establish, then, is that there are different temporal and spatial contexts in which destabilising events occur and that the instability score for any given change or challenge event, should be measured as a deviation from the system specific or 'normal pattern' obtaining in the particular system under consideration during the preceding time period. We have also argued that the 'frequency' approach wrongly assumes that context is irrelevant and that instead there is a single universal 'normal pattern' of 'non-occurrence' rather than a multiplicity of spatio-temporal system specific normalities. Clearly, having rejected the utility of raw frequency we must now offer some alternative method of contextualising change and challenge events; that is to say we must offer an alternating method of assessing the severity of destabilising events by reference to the differing normalities of the systems (and time periods) in which they occur.

One method of assessment would be to seek the advice of experts on each of the individual countries under analysis. On the basis of his own theoretical knowledge of the political system in question, each expert could be asked to evaluate the severity of each destabilising event on, say, a 10 point judgemental scale. A score of 10, for example, would indicate the most extreme departure from the normal pattern of political interaction within that system. While such an approach would permit great flexibility in the identification of different 'normal patterns', it would also have two considerable disadvantages. Firstly, given the need for comparative analysis to compare a large number of systems, it would be extremely difficult to obtain the assistance of a sufficient number of 'experts' to make the exercise logistically feasible. Secondly, and more importantly, the inherent subjectivity involved in such a judgemental approach would inevitably leave any analysis which sought a statistical explanation of the judgemental scores wide open to the (well-founded) accusation of unreliability.

A second method of assessment would be one which attempts to identify a set of uniform *objective* criteria by which the relative severity of destabilising events could be evaluated. It is an approach of this sort which we now attempt to specify.

A general method of identifying deviations from 'normal' event patterns

We have argued that any given change or challenge event should be evaluated by reference to the prevailing 'normal' event pattern of the system in which it occurs. In order to avoid the assumption that greater *'frequency'* is necessarily equated with greater instability, the 'system specific' conditions of each country need to be taken into account. We have also seen that any attempt to contextuate events on the basis of a detailed and substantive knowledge of individual systems would be confronted by unsurmountable problems of logistics and of subjectivity. The method which we in fact propose is fundamentally a *statistical* one, and consequently it is a method which enables us to apply the same set of criteria of contextuation to an infinite variety of systems, time periods and change and challenge events.

The general assumption upon which the method is based is that the system specific 'normal' event pattern of a change or challenge event, x_t, in system A during a given time period T, can be defined by *some postdictive linear or non-linear least squares function of time itself*: for the ith occurrence of x_t, a deviation (residual) from that function, since it represents a deviation from the system specific normal pattern of system A, in turn defines the level of instability associated with that ith occurrence of x_t.

It should be noted that we have defined x_t as any given *change or challenge event*. What we are suggesting, therefore, is that once the indicators of, say, regime change have been specified (and we in fact did this in Figure 4.1), each indicator series should be subjected to the method of contextuation which we identify below. It is only when this contextuation has been achieved that the indicators can be aggregated into a single regime change instability index.

Clearly, however, the crucial element in this general assumption which we have *not* yet really touched upon is the idea of a 'postdictive . . . function of time . . .' In order to explain what, in principle, is meant by this term, we will provide a simplified hypothetical example of a 'normal pattern' which is best described by a simple trend function. This is not to say, however, that this is the actual method of contextuation employed – we will return to that in detail after the general principle has been established.

Consider, then, the series x_t which is defined by Figure 4.4. It is clear that a positive linear trend function of time can be fitted to the scatter of dots defined by the coordinates of x_t and time. (For reasons which we will specify later, such a trend cannot be fitted to the early part of the function.) The method we are proposing suggests that in this context, since x_t is tending to increase regularly

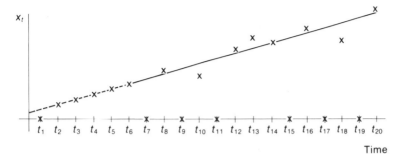

FIGURE 4.4   Coordinates of hypothetical x_t plotted against time

over time, the destabilising impact of each occurrence or non-occurrence of x_t should be measured as a least squares residual off the positive linear trend function defined by the relationship between x_t and time. In other words, we are arguing that in the time period in question it is 'normal' not only for some minimum level of x_t to occur, but also *for x_t to increase secularly over time.* Moreover, because (as we argued earlier) what is 'normal' for any particular system in a given time period should not be regarded as constituting instability, it is the deviations from normality (the residuals off the time function) which define the level of instability associated with x_t at different points in time.

Consider, for example, the scores at t_8, t_{12}, t_{13}, t_{16} and t_{20}. Given the function we have defined, they provide *positive* residuals: they represent relatively high levels of instability, and indeed, the further they are above the trend function, the greater the level of instability which they denote. Given our definition of instability as a deviation from 'normality', the level of instability at t_{16} (for example) is less than at t_{13}, even though in raw frequency terms x_t is higher at t_{16} than it is at t_{13}.

Similarly, the residuals at t_{10} and t_{18} provide *negative* residuals: the further they are below the trend line, the greater *stability* which they represent. As with the 54 political deaths in Colombia in 1950 which we cited earlier, the scores on x_t at t_{10} and t_{18} denote lower levels of instability than might have been expected on the basis of the previous x_t pattern within the system. Superficially, the idea of actual occurrences of x_t denoting relative stability (even if such occurrences do represent points below the overall trend – below the expected level of instability which immediate past experience suggests) seems illogical. However, it should be noted that the *non-occurrences* of x_t (at t_7, t_9, t_{11}, t_{15}, t_{17}, t_{19}, in our example) represent even *greater* negative residuals, and consequently, they denote even higher levels of (relative) stability than the residuals at t_{10} and t_{18}.[13] The fact that the residuals at t_{10} and t_{18} provide (in numerical terms) negative scores, is of itself unimportant. Since, as we suggested earlier, instability/stability is a *relative* concept, it follows that the positive or negative status of the instability scores is irrelevant. (It makes no difference to any correlative procedures whether a variable ranges from -20 to $+10$ or from 0 to 30). All that matters is that the relative magnitudes of the instability scores are measured as deviations from the same 'normality'.[14]

The principle of taking residuals off functions of time, then, enables us to modify the frequency scores of those x_t events which do occur on the basis of the underlying trend which is operating over a particular time period. Implicit in such an approach, of course, is the additional assumption that the non-occurrence of x_t may, in different circumstances, be of differential importance. The negative residual score at t_{19}, for example, will be higher than the negative residual score at t_7 although in both cases no occurrences of x_t were observed. Again, while this might seem superficially to be illogical, it in fact makes very good intuitive sense: prior to t_7, the overall level of x_t is much lower than it is prior to t_{19}. The period of relative peace denoted by the zero score at t_{19} in consequence represents a greater degree of relative stability than that denoted by the zero score at t_7.

To summarise, then, the *principle* involved in the method of contextuation which we are proposing consists in describing any given series of change or challenge frequency scores as some function of time, and measuring the level of instability associated with each observed case of that event variable as a least squares residual off that function. As we suggested before, however, this simplified outline of principle does not actually constitute the method proposed. Partly because of the refusal of reality to fit simple linear trends and partly because of the necessity of assessing the size of the residual for x_t at t_n only on the basis of the x_t pattern for the period t_1, . . ., t_n, the method itself is rather more complicated. Before it can be broken down and presented as a discrete sequence of procedures, however, several preliminary qualifications need to be made.

First, as we stated earlier, our analysis is conducted on monthly time series data across 136 countries for the period 1948–67, using data derived from the *World Handbook II* and Blondel time series data-sets. (The actual change and challenge event variables which we examined were identified in Table 4.1.) In relation to any particular country, therefore, the starting point for our method of contextuation is a series of raw frequency scores on a given event variable (x_t) derived from these sources. Since the scores are recorded at monthly intervals for the period 1948–67, the total number of time points, T, is (at least initially) 240.

Secondly, as we have also suggested, in order to assess how far any given occurrence of x_t deviates from the previous 'normal pattern' of x_t, we must first attempt to fit some function of time to the series of x_t. What this means in practice is that if the occurrence of x_t in question occurs at, say, t_{20}, it only makes sense to consider the *previous* 'normal pattern'; that is to say, in this instance, instead of operating on all 240 points, we would only want to consider the period from t_1 to t_{20}. Anything which occurs *after* t_{20} is irrelevant to our assessment of the destabilising impact of the event which occurs at t_{20}. It is also the case, however, that in order to estimate 'some function of time', a minimum number of observations are necessary in order to give the computations a sound statistical basis. In other words, we have to balance on the one hand the need for some minimum number of observations which is necessary before any 'previous normal pattern' can be identified, with, on the other hand, the need to consider the events at t_n only on the basis of the pattern prior to t_n.

The minimum number of observations which we propose to employ for this study is $T = 60$ (i.e. 60 months = 5 years). The reasons for this choice are partly substantive (we are assuming that it takes at least five years for a 'normal pattern' to emerge), but mainly technical: given the number of independent (time) variables which we utilise below, $T = 60$ is the smallest sample size which provides sufficient degrees of freedom to make significance testing a realistic exercise; and as we will see, significance testing is a vital part of our operational procedure.

Ideally, then, for any given x_t the first stage of our procedure would be to confine ourselves to an examination of the first 60 time points of the series (i.e. $T = 60$). We would then attempt to assess how far the occurrence or non-occurrence of x_t at t_{60} deviates from the previous 'normal pattern'. The resultant 'deviation score' would constitute our operational instability score for x_t at t_{60}. We would not be able to estimate *any* instability scores on x_t for the preceding 59 time points. The second stage of our procedure would then involve an examination of the first 61 time points ($T = 61$); the resultant 'deviation score' would provide an instability score for x_t at t_{61}. It would then be necessary to reiterate the sequence of operations for $T = 62, 63, 64, \ldots, 240$.

Such a procedure, however, raises three important problems. Firstly, it means that the 'normal pattern' upon which the deviation scores are based covers a progressively longer period as T increases; secondly, it means that out of every 240 observations available at the outset of the investigation, 59 are lost; and thirdly, the 180 reiterations of the process for each x_t series would require enormous machine resources, resources which were not available for this study. The first problem cannot be resolved: to reduce the period over which the 'normal pattern' is estimated to a uniform $T = 60$ would result in an unnecessary loss of information at higher values of T; and given the general paucity of cross-national information we assume that it is better to use that information which *is* available to the maximum possible extent.

We propose to circumvent the second two problems, however, by partially violating the principle of only considering the occurrence of x_t at t_n as a deviation from the pattern of x_t prior to t_n. Indeed, in relation to the second problem, we will take the residuals from the pattern observed up to t_{60}, for *all* the cases of x_t from t_1 through to t_{60} *not* just for t_{60} as the 'ideal' method outlined above suggested. Similarly, in relation to the third problem, instead of reiterating the contextuation process at monthly intervals of $t = 60, 61, \ldots, 240$, we will reiterate on an *annual* basis at $T = 60, 72, 84, 96, \ldots, 240$. (This in fact reduces the number of reiterations per x_t from 180 to 15.) Clearly both of these expedients will mean that to a limited extent any given 'deviation' score may be based on a consideration of events which were not temporally antecedent to it. Figure 4.5 describes an example of such an eventuality. The precise form of the trend function described by Figure 4.5 is determined partly by what happens at t_{62} to t_{72} and, in consequence, the residual at t_{61} is also partially so determined. In estimating the residual value at t_{61} using all the time points up to t_{72}, we are therefore indulging in a partial violation of our definition of the destabilising impact of any given occurrence of x_t as a deviation from the *previous* 'normal pattern'. However, since this can never involve more than eleven observations for any

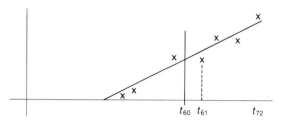

FIGURE 4.5

given estimated function, we would argue that such a violation is not too serious, particularly in view of the fact that it is only through the use of this expedient that the operationalisation of the principle of 'deviations' becomes technically feasible.

The final qualification which we need to make relates to the nature of the 'functions of time' which our method of contextuation employs. In the empirical part of this study two sorts of function were investigated, in order to identify the 'normal' pattern of any given event series: cyclical and (linear and non-linear) trend functions. Allowance was made for the fact that any given 'normal' pattern could be composed of a combination of (several) cyclical and (one) trend functions.

The *cyclical* functions were estimated using a form of periodogram analysis. For each time period examined, this involved the generation of cycles of 6, 12, 18, . . ., 36 months duration: the dependent variables (the x_t series) were then regressed on these generated cyclical variables. Where a cyclical pattern was found to exist, residuals were taken from the relevant cyclical function.[15] The criterion of demarcation for the 'existence' of a cycle was the null hypothesis significance (t) test: for any given cyclical function, the assumption was made that if the relevant t statistics were less than the required critical value, the null hypothesis that $B_k = 0$ could not be rejected, thereby implying that there was no relationship between that function and the x_t series in question.

The *trend* functions which we examined were somewhat different from the polynomials in time which are usually employed in time series detrending procedures. It was considered that greater flexibility of estimation could be obtained by the use of a series of slope shift interaction terms which enable the estimation of a wide range of non-linear models.[16] The various trend functions were estimated on the basis of the assumption that, in attempting to identify a 'normal pattern' for any given x_t, a relatively simple function is preferable to a more complex one. Accordingly, the following sequence of trend function models was estimated; the first model to provide significant parameters and a non-trivial $R^2 (R^2 \geq 0.10)$ was assumed to describe the 'normal' (cyclical) pattern of the given x_t series.

(i) Simple linear pattern trend: slope constrained to be either positive or negative

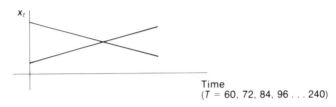

Time
$(T = 60, 72, 84, 96 \ldots 240)$

FIGURE 4.6(a)

(ii) Series divided into 2 equal parts: the model permits each part of the series to have its own (empirically determined) slope

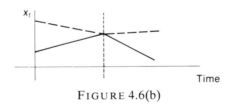

FIGURE 4.6(b)

(iii) Series divided into 3 equal parts

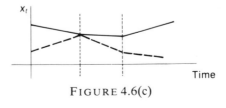

FIGURE 4.6(c)

(iv)   Series divided into 4 equal parts

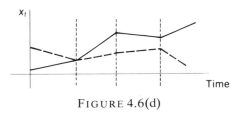

FIGURE 4.6(d)

(v)   Series divided into 5 equal parts

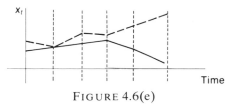

FIGURE 4.6(e)

A method of contextuation operationalised

Having specified the general nature of the functions of time which our method employs, we can provide a detailed outline of the process which we propose, of identifying functions and taking deviations from them. The results of that process constitute our operational definition of instability for the ith change or challenge event. (It should be stressed however, that the method suggested is only one of a number of possible alternative models which could be devised on the basis of the 'deviation from normality' principle.)

Consider, then, for a given country, a series of 240 raw frequency scores which describe some change or challenge event, x_t. Our operational method of contextuation suggests that we define the destabilising impact of the ith occurrence of x_t as follows.

(i)   Subset the first 60 observations of x_t ($T = 60$).
(ii)   Regress x_t on a series of generated cyclical variables representing cycles of 6, 12, 18 . . . 36 months duration.
(iii) Regress x_t on those cyclical functions which provide significant parameters at (ii).
(iv)   'Decycle' the series on the following principle:
       (a) where the original x_t score was zero, let x_t^* (the 'decycled' series) also score zero;

(b) where the original x_t score was not zero, let x_t^* equal the *absolute value* of the residual from the cyclical function defined at (iii).

It should be noted that (a) implies that non-occurrences of x_t at different time points are *not* of differential importance. The reason for this temporary violation of one of our original assumptions is a methodological one: if a cycle is significant but relatively weak, and consists principally in the regular occurrence of a single event, as in Figure 4.7, taking residuals from the cycle can in fact generate a cyclical effect in the zero values of x_t which is of greater intensity than the cycle which we are trying to remove. In any case, stage (vi) below permits different non-occurrences of x_t to produce differential instability scores.

(v)   Whether or not a cyclical function is found to exist at (ii), that is to say, whether or not the generated cycle variables furnish significant parameters, *standardise the series*, thereby giving it a mean of zero and a standard deviation of unity. Call this standardised variable x_t^{**}.

The reason for this procedure is that it provides an additional method of contextuating x_t on the basis of the x_t 'pattern' within the country under analysis, *even if that 'pattern', or configuration, is itself unpredictable*, either by cyclical or trend functions. Consider, for example, the x_t 'patterns' in two different countries, A and B, which are described in Figure 4.8. Both of the scatterplots in this figure are intended to denote *random* relationships between x_t and time. Clearly, however, even though both random 'patterns' are, by definition, unpredictable either by cyclical and/or trend functions, any one occurrence of x_t in system A is far more unusual (that is to

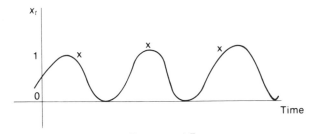

FIGURE 4.7

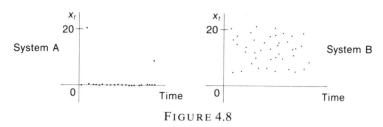

System A

System B

FIGURE 4.8

say, it represents a far greater deviation from what is normal) than any given occurrence of x_t in system B. By standardising x_t in each system, therefore, we measure each occurrence or non-occurrence of x_t as a deviation from the same mean of zero. In our example, standardised versions of the original x_t score of 20 for system A would consequently be greater than the standardised version of the same score for system B. In short, the standardisation procedure is a safety net which enables us to modify frequency scores on the basis of the overall level of x_t even when there is no predictable pattern in x_t.

(vi) (a) Estimate the linear relationship between x_t^{**} and time by regressing x_t on time. If the model furnishes significant parameters, detrend the series by taking the residuals from the equation, calling them x_t^{***}.

(b) If (a) does not provide a significant trend, estimate a *non*-linear relation between x_t^{**} and time by allowing the function to have two different slopes above and below $t = T/2$ (in this case since $T = 60$, this point is t_{30}). If the model furnishes significant parameters, detrend the series by taking the residuals from the estimated equation. The deviations are denoted x_t^{***}.

(c) If (b) fails to provide a significant trend, estimate a more complex non-linear relationship between x_t^{**} and time by allowing the function to have three different slopes as in Figure 4.6(c). If the model furnishes significant parameters, detrend the series by taking the residuals from the estimated equation. The deviations are denoted x_t^{***}.

(d) If (c) fails . . . allow the function to have four different slopes . . .

(e) If (d) fails . . . allow the function to have five different slopes . . .

(f) If (e) fails, rename x_t^{**} as x_t^{***}.

(vii) Since x_t^{***} is now our contextuated series, at least up to t_{60}, that is to say, since the modified x_t^{***} scores represent the deviations from the prevailing system pattern of x_t, we now make a permanent record of this contextuated series ($T = 60$).

(viii) Subset the first 72 observations ($T = 72$).

(ix) Repeat stages (ii) to (vi). x_t^{***} is now our contextuated series, at least up to t_{72}. However, we already have a record of x_t^{***} up to t_{60} (which correctly ignores the x_t pattern between t_{60} and t_{72}), and therefore we make an additional permanent record of only the last 12 observations (t_{61} to t_{72} inclusive) of the newly contextuated series.

(xi) Subset the first 84 observations.

(xii) Repeat stage (ix).

(xiii) Make an additional permanent record of only the last 12 observations (t_{85} to t_{96} inclusive) of the newly contextuated series.

(xiv) Reiterate the process of (xi) to (xiii) for $T = 96, 108, 120$ . . . 240.

The end result of this procedure is a series of 240 instability scores, x_t^{***}, which (given the qualifications that have been made) represent the deviations from the prevailing system normalities of x_t; 'normali*ties*' because the specific cyclical and trend functions which our method of operationalisation identifies for any given x_t may vary over time. For any given system, and for any given change or challenge event, x_t^{***} constitutes our operational measure of instability at time t. In this context, since we are operating on monthly time series data, t equals one calendar month. This is not to say that we cannot measure 'instability' over a period of time longer than one month – this can be achieved by additively aggregating monthly scores – but simply that because the stability of any given system can vary considerably over time, the measurement of the instability of relatively short term political situations is an essential prerequisite to any analysis of instability over a longer time period. Indeed, in subsequent chapters, we will examine instability at three different levels of temporal aggregation: part of our analysis will consider monthly data, part of it will consider annual data and part will examine twenty-year aggregates.

Finally, it is necessary to point out that the above procedure was carried out (for each country) on each of the eleven change and challenge event variables defined by Table 4.1. In order to obtain composite government change, regime change, violent challenge and peaceful challenge indices for each country month, the transformed deviation scores on the component indicators of each index were additively aggregated.

SUMMARY

We have argued then that instability/stability should be regarded as a continuous, relative phenomenon which occurs to varying degrees in different systems at different points in time (as we suggested before, stability and instability are relative tendencies rather than discrete stases); and that the behaviours which denote instability can be divided into (government, regime and community) *changes* and (violent and peaceful) *challenges*. We have also suggested that any attempt to measure instability should focus, at least initially, on short run political situations, which we defined to be of one month's duration.

The most critical part of our definition, however, is the notion of deviations from some 'normal' system specific pattern. Essentially, what we have argued in this context is that (1) regularity (in the form of some time function) enables prediction; (2) prediction enables the estimation of 'normality'; (3) the identification of 'normality' makes it possible to measure deviations from that 'normality'; and (4) it is the magnitude of these deviations which defines the relative level of stability or instability for each time point. Instability, in short, consists *in* 'deviations from normality'.

It should be noted, however, that 'prediction' in this context really implies 'postdiction', and that at this stage in our analysis we are only concerned with pre- or postdiction in so far as it enables us to make a satisfactory *description* of instability at any given time. (We are not at present interested in any *causal* determinants of instability.) To reiterate, we have used the concept of postdiction to enable us to identify 'normal' system specific patterns of change and challenge events. For any given time point, we have assumed that what is 'normal' in a particular system can be identified by reference to the regularities in the occurrences of that event which are observed over time. We have also assumed that, in so far as a series of observations on a specific event variable exhibits *regularity*, it is possible to use (some postdictive function of) time itself to describe that regularity. The appropriate function of time, therefore, since it describes what is 'regular', also describes what is 'normal'; and the extent to which the *i*th occurrence of the series in fact deviates from this function (i.e. the extent to which it deviates from 'normality') determines its instability score.

Given the applicability of these assumptions, our definition of instability has two distinct advantages over previous definitions. First, by contextuating events in terms of their predictability, it moves some way towards the commonly held 'journalistic' notion of instability as uncertainty. To the extent that a 'political situation' in a given system is not dissimilar to previous 'political situations' in that system, a political journalist is likely to be relatively certain as to its outcome, and in consequence he is unlikely to describe it as being 'unstable': it is only when the current 'political situation' is very different from previous 'situations' that the current situation is likely to be characterised as uncertain or 'unstable'. Similarly, with our own definition, in so far as a particular event represents a continuation of some discernable regular sequence, it will not, on the basis of our operationalisation, be regarded as constituting a high level of instability: it is only when an event deviates dramatically from the previous system pattern that it is associated with a relatively high level of instability.

The second, and most important, advantage of our definition, however, is that unlike previous definitions it recognises the existence of different 'normalities', that is to say, it recognises that what is a 'normal' part of the pattern of political interaction for one system and one time period is not necessarily a 'normal' occurrence for another. Indeed, the definition which we have proposed makes full allowance for the possibility that what is 'normal' not only varies from system to system, but also that even within the same system it varies over time. While the operational method of identifying 'normalities' which we have outlined here is admittedly not an ideal one, we would contend that given current machine and data constraints, our operational method constitutes a reasonable approximation to the theoretical definition of instability which we have proposed.

We are now in a position to depart from questions of pure definition, and we therefore turn to examine a series of hypotheses and models which purport to 'explain' cross-national patterns of political instability. In subsequent chapters, all of the measures of instability which we utilise will be based upon the operational method which we have defined here.

Before we embark on our empirical investigation of cross-national patterns of instability, however, one final qualification is necessary. It needs to be recognised that while the instability measures derived from our operational method are monthly *time series* scores, part of our later analysis is *cross-sectional*. For any given instability dimension, therefore, this necessitates the *aggregation* of these monthly scores for each country, to form a single composite instability measure for the period 1948–67. The method of aggregation which was employed was in fact a simple additive one: for each country and for each dimension, the 240 'deviation from normality' instability measures were arithmetically summed. Given the considerable importance of region as a control variable in quantitative cross-national research,[17] these composite instability measures were then standardised on a region by region basis. This means, for example, that for the Western Europe/North America region, the composite instability scores on any given instability dimension were transformed so as to measure the relative total instability of each Western Europe/North America system as a deviation from the *average* Western Europe/North America level of instability. The 'twenty-year aggregate' instability scores which are reported in Appendix 1, therefore, are not only *system specific* scores in the sense that they define the destabilising impact of any given event in terms of the extent to which it constitutes a deviation from the previous system normality, but they are also *regional specific* scores in the sense that they define the 'total' level of instability of any given system in terms of the extent to which its composite system specific instability score is *abnormal* in the context of the region in which it occurs. The instability measure specified in Appendix 1 should consequently be interpreted as follows: given the 'normal' change or challenge event pattern in country *A* during the period 1948–67, and given that country *A* is in region *B*, the magnitude of regime change, government change, violent challenge or peaceful challenge instability in country A over the period 1948–67 was x (where x is the instability score for any particular country reported in Appendix 1). This may seem somewhat convoluted, but we would argue that since what is part of 'normal' political process varies both from system to system and from region to region, such controls are essential if the level of instability of any given system is to be adequately defined. Anything less complex would entail oversimplification.

5 Interrelationships between the Dimensions of Political Instability

In an earlier chapter we identified four key dimensions of political instability – regime and government changes and violent and peaceful challenges[1] – and provided operational definitions for each of them. In this chapter we seek to provide answers to two sets of questions concerning their interrelationships. The first is concerned simply with the degree of *association* between the various dimensions: do countries which exhibit relatively high scores on the regime change index, for example, also tend to have relatively high levels of government change and/or violent and/or peaceful challenge? The second set of questions is concerned with whether or not there is any evidence to suggest that *causal* linkages exist between the four instability dimensions: is it the case, for example, that violent challenges lead to changes in regime, or that peaceful challenges tend to escalate into more violent forms of behaviour?

The questions which relate to degrees of *association* are, at first sight, relatively easy to resolve since Pearson product moment correlation coefficients can be employed in order to estimate the (linear) strength of any bivariate relationship.[2] As we will demonstrate later, however, the problem of association is complicated by the fact that data at different levels of temporal aggregation provide somewhat conflicting results as to the magnitude of the correlations.

Questions relating to *causal linkages* between variables, on the other hand, are far more contentious than those which are concerned with association. As we pointed out in Chapter 2, there is no logical relationship between an empirical correlation and a causal effect, although this problem is frequently circumvented by hypothesising the existence of unidirectional causation between any pair of variables under consideration, and arguing that whatever empirical correlation is found to exist represents corroboration for that hypothesis. As we also argued in Chapter 2, however, such an empirical correlation is also consistent with the proposition that the causal effect (in so far as it exists at all) operates in the reverse direction to that which was originally hypothesised. With regard to the dimensions of instability which we have identified, it makes very little sense to argue that empirical correlations only support unidirectional causal hypotheses, since from a theoretical perspective it seems just as likely that regime change, for example, could produce violent challenge behaviours as it is that violent challenges could produce a change in regime. What we really need, therefore, is some empirical means of establishing the direction(s) and magnitude(s) (either reciprocal or non-reciprocal) of those causal linkages between our instability dimensions which do exist, which does not espouse the simple corroborative principles of the hypothetico-deductive paradigm. Broadly (as we also pointed out earlier), there are two ways of estimating such causal effects: (1) by the use of non-recursive causal modelling techniques on cross-sectional data; or (2) by the use of time series data where the time intervals are sufficiently small to enable the detection of significant lagged relationships; and in this chapter we will employ both of these forms of analysis.

The chapter as a whole is divided into four sections. We will begin by examining three general scenarios which purport to describe the interrelationships between the dimensions of political instability and attempt to specify the predictions which they imply for our data. We will then address the question of degrees of association, that is to say, the question of the relative strengths of the interrelationships between the dimensions of instability, using (at least initially) three different types of data: twenty-year aggregate cross-section, annual time series and monthly time series. Thirdly, we will turn more directly to the question of causality between the dimensions and examine possible reciprocal relationships using non-recursive modelling techniques; although given the qualifications which were made in Chapter 2 concerning Hibbs' use of temporally aggregated event variables, we shall not lay great stress upon the general applicability of these findings. Finally, by examining annual and monthly time series data we will attempt to specify the dominant directions of those causal effects which appear to exist between the dimensions of instability emphasising the considerable regional differentials which our results suggest.

THREE ALTERNATIVE SCENARIOS: SYNDROME, SAFETY VALVE AND HIBBS

As we suggested before there are broadly three scenarios which attempt to describe the interrelationships between the dimensions of political instability. The most pervasive is what we will characterise as the *instability syndrome*.[3] While recognising that, analytically, there may be several different types of instability-related behaviours, this approach tends to regard instability empirically as a monolithic all-pervading phenomenon; unstable systems tend to experience relatively high levels of all forms of destabilising behaviours, which is precisely why they are characterised as unstable. The syndrome approach prescribes, therefore, that all destabilising event variables will tend to be strongly interrelated, that is to say, in the terminology which we advanced in Chapters 3 and 4, the higher the level of (say) regime change instability which a country experiences, the probability is that it will also experience relatively high levels of governmental change, and relatively high levels of violent and peaceful challenges. In other words, all the change and challenge dimensions of instability which we identified earlier should be highly and positively intercorrelated (see Figure 5.1a).

The second scenario is rather more discriminating. It is claimed that, in Western systems in particular, certain types of instability-related behaviours (notably peaceful political protest) can actually serve to reinforce the stability of governments and/or of regimes by acting as 'safety valve' mechanisms which allow political resentments and dissatisfaction to be directed through legitimate institutionalised channels.[4] The safety valve thesis, therefore, implies that peaceful challenges at least, since they serve to reinforce other forms of stability, should (particularly in Western systems) be negatively correlated with the other three types of instability under examination (see Figure 5.1b).

A third, empirically based, scenario derives from Hibbs' analysis of violence, protest and *coups d'état* which we mentioned in Chapter 2. The implications of Hibbs' conclusions for the interrelationships between our four dimensions of instability are not entirely clear, however, partly because Hibbs ignores the governmental change dimension of instability and partly because he only examines the Internal War-Collective Protest relationship via the mediating influence of sanctions. Nonetheless, in the sense that Hibbs' *coups* variable can be equated, to a limited extent, with

(a)

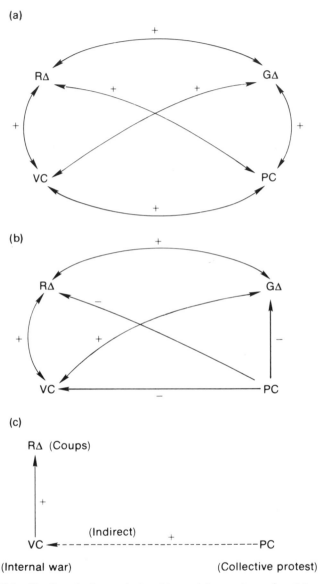

(b)

(c)

RΔ (Coups)

VC
(Internal war)

(Indirect)

PC
(Collective protest)

FIGURE 5.1 Predicted interrelationships: (a) syndrome*; (b) safety valve; (c) Hibbs

*The diagrams presented here follow normal path analysis conventions: (a) curved arrows indicate a (non-directional) correlation where the contention is simply that the variables should be associated; (b) straight arrows indicate directional linkages; and (c) signs indicate whether a relationship should be positive (+) or negative (−).

our regime change index,[5] and since (as we pointed out in the previous chapter) his Internal War-Collective Protest distinction is similar to our violent challenge-peaceful challenge one, Hibbs' final model does in fact suggest some predictions for the interrelationships between our measures. As Figure 5.1c suggests, certain empirical tendencies should be apparent within our data: peaceful challenges (PC) should be highly and positively correlated with violent challenges (VC) and, when time series data are employed, should tend to precede them;[6] similarly, PC should tend to precede and be positively correlated with our index of regime change (RΔ) instability.

Having identified the implicit predictions which these three alternative scenarios make, we are now in a position to see how far they are consistent with our data. The syndrome approach, since it basically prescribes that there should be high intercorrelations between the various dimensions of instability, is principally concerned with strength of association rather than with the direction of causality. Consequently, our main attempts to evaluate it will be confined to the section below, where the question of degrees of association is explicitly addressed. The Hibbsian and safety valve theses, on the other hand, since they directly confront this question of causality, will be evaluated mainly in the sections on pages 106 and 109. Additionally, of course. we will be interested in any alternative conclusions which our data analysis might suggest.

DEGREES OF ASSOCIATION

Given the models which we described in Figure 5.1a–c, it would seem relatively easy to assess how far our own data, at least in terms of the strength of association between the various instability dimensions, were consistent with the implied predictions of the three scenarios which we outlined. Complications arise, however, when the somewhat conflicting results presented in Table 5.1 are considered: the table reports the different values of Pearson's r for three different levels of temporal aggregation: a twenty-year aggregate cross-section, annual time series and monthly time series.

Table 5.1 in fact suggests three general conclusions: (1) there are significant regional variations in the magnitudes of the coefficients; (2) there is a tendency, independent of region, for the coefficients to become inflated as the size of the temporal unit

TABLE 5.1   Bivariate correlations (Pearson r) between dimensions of instability, at three levels of temporal aggregation

		20 year cross-section			Annual $t - s$			Monthly $t - s$		
Middle East	VC	0.54			0.16			0.06		
	GΔ	−0.25	0.35		0.17	0.16		0.09	0.12	
	PC	−0.07	0.38	0.68	0.13	0.40	0.22	0.09	0.28	0.12
		RΔ	VC	GΔ	RΔ	VC	GΔ	RΔ	VC	GΔ
	N	13			260			3120		
Atlantic	VC	0.06			0.08			0.0		
(W. Europe/	GΔ	−0.10	0.54		0.07	0.27		0.02	0.28	
N. America)	PC	−0.04	0.30	0.15	0.00	0.44	0.24	0.01	0.37	0.23
		RΔ	VC	GΔ	RΔ	VC	GΔ	RΔ	VC	GΔ
	N	22			440			5280		
Africa Sub-	VC	0.30			0.16			0.05		
Sahara	GΔ	0.26	0.75		0.11	0.69		0.06	0.55	
	PC	0.29	0.54	0.91	0.20	0.32	0.60	0.11	0.16	0.51
		RΔ	VC	GΔ	RΔ	VC	GΔ	RΔ	VC	GΔ
	N	36			720			8640		
Latin America	VC	0.07			0.18			0.04		
	GΔ	−0.04	0.45		0.16	0.37		0.08	0.14	
	PC	0.08	0.05	−0.04	0.13	0.52	0.37	0.00	0.36	0.14
		RΔ	VC	GΔ	RΔ	VC	GΔ	RΔ	VC	GΔ
	N	23			460			5520		
Far East	VC	0.09			0.00			0.00		
	GΔ	0.05	0.17		0.17	0.24		0.08	0.09	
	PC	−0.22	0.24	0.88	0.03	0.26	0.17	−0.01	0.11	0.07
		RΔ	VC	GΔ	RΔ	VC	GΔ	RΔ	VC	GΔ
	N	19			380			4800		
Eastern	VC	0.23			−0.04			0.00		
Europe	GΔ	−0.05	0.21		0.08	0.44		0.01	0.19	
	PC	0.59	0.13	0.42	−0.02	0.64	0.40	0.00	0.51	0.22
		RΔ	VC	GΔ	RΔ	VC	GΔ	RΔ	VC	GΔ
	N	9			180			2160		

increases; and (3) there is a marginal tendency for governmental change (GΔ), VC and PC to be relatively highly intercorrelated and for each of them to be relatively weakly correlated with RΔ. These general conclusions, however, require considerable elaboration and qualification.

First, it should be noted that the varying magnitudes of the correlation coefficients which are observed for the different levels of temporal aggregation are basically generated in two ways. On the one hand, when data are in time series form, any estimates of strength of association are in danger of being distorted by serially correlated error, a phenomenon which, by definition, violates the usual OLS assumptions about the independence of the residuals; although in this study serially correlated error was *not* a problem – GLS estimates of the standardised regression coefficient, B_{GLS}, proved virtually identical to the Pearson r coefficient in all cases. The second source of differential estimates of strength of association lies in the fact that if the magnitude of a coefficient between two variables is to be maintained at different levels of temporal aggregation, the smaller the size of the temporal unit, the greater the necessity that the co-occurrences of the two variables coincide temporally. Consider the hypothetical example described in Figure 5.2, in which data are available for country A on two variables on a monthly basis over a period of thirty months. Clearly, these data can be viewed in at least three ways.

(1) If we were to regard these data as a cross-section, we would not actually be able to calculate any measure of association between the two variables because there would be only one case or observation. None the less, we would be able to use these aggregate scores on variable X ($= 9$) and variable Y (also $= 9$) for cross-sectional correlative procedures provided that we had similar aggregative data for a number of other countries; (and the fact that variables X and Y both have the same score within country A would undoubtedly increase the probability of a positive cross-sectional correlation between X and Y being observed).

(2) If the data presented in Figure 5.2 are aggregated into six-month time *series* units, however, a correlation coefficient (albeit an exaggeratedly high one with limited degrees of freedom) *can* be computed, since, as Table 5.2 indicates, we now have five observations for each variable.

(3) If the data presented in Figure 5.2 are considered in their original monthly time-series form, however, the magnitude of the correlation between them *at time t* is drastically weakened; indeed, the correlation disappears altogether.

Now although the example cited here is both hypothetical and extreme, we hope the general point is made: for any given joint distribution of two variables measured over time, the magnitude of the correlation between them varies with the size of the time units which are employed. There have, in fact, been several econometrically-oriented investigations of the effects of temporal aggregation on measures of association, but their main conclusion is that there is no *systematic* relationship involved, a tendency which is reflected in our own data.

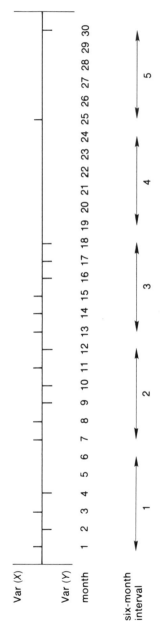

FIGURE 5.2 Hypothetical occurrences/non-occurrences of two variables, X and Y, over a period of thirty months

TABLE 5.2   Six-monthly time-series data derived from Fig. 5.2

		Variable X	Variable Y
(Six-month interval)	t_1	2	2
	t_2	3	3
	t_3	3	3
	t_4	0	0
	t_5	1	1

But if there is no systematic relationship between the various coefficients presented in Table 5.2, how are the coefficients themselves to be interpreted? Which level of temporal aggregation (if any) offers the most adequate (or, perhaps, the least inadequate) description of the interrelationships between the dimensions of political instability? These questions cannot be answered definitively, but two general sorts of solution can be offered: either (a) the coefficients can be interpreted as representing distinct short term, medium term and long term effects; or (b) the coefficients which employ the most stringent tests of association and prediction can be adopted and the remainder ignored.

(a)   **Interpreting the different coefficients as constituting short term, medium term and long term effects**

The first solution (though this is one which we will, in fact, reject) is to argue that the different coefficients obtained from the use of different sized time units can be reconciled by reference to the conclusion reached by Kuh and Meyer; that '. . . cross-section data tend to measure long run and other effects that are not observable . . . in short period . . . time series variations'.[7] It follows from this argument that each set of coefficients can be regarded as representing a particular type of relationship. In this context, the monthly time series results would represent comparatively short term relationships, whereas the annual time series would represent medium term, and the twenty-year cross-section, long term relationships. The implication of this interpretation of the observed relationships, of course, is that for each bivariate relationship the three sets of coefficients (monthly, annual, cross-sectional) do not necessarily imply theoretically inconsistent conclusions; they simply

imply that the three different levels of temporal aggregation enable descriptions to be made of three different types of effect. In this regard, the patterns of intercorrelation presented in Table 5.1 would appear to suggest that (with some exceptions) the degree of association between the dimensions of instability is, in general, greater in the long term than it is in the medium term, which is in turn greater than the degree of association in the short term.

This argument, however, is based upon an important fallacy. The claim that aggregated cross-sectional correlations measure long-run effects may be empirically true, but it does not follow logically from the measurement procedure itself. Consider, for example, a long-run relationship in which the level of peaceful challenge at time t_1 (where t is, say, 1 year) really does influence the level of governmental change in some later time period, say at t_{10}. The correct, and indeed obvious, way to estimate the strength and/or form of this relationship would be to use time series data in order to compare the level of PC at t_1 with the level of GΔ at t_{10} over as large a sample of nations and time periods as possible.[8] One would expect, in this context, to find a high correlation between PC_{t1} and $GΔ_{t10}$. To estimate the strength of the aggregated relationship for the whole ten-year period is an entirely different procedure; correlating ten-year aggregates simply does not measure the kind of long-run effect which we described above. The spurious nature of the argument which claims that such aggregates do measure long-run effects originates, I think, in a semantic confusion. The argument fails to distinguish between, on the one hand 'a long-run effect', which as we have indicated clearly requires time series data for its evaluation, and on the other hand 'an average relationship over a long period', which *can* be reasonably evaluated by reference to a temporally aggregated cross-section. The second interpretation does not have the same wide-ranging theoretical implications as the first, but it in fact represents the only satisfactory description which can be made of a correlation coefficient (or of any summary statistic) generated from a temporally aggregated cross-section.

To recognise this limitation of aggregated cross-sectional data is, of course, to expose the pointlessness of examining the intercorrelations derived from such data when more precise time series data are available: where, we might ask, is the logic in examining an 'average relationship over a long period' when a 'non-average' (monthly or annual time series) examination over the same long period can be undertaken? This is not of course to deny the utility of cross-sectional data in all contexts – cross-sectional analysis is entirely suitable, for example, with regard to the possible socio-economic and structural correlates of instability, since the relevant data often only exist in cross-sectional form, do not vary much in the short-run and are certainly not available as monthly time series – but simply to re-emphasise its limitations in describing the interrelationships between event variables such as our instability measures, which vary considerably from month to month.

(b) Adopting the most stringent test of association and prediction

It would appear to be the case, then, that the three types of coefficient presented in Table 5.1 do not furnish theoretically consistent conclusions, but rather that the cross-sectional, and perhaps (though to a lesser extent) even the annual, correlations presented in the table provide somewhat misleading conclusions as to the strength of association between the dimensions of instability. In this context, it seems logical to conclude that the *monthly intercorrelations provide the least inaccurate indication of the 'real' interrelationships between the dimensions*, since those data impose the most stringent requirements of co-occurrence upon the event variables to be correlated, and we take it as axiomatic that when hypotheses are being evaluated or generalisations inductively derived, the most rigorous tests possible should be applied to the data.

Of course, it could be argued that since it is possible, for example, for $R\Delta$ at t (where $t = 1$ month) to be a function of, say, VC at $t - 1$, $t - 2$ and $t - 3$, the measures of association based upon the annual time series, and perhaps even the cross-section data (though they may not actually provide direct measurements of long-run effects), can take some account of these lagged effects, while monthly correlations at t (like those provided in Table 5.1) cannot. While this argument may be partly true, we reject it for two reasons. Firstly, as I have demonstrated in an earlier study, the use of temporally aggregated data necessarily involves making assumptions which may not be justified about the structure of $t + n$ and $t - n$ correlations. Secondly (and more importantly), in subsequent sections of this chapter we will in fact explicitly investigate a series of lagged relationships between our dimensions of instability; and, as we will see, in most cases these lagged effects do not significantly increase the degrees of association between the various instability dimensions beyond the levels described in Table 5.1.

There is an additional reason, however, for regarding the monthly intercorrelations as the best indicators of the strength of association among the dimensions of instability, a reason which is related to the more general question of the nature of the predictions which any given political analyst is trying to make.

Consider, for example, a situation in which, using a twenty-year aggregate cross-section (and making suitable controls for other variables), we obtain a significant standardised regression coefficient (say $B = 0.4$) between two event variables X and Y. Suppose that we now decide to use our knowledge of B in order to predict the likely course of events in a particular country, and suppose further that shortly after we begin our observation of this country, X increases by 1 unit. Presumably, using our knowledge of B, we will predict a 0.4 increase in Y. But at what point in time will we predict this increase to occur? Immediately? Or in six months? Or 'some time over the next twenty years'? Quite clearly, the weakness of a prediction about event variables based on a twenty-year cross-section is that the only conclusions *which can be derived from the data* (that is to say, discounting common sense and imagination) is that there will be a 0.4 increase in Y 'some time over the next twenty years'; and, equally clearly, this is not a particularly useful prediction. While it should be acknowledged that this limitation does not have the same implications for (socio-economic and structural) *non*-event variables (since these variables may take ten or twenty years to change significantly anyway), we would argue that, if meaningful predictions about the interrelationships between event variables are to be made, a greater degree of temporal precision should be possible. (If X changes now, we should be able to predict what will happen to Y, preferably within the next month or two, but at least within the next year.) We would also argue that such precision is only possible if the level of temporal aggregation is considerably smaller than twenty years. Indeed, given that political scientists should be aiming for as great a degree of precision as possible, the smaller the size of the temporal unit, the better. It is precisely for this reason that in attempting to assess the degree of association between our instability dimensions, we will emphasise the monthly correlations: it is these correlations which not only make the most stringent demands upon co-occurrence but which also provide the most precise basis for future prediction.

Implications of the monthly correlations

Having established, then, that our best indications of the strength of association between the dimensions of instability are to be derived from the *monthly* time-series correlations, we are now in a position to examine the implications of those correlations. The most obvious conclusion to be drawn is that there appears to be no support for either the syndrome or the safety valve theses as we stated them: with regard to the syndrome thesis, our regime change index consistently fails to be related to any of the other dimensions of instability ($r < 0.1$ in all cases except for the RΔ-PC relationship in Sub-Saharan Africa where $r = 0.11$); and with regard to the safety valve thesis, peaceful challenges, in so far as they are related to the other dimensions at all, tend to be positively, rather than negatively, correlated with them. However, as we hinted earlier, the VC, GΔ and PC dimensions of instability *do* tend to be intercorrelated (with the exception of Far East) across all regions, although only three of these correlations are above $r = 0.5$ (GΔ-VC and GΔ-PC in Sub-Saharan Africa, and PC-VC in Eastern Europe), and most are below $r = 0.3$. Making allowance for the fact that the tendencies are relatively weak, therefore, there is a limited amount of evidence to support a reduced or circumscribed version of the syndrome thesis; that PC, VC and GΔ tend to be weakly correlated (on a month by month basis) in nearly all of the regions analysed.

Within the general context of this reduced syndrome interpretation, however, several additional qualifications about the interrelationships between the dimensions of instability need to be made. It should be noted firstly that, in the Far East, even this interpretation is inadequate, since in this region only the PC-VC relationship provides a correlation (and then only marginally) above $r = 0.1$: in the Far East there would appear to be virtually no relationship between the dimensions of instability at all. Secondly, with the exception of Sub-Saharan Africa, the highest correlation within each region is the coefficient for the PC-VC linkage, although, as we suggested before, these correlations are not particularly high. Finally, it is interesting to note that, within each regional grouping, the GΔ-VC and GΔ-PC correlations tend to yield similar values. (In the Middle East, $r = 0.12$ for the GΔ-VC and GΔ-PC relationships; in Atlantic, $t = 0.28$ and 0.23 respectively; in Sub-Saharan Africa, $r = 0.55$ and 0.51 respectively; in Latin America, $r = 0.14$ and 0.14 respectively; and in Eastern Europe, $r = 0.19$ and 0.22 respectively.) Although the values of the coefficients vary from region to region, the remarkable consistency of the tendency suggests that, independently of region, governmental change has a similar relationship with both violent and peaceful challenges.

To summarise, with regard to the overall degree of association between the dimensions of instability, the evidence seems to suggest that while there are regional variations in the levels of intercorrelation (which are all fairly low), the *pattern* of those intercorrelations is reasonably consistent: across nearly all regions (1) regime change does not appear to be related to the other instability dimensions, (2) the highest correlation is between the VC and PC indices, and (3) governmental change correlates equally well (or badly) with the two sorts of challenge behaviour.

We are now in a position to move away from questions of mere association and can approach the more problematic issue of causality. As we suggested before, in attempting to evaluate the three scenarios which were outlined in the first Section of this chapter, we will approach this question in two ways. We will begin by examining (using cross-sectional data) a non-recursive model of the interrelationships between the instability dimensions, which, in the first instance, assumes that reciprocal linkages exist between each pair of dimensions. We will then turn to investigate a series of lagged models, in order to see if, for any given two-variable relationship, time-series data suggest any alternative conclusions about the direction of causality.

THE DIRECTION OF CAUSALITY: USING NON-RECURSIVE MODELLING TECHNIQUES AND CROSS-SECTIONAL DATA

It may seem rather perverse to use cross-sectional data (albeit in conjunction with non-recursive techniques) in order to examine the notion of *causality* between event variables, when in the immediately preceding section we dismissed this type of data as being unsuitable for the accurate identification of the strength of association between such variables. The perversity is only superficial, however, when the full implications of a non-recursive model are considered. Non-recursive (and indeed recursive) models enable the estimation of the effect which X has upon Y, *controlling for the effects of other variables*; and since these 'other variables' which are relevant in this context are only available in cross-sectional form, if the appropriate controls are to be made, it is inevitable that cross-section data must be used. It is not necessary to describe the estimation and identification procedures of non-recursive modelling here, since detailed treatments of the subject exist elsewhere. It is sufficient to point out here that its purpose is to enable the estimation of

(i) the effect on X of a unit change in Y, controlling for everything else which is known to influence X, and

(ii) the effect on Y of a unit change in X, controlling for everything else which is known to influence Y.

In short, a two-stage least squares (2SLS) non-recursive model enables the simultaneous estimation of reciprocal causal effects. Figure 5.3a reports our non-recursive estimates of the linkages between the dimensions of instability. Figure 5.3b reports the *significant* linkages identified in Figure 5.3a.

As can be seen from a comparison of Figure 5.3b and Figure 5.1a (which describes the predictions generated by Hibbs' final model), *Hibbs'* conclusions derive no support from the analysis undertaken in this part of our study: while Hibbs' conclusions imply that peaceful challenges should serve to encourage (albeit indirectly) violent challenges, according to our 2SLS estimates it would appear that VC has no effect on PC instability whatsoever. In addition, the RΔ → VC arrow in Figure 5.3b ($B = 0.19$) contradicts the direction of the regime change (*coup*) – violent challenge (internal war) relationship which Hibbs specifies.

Figure 5.3b also contradicts the idea of a peaceful challenge *safety valve* mechanism. As Figure 5.1b predicts, if the safety valve thesis is correct, then peaceful challenge should be seen to have a reductive impact upon (at least one of) the other dimensions of instability. Figure 5.3b demonstrates that this is clearly not the case: on no occasion does PC vary negatively with another variable. Finally, it is worth mentioning that Figure 5.3b also . provides very little support for the syndrome thesis: only three of

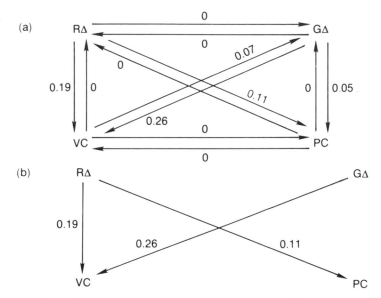

FIGURE 5.3   Non-recursive estimates of (a) reciprocal linkages between each pair of instability dimensions, and (b) between instability dimensions: significant relationships only.

The exogenous variables employed in order to obtain these estimates are derived from the 'best models' which we report in Chapter 8. They are explicitly identified in Tables 8.1–8.4.

the twelve possible linkages between the dimensions of instability were found to be positive and significant.

The non-recursive estimates, however, not only imply virtually no support for our three original scenarios: the very low levels of statistical explanation identified in Figure 5.3b also preclude the possibility of offering an alternative theoretical interpretation of the data at this stage. Moreover, since (as we pointed out in Chapter 2) estimates of linkages between event variables derived from cross-section data tend to be somewhat unreliable in any case, it would seem advisable to conclude that these non-recursive results, quite simply, do nothing to confirm any of our initial predictions about the interrelationships among the different dimensions of instability. In consequence, we now proceed to examine those interrelationships using *time series* data: in the following section, our principal objective will be the identification of contexts in which one type of instability consistently tends to precede one or more others.

THE DIRECTION OF CAUSALITY: USING LAGGED RELATIONSHIPS AND ANNUAL AND MONTHLY TIME-SERIES DATA

Whereas in the preceding section it was not really feasible to examine the potential effects of region upon each dimension of instability because of the comparatively small number of cases within each regional grouping, because (with annual data) we now have twenty observations per country[9] (and, with monthly data, 240 cases per country), the number of cases is in fact sufficient to permit the examination of distinct regional subsets. Given the clear regional variations which we identified in Table 5.1, and which have been reported elsewhere, this will obviously enable us to undertake a more sensitive investigation of the patterns of interrelationship between government and regime changes and violent and peaceful challenges than we have so far made. Nonetheless, as we suggested before, in comparison with our 2SLS estimates, the introduction of time-series data also implies a loss of information in the sense that the estimates presented in Figures 5.3a and 5.3b explicitly controlled for a number of exogenous variables which also appear to influence each of the four dimensions of instability. This disadvantage is outweighted, however, by the fact that time-series data enable us to search for (statistically) *significant lagged relationships*, that is to say, relationships in which one variable at $t - 1$ (say) can be used to predict another at t.

The importance of such relationships lies in the fact that they enable us to address the problem of the relationship between causality and correlation with rather more sophistication than we would be able to if we simply made blanket reference to the hypothetico-deductive paradigm. As we pointed out earlier, with cross-sectional data, a strong correlation between two variables A and B is consistent with at least two hypotheses: (1) A causes or influences B; and (2) B causes or influences A. (In such a context the empirical correlation can be cited as corroboration for either of these hypotheses.) As we also pointed out, however, it has been shown that even technically sophisticated attempts to identify the dominant direction of various causal linkages using cross-sectional event data produced somewhat unsatisfactory results. What we would argue, therefore, is that the identification of significant lagged relationships represents a rather less suspect method of specifying the probable direction (or dominant direction) of the linkage between any pair of variables.

Consider then, for example, the RΔ and VC dimensions of instability. In general, four types of lagged relationship could exist between the two variables:

(i) RΔ_{t-1} predicts VC$_t$ but VC$_{t-1}$ does not predict RΔ_t;

(ii) VC$_{t-1}$ predicts RΔ_t but RΔ_{t-1} does not predict VC$_t$;

(iii) VC$_{t-1}$ predicts RΔ_t and RΔ_{t-1} predicts VC$_t$;

(iv) VC$_{t-1}$ does not predict RΔ_t and RΔ_{t-1} does not predict VC$_t$.

Clearly, types (iii) and (iv) do not allow any conclusions to be drawn as to the direction of causality between violent challenges and regime change, since in both cases there is a symmetry of lag and lead effects (iii) or non-effects (iv) which effectively cancel each other out and which probably denote a balanced reciprocal relationship. Types (i) and (ii), however, *do* permit some conclusions to be drawn. If *A* consistently tends to precede *B*, then if there is any causal connection between them, it seems reasonable to argue that *A* has a causal influence upon *B*, rather than that *B* has a causal influence upon *A*. Wherever relationships of type (i) or type (ii) exist, we would argue that this constitutes sufficient evidence for the dominant direction of causality to be identified. Using this general principle, Table 5.3 reports, by region, all the significant lagged effects which were found to exist in our annual data between the dimensions of instability.

Before we can comment upon these annual findings, however, it is necessary to mention briefly the equivalent findings which were derived from our monthly data. (We do not report these findings in detail here because of the limited conclusions which they suggest.) Using monthly data, lag and lead regression coefficients (between X_t and Y_t) were estimated for X_{t-1}, X_{t-2}, ..., X_{t-6} and X_{t+1}, X_{t+2}, ..., X_{t+6} for each pair of instability dimensions. In almost every region, the lag and lead coefficients (estimated either individually or in combination) proved to be non-significant. The only exception was in Latin America, where VC at $t - 1$ and PC at $t - 1$ consistently tended to precede GΔ at t; and even then, the levels of statistical explanation were relatively low. Given that these monthly data provide virtually no basis for predicting into the future, that is to say, given that knowledge of what happened this month (or even during the last six months) is not much use for

Significant lagged relationships derived from annual data

Region	Dependent variable	Significant predictors of dependent variable at t*	R^2	Conclusions
Atlantic	$R\Delta_t$	PC_{t-2}	0.037	(1) $R\Delta \leftarrow PC$ (2) $G\Delta \leftarrow VC$
	VC_t	$G\Delta, PC, PC_{t-2}$	0.23	
	$G\Delta_t$	VC, PC, VC_{t-1}	0.095	
	PC_t	$VC, G\Delta, VC_{t-1}, VC_{t-2}$	0.215	
Middle East	$R\Delta_t$	$VC, G\Delta, VC_{t-2}$	0.05	(1) $G\Delta \leftarrow PC$
	VC_t	$R\Delta, PC, PC_{t-1}$	0.177	
	$G\Delta_t$	$R\Delta, PC, PC_{t-1}$	0.08	
	PC_t	$VC, G\Delta, VC_{t-1}$	0.20	
Far East	$R\Delta_t$	$G\Delta, G\Delta_{t-1}, G\Delta_{t-2}, VC_{t-2}$	0.06	(1) $R\Delta \leftarrow VC$ (2) $R\Delta \leftarrow G\Delta$ (3) $VC \leftarrow PC$
	VC_t	$G\Delta, PC, G\Delta_{t-1}, PC_{t-1}$	0.12	
	$G\Delta_t$	$R\Delta, VC, PC, VC_{t-1}, PC_{t-1}, PC_{t-2}$	0.13	
	PC_t	$VC, G\Delta, G\Delta_{t-1}, G\Delta_{t-2}$	0.11	
Sub-Saharan Africa	$R\Delta_t$	$VC, G\Delta, PC, VC_{t-1}$	0.07	(1) $R\Delta \leftarrow VC$
	VC_t	$R\Delta, G\Delta, PC, G\Delta_{t-1}$	0.50	
	$G\Delta_t$	$R\Delta, VC, PC, VC_{t-1}, PC_{t-1}$	0.64	
	PC_t	$R\Delta, VC, G\Delta, G\Delta_{t-1}$	0.401	
Latin America	$R\Delta_t$	$VC, G\Delta, VC_{t-1}$	0.05	(1) $G\Delta \leftarrow VC$ (2) $VC \leftarrow PC$
	VC_t	$R\Delta, G\Delta, PC, PC_{t-1}$	0.34	
	$G\Delta_t$	$R\Delta, VC, PC, VC_{t-1}$	0.21	
	PC_t	$VC, G\Delta,$	0.314	
Eastern Europe	$R\Delta_t$	—	0	(1) $PC \leftarrow G\Delta$
	VC_t	$G\Delta, PC,$	0.45	
	$GΔ$	$VC, PC,$	0.23	
	PC	$VC, G\Delta, G\Delta_{t-2}$	0.43	

*Coefficients for all cited independent variables were more than twice their respective standard errors. All coefficients were positive.

predicting what is likely to happen next month, it seems sensible to explore the possibility of employing knowledge of what happened this *year* as a means of predicting what might happen next year. It is in this context that the results presented in Table 5.3 assume relevance.

The table, in fact, suggests a number of general conclusions. Firstly, with regard to the levels of statistical explanation (the R^2 values), the pattern follows the observations which we made in an earlier section of this chapter when we discussed the question of strength of association: (1) the RΔ index consistently bears little or no relation to the other dimensions – all the R^2's are below 0.07; (2) the equations for the remaining instability dimensions generally exhibit similar values of R^2, which is consistent with the 'limited syndrome' scenario which we sketched earlier (although the GΔ equations for Atlantic and Middle East disavow this tendency); and (3) the relationships are strongest in Sub-Saharan Africa ($R^2 = 0.07$ for the RΔ equation; 0.50 for the VC equation; 0.64 for the GΔ equation; and 0.40 for the PC equation) and weakest in the Far East ($R^2 = 0.06$ for RΔ, 0.12 for VC, 0.13 for GΔ, and 0.11 for PC).

The second set of conclusions are concerned with the extent to which the results presented in Table 5.3 are consistent with the Hibbsian and safety valve theses which we outlined earlier, and with the results of our own non-recursive model. The applicability of the safety valve thesis can be dismissed immediately, since none of the relationships specified in Table 5.3 is negative. The Hibbsian model, however (which, it will be recalled, predicts that PC → VC → RΔ), does derive some support in certain regions: in sub-Saharan Africa and in the Far East, VC consistently tends to precede RΔ (that is to say VC → RΔ); and in the Far East and in Latin America, PC consistently precedes VC (that is to say PC → VC). Clearly, since our non-recursive model contradicted Hibbs' findings concerning the interrelationships between PC, VC and RΔ, the fact that Hibbs' model receives partial support from our annual time series data necessarily implies that these time series results contradict our non-recursive conclusions: the most notable contradictions are the RΔ-VC relationship (the time series direction is VC → RΔ in those cases where it is significant, whereas the non-recursive direction is RΔ → VC) and the VC-PC relationship (the time series direction is PC → VC, whereas in the non-recursive model there is no relationship between VC and PC).

The final and most important implications of Table 5.3 are summarised in the 'conclusions' column in that table, which identifies the dominant direction of each of the causal linkages for which evidence exists. Seven out of the ten linkages are concerned with relationships between change and challenge dimensions: in six of these cases the *change* variable is dependent.[10] In other words, it would appear to be the case that, in general, challenge behaviours tend to precede changes in either government or regime, that is to say challenge behaviours tend to be aimed at the old regime or government, rather than the new. The notable exceptions to this pattern occur in Eastern Europe where governmental change tends to precede peaceful challenges rather than follow them – the challenge is aimed at the new government rather than at the old – although given the supervisory role which the Soviet Union has adopted for itself in the internal politics of the Warsaw Pact countries (one thinks particularly of the enforced governmental changes in Czechoslovakia in 1948 and 1968, and in Hungary in 1956), this countervailing tendency is hardly surprising.

Despite this general tendency for challenge behaviours to precede government or regime change, however, the specific pattern of significant lagged relationships varies from region to region. These variations, which in the final analysis constitute our most important generalisations about the interrelationships between the dimensions of instability, are summarised in Table 5.4. We have already established how far these generalisations are consistent with our own previous findings; the question we must now ask is whether or not there is some kind of simplifying logic

TABLE 5.4 Summary of findings derived from annual time-series data

---

(i) In the Atlantic area, peaceful challenges tend to precede regime changes, violent challenges tend to precede governmental changes.

(ii) In the Middle East, peaceful challenges tend to precede governmental changes.

(iii) In Eastern Europe, government changes tend to precede peaceful challenges.

(iv) In the Far East, peaceful challenges tend to precede violent challenges, violent challenges tend to precede regime changes, governmental changes tend to precede regime changes.

(v) In Sub-Saharan Africa, violent challenges tend to precede regime changes.

(vi) In Latin America, peaceful challenges tend to precede violent challenges, violent challenges tend to precede governmental change.

underlying them. Of course, we could argue that the different tendencies which we have just described simply constitute a series of 'regional effects', which are themselves a function of the different cultural and historical conditions which operate within each of the regions. This interpretation is perfectly satisfactory when no simpler, unifying pattern is observable. In relation to the ten generalisations which we described above, however, there *would* seem to be a simpler pattern. In each of the Third World regions (Middle East, Far East, Sub-Saharan Africa and Latin America) there is a marked tendency for 'less severe' forms of instability (once they have occurred, for whatever reason) to generate an internal dynamic of their own, and to *escalate* into 'more severe' forms of instability. Now, clearly, this latter statement requires qualification. What it assumes is that while the four dimensions of instability which we have identified are analytically distinct, certain of those dimensions are more disruptive for the political system as a whole than others. Figure 5.4 describes a possible rank ordering of the instability dimensions on this implied 'disruption' scale

Given the system of orderings specified in Figure 5.4, the meaning of the term escalation now becomes clear: escalation exists (a) when PC leads to GΔ or VC, or (b) when GΔ or VC lead to RΔ. Moreover, as the results presented in Table 5.4 indicate, there is such a tendency for escalation to occur, in the Third World at least: (1) peaceful challenges tend to escalate into violent challenges in the Far East and Latin America; (2) violent challenges tend to escalate into regime change in the Far East and in Sub-Saharan Africa; (3) peaceful challenges tend to escalate into governmental changes in the Middle East; and (4) governmental changes tend to escalate into regime change in the Far East.

In the Atlantic and East European regions, however, there is no such tendency towards escalation: in Eastern Europe (as we indicated earlier) peaceful challenges tend to follow rather than precede governmental changes; and in the Atlantic area, violent challenges are likely to lead to governmental change rather than to regime change, while peaceful challenges show a marginal tendency to lead directly to changes in regime.

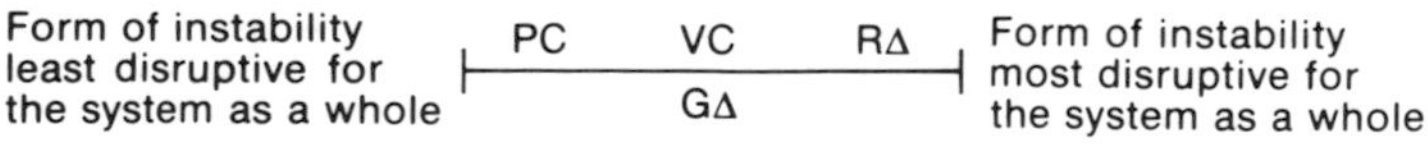

Form of instability least disruptive for the system as a whole	PC	VC	RΔ	Form of instability most disruptive for the system as a whole
		GΔ		

FIGURE 5.4   Rank ordering of instability dimensions

This difference between the Third World and the developed World, with respect to the question of escalation, clearly requires some sort of explanation; although, given the plethora of literature devoted to the general issue of political development, an adequate explanation is not particularly difficult to find. The most appropriate concept to cite in this context would in fact seem to be Huntington's notion of *institutionalisation*, the development of strong and stable political institutions (which exhibit adaptability, autonomy and coherence) capable of absorbing the divisive effects of social and economic change and the consequent demands for political participation which such change can generate.[11] The implications of the concept of institutionalisation for the escalatory tendencies which we identified above are fairly obvious: in general, strong and stable political institutions prevent escalation. Specifically, this implies that in the Third World regions, the available political institutions are not sufficiently autonomous, adaptable or coherent to channel the less severe forms of instability (particularly PC) through conventional and/or legal mechanisms. It is the inability of less developed systems to provide such mechanisms which creates the internal dynamic of the escalatory process: in Third World systems there is less of an institutional cushion to prevent (say) peaceful challenges from escalating into (say) violent challenges.[12]

In the Atlantic and East European regions, however, it would appear to be the case that the level of political institutionalisation *is* sufficient to break the escalatory sequence. While in Eastern Europe it is probably the coercive power of the state which is the main source of this sufficiency, in virtually all of the Atlantic systems, peaceful challenges at least are an accepted and integral part of the political process: the fact that these relatively non-disruptive behaviours can be channelled through conventional, institutionalised mechanisms is not only a reflection of the institutional strength of the system as a whole, but, more importantly, it prevents the development of an escalatory dynamic. In short, escalation seems to occur only where political institutions are weak.

SUMMARY AND CONCLUSIONS

In this chapter we have been concerned with two main questions: (1) the relative strengths of association and (2) the possible causal interrelationships among the dimensions of political instability which we identified in Chapter 4. The starting point for our analysis was the identification of three 'scenarios' which purport to describe those interrelationships: the 'syndrome' thesis which suggests that unstable countries tend to experience all forms of instability; the 'safety valve' thesis which argues that peaceful challenges can actually serve to inhibit other forms of instability; and the (empirical) 'Hibbsian' model which predicts that peaceful challenges should tend to lead to violent challenges, and that violent challenges should themselves tend to produce regime change.

With regard to the question of degrees of association, we reported (by region) the (conflicting) bivariate intercorrelations among dimensions using data at three levels of temporal aggregation: a twenty-year aggregated cross-section (where the overall levels of correlation were highest), an annual time series, and a monthly time series (where the overall levels of correlation were lowest). We argued that the *monthly* correlations in fact offered the least inaccurate and indeed most meaningful representations of the relative strengths of association between instability dimensions. The basis of this argument was, firstly, that since estimates of strength of association derived from twenty-year aggregates (and to a lesser extent estimates derive from annual time series) can only describe *average* relationships over a long period, monthly correlations impose the most stringent requirements of co-occurrence upon the (event) variables to be correlated, and, as we suggested, when any attempt to evaluate a generalisation is being made, the rules of scientific enquiry demand that the most rigorous tests possible are applied to the available data. The second main reason for focussing on the monthly findings was that because results derived from twenty-year aggregates generate temporally non-specific predictions about the interrelationships between event variables, and because temporal specificity in the context of such variables is a prerequisite of meaningful prediction, the strength of association between event variables is optimally estimated using data at the lowest possible level of temporal aggregation, which in this study, of course, is represented by our *monthly* data.

The conclusions which our monthly data suggested, however, were rather limited: while there was some support for a reduced version of the syndrome thesis (excluding the RΔ dimension of instability), most of the correlations were below $r = 0.3$, a level of association which does not permit definitive statements about the relationships between dimensions to be made, apart from the rather general observation that *in most regions PC, VC and GΔ tend to be weakly intercorrelated*.

We addressed the question of *causality* in two ways: (1) by developing a 2SLS non-recursive causal model using the twenty-year aggregate cross-section; and (2) by searching for statistically significant lagged relationships in the annual and monthly time series data-sets. The non-recursive model, which permitted the simultaneous estimation of all the possible reciprocal linkages between the dimensions of instability, suggested two general conclusions. Firstly, it provided no support for either the Hibbsian, syndrome or safety valve theses. Secondly, the level of statistical explanation was so low that the model appeared to offer no support for any alternative theoretical interpretation.

In the second part of our discussion of the question of causality, we searched our time series data for relationships where one variable consistently tended to precede another, by examining the structure of $t + n$ and $t - n$ correlations (by region) for each bivariate relationship. The *monthly* data, however, failed to suggest any conclusions about the direction of causality, apart from in Latin America, where governmental changes were consistently preceded by peaceful and violent challenges. Because the monthly data revealed so little, we proceeded to examine the pattern of (lag and lead) *annual* time-series correlations, and although there were significant regional variations in the conclusions which the data suggested, there was a general tendency in the Third World regions towards *escalation*. This tendency was not apparent, however, in the (comparatively developed) Atlantic and East European regions, and we consequently argued that the escalation phenomenon was probably a function of the lower levels of political institutionalisation which exist in less developed systems.

Having mapped out the different sets of regional inter-relationships among the dimensions of instability, and having attempted to reduce them to the operation of a more general process, we are now in a position to widen the focus of our analysis and look for *exogenous* causal influences upon each of our dimensions of instability. Ideally, we would wish to conduct this search using time-series data, but as we have repeatedly asserted, many of these exogenous variables are available only in cross-sectional form. In consequence, we are forced, in subsequent analyses, to use temporally aggregated cross-sectional data. While this does not mean that our conclusions will be subject to the same criticisms as the cross-sectional analysis carried out in this chapter (those criticisms were confined to aggregated cross-sectional investigations where both dependent and independent variables were concerned with political *events*), it does imply that it will not be possible to incorporate the conclusions which we draw in subsequent chapters and the conclusions which we have drawn in this chapter into the same overall (statistical) model. In this sense, the next three chapters mark a considerable departure both from the issues which we have attempted to cover, and from the methodology which we have employed, in this chapter.

6 Potential Exogenous Correlates of Political Instability: Some Theoretical Considerations

In this and in the next chapter we examine a series of exogenous variables which have at different times been postulated as influences upon the level of political instability. We undertake this task for three main reasons. First, despite the plethora of empirical findings concerning the determinants of instability which were outlined in Chapter 2, many of those studies (as we saw) yielded mutually contradictory conclusions: in the next two chapters we will attempt to impose some order upon the consequent confusion. Secondly, while previous causal analyses (with the notable exception of Hibbs' analysis) have tended to view instability as a unitary phenomenon, we have sought to regard it as a multi-faceted one; and as we will see, the four instability dimensions which we identified in Chapters 3 and 4 relate to the various exogenous variables in very different ways.

The third and principal justification for examining the impact of these exogenous variables, however, is related to the general technique for operationalising political instability which we advanced in Chapter 5; a technique which (it will be recalled) avoids the fallacious assumption that, regardless of context, greater *frequency* (of destabilising events) necessarily denotes greater instability, and is instead based upon the assumption that the destabilising impact of any given event should be assessed in terms of the extent to which that event constitutes a deviation from the previous system norm. The direct implication of the use of this technique is that the four sets of temporally aggregated instability scores which we employ as dependent variables (which correspond to our four instability dimensions) are by definition very different from the temporally aggregated instability scores which previous (frequency-oriented) analyses have utilised; in the next two chapters we will be interested to see whether or not these new measures indicate any alternative patterns of interrelationship between instability and its (exogenous) socio-economic and structural correlates.

The exogenous variables which we examine fall into two broad categories. The first set of variables is concerned with what we will refer to as *paradigms of political change*: the two (competing) paradigms which we investigate – 'development' and 'dependency' – attempt to provide general theoretical frameworks within which the process of political change in specific political systems (and indeed, in political systems in general) can be analysed. The second set of exogenous variables is concerned with the *structural characteristics* of political systems, in relation to which we investigate the role of 'governmental coercion' (actual and potential), 'structured inequality' (inequalities in income and land ownership) and 'structured division' (notably primordial cleavages).

In this chapter we examine the theoretical background of each of the above five groups of exogenous variables, and develop a series of hypotheses which directly relate those exogenous variables to political instability. In the next chapter, we attempt to assess how far these hypotheses are consistent with our data by examining, firstly, the overall (global) levels of correlation relating to each hypothesis, and secondly, various non-linear and regional variations in those levels of correlation. In Chapter 8, we attempt to synthesise all these findings in a series of single equation predictive models.

PARADIGMS OF POLITICAL CHANGE: 1 DEVELOPMENT

The notion of 'development' is one of the most widely used – and also one of the most extensively abused – concepts in comparative politics. Before we can discuss its specific implications, however, it is necessary to draw two distinctions, both of which tend to be ignored, to varying degrees, by critics of the developmental model.

The first of these is the distinction between development as an achieved *stasis* and development as an on-going *process*. All development theorists to some extent use both of these notions, since even if one attempts to discuss development exclusively as a process, the question of 'development towards what?' is inevitably begged. The *balance* of emphasis between process and stasis, however, varies from study to study. The stasis-oriented investigations of Rustow and of Almond and Powell, for example, tend to focus mainly upon the structural characteristics of (what these authors define to be) the 'developed' western liberal democracies in order to produce their respective characterisations of what constitutes a 'developed' system.[1] It is then argued that other nations are moving inexorably (though at differential rates) towards this optimal stasis. The more recent exponents of the development thesis (and in particular, the 'crisis theorists'), on the other hand, specifically identify development as a process which has no *single* goal or end-state.[2]

This does not mean, however, that the propounders of this model fail to answer the question 'development towards what?' It simply implies that they recognise that changes in, and interactions between, what they characterise as the components of the 'development syndrome' – 'capacity', 'equality', and 'differentiation'[3] – will not produce a unidirectional form of change. Rather, such changes in the components of the development syndrome are regarded as being capable of producing a multiplicity of types of political system, since it is possible, in principle, for any given system to change in relation to any one of the syndrome components, and to fail to change in relation to one or more others. Development consists in movement (away from the origin) along *any* of the dimensions or components identified in Figure 6.1.

A second distinction which needs to be drawn is that between *socio-economic* development and *political* development. Although these two types of change may well be empirically related, it is nonetheless made quite clear by most development theorists that they are *analytically* distinct and that they accordingly merit separate investigation: political development is associated with changes (of the type specified above) in political structures and processes, whereas socio-economic development is concerned with the capacity, or with changes in the capacity, of any given society to create and sustain the consumption of material goods.

Given these distinctions, the concept of socio-economic development at least can be defined and operationalised relatively easily. Table 6.1 identifies the component dimensions of

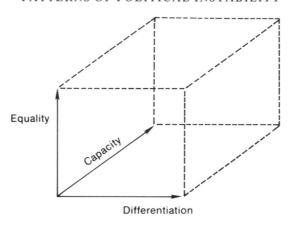

FIGURE 6.1   Diagrammatic representation of the crisis theorists' concept of development (movement along any of these dimensions constitutes development)

socio-economic development (defined as both a process and a stasis) which we propose to use in our subsequent analysis. The table also identifies the operational referrents of each of the component dimensions which we will employ; it seems to be self-evident that these indicators measure the level of, and changes in the level of, socio-economic development.

The specifically political aspects of development, on the other hand, are somewhat less easy to define and measure. We have already referred to the analyses of Rustow, of Almond and Powell and of the 'crisis theorists'. There are, however, several additional ways of conceptualising development. Apter, for example, equates development with an expansion in the range of political and economic choices available to the individual within a given system;[6] Huntington views it primarily in terms of the emergence of strong and stable political institutions capable of absorbing the devisive impact of social change;[7] and Pye, in attempting to review a number of previous analyses, cites ten alternative definitions.[8] Despite the imaginative possibilities of many of these definitions, we would, nonetheless, argue that the crisis theorists' notion of development as the expansion of (or the achievement of relatively high levels of) equality, differentiation and capacity provides the most adequate theoretically-oriented definition, for two main

TABLE 6.1   Dimensions and indicators of economic development: (a) as a stasis, and (b) as a process[4]

(a) *Level of economic development*

(i) Income
  – GNP per capita

(ii) Health
  – calories per capita
  – infant mortality as proportion of live births
    (indicator used inversely)   } aggregated to form 'Health' Index
  – physicians per capita

(iii) Education
  – expenditure on education as percentage GNP
  – primary and secondary as proportion school age population } aggregated to form 'Education' Index
  – percentage literate

(iv) Urbanisation
  – composite index based on proportion of population living in cities over 25,000 and 100,000 inhabitants

(v) Communication
  (1) Messages
    – newspapers per capita
    – telegrams per capita
    – telephones per capita
    – mail per capita
    – radios per capita
    – television per capita   } aggregated to form 'Communications' Index
  (2) Transport infrastructure
    – highway vehicles per capita
    – railroad mileage per capita
    – rail passenger miles per capita
    – rail ton-miles per capita

TABLE 6.1 (*cont.*)

(vi) Industrialisation
   (1) Energy
      – energy production per capita
      – energy consumption per capita
   (2) Industrial raw material production
      – steel production per capita
      – cement production per capita
   (3) Labour force
      – percentage workforce in industry

} aggregated to form 'Industrialisation' Index

(b) *Changes in the level of economic development*[5]
   (i) Income Δ
      – changes in GNP per capita
   (ii) Education Δ
      – changes in the level of primary and secondary education
   (iii) Urbanisation Δ
      – changes in the proportion of the population living in cities of over 100,000 inhabitants
   (iv) Communication Δ
   (1) Messages
      – changes in the number of telephones per capita
   (2) Transport
      – changes in the number of highway vehicles per capita

reasons. Firstly, as we suggested before, by viewing development as a multi-dimensional process with no single end-state, it seeks to avoid those accusations of 'league-table building' which *can* be reasonably well directed at many of the alternative development formulations. Secondly, it offers an admirable synthesis of the more important features of the development process which have been identified by previous analyses: although it is beyond the scope of this analysis to provide a detailed elaboration of the way in which this synthesis is effected, Table 6.2 outlines the principal similarities which exist between the crisis theorists' concept of development and earlier ones.

The major problem associated with the crisis theorists' definition of development, however, is one of quantitative operationalisation. The data necessary to effect precise cross-national measurements of equality, capacity and differentiation are simply not available at present. In order to operationalise the *capacity* dimension of development we propose to use the *National Government Revenue Per Capita* index provided by A. S. Banks, since this variable appears to offer the best indication of the extent to which the political system has *penetrated* society and economy. Our attempt to operationalise the equality and differentiation components, however, is even more severely affected by the paucity of data, and in fact we are forced to employ a single indicator for both of these dimensions – the CCPR 'polyarchy' or 'democratic performance' index.[9] While this index does not *explicitly* measure either 'equality' or 'differentiation', its value as a surrogate is derived from the fact that the countries which exhibit relatively high polyarchy scores (notably the western liberal democracies) are precisely those countries which the crisis theorists refer to as being relatively highly developed in terms of their levels of 'equality' and 'differentiation'; conversely, the countries which the crisis theorists characterise as having relatively low levels of equality and differentiation (notably the third world nations) also tend to exhibit relatively low scores on the polyarchy index. Table 6.3 summarises our operational measures of political development, both as a stasis (the *level* of political development) and as a process (*changes* in the level of political development), although, as the table indicates, lack of data means that we can only examine the capacity dimension of development as a process.

The question which we now need to address is how far the concept of development can be used in order to explain

TABLE 6.2 Alternative definitions of political development

Almond and Powell	Cutright	Neubauer	Pye	Packenham	Huntington	Rostow and Ward	Crisis Theorists
Sub-system autonomy					Autonomy		
	Competitiveness of party system	Electoral competition					
			Westernisation = modernisation / Building of democratic inst.				
Structural differentiation			Admin. legal development	Admin. devt. legal–formal	Coherence complexity	Differentiation	Differentiation Differentiation
Cultural secularisation		Equality of represent.	Mass participation	Social systems that facilitate participation / Participant Political Culture		Cultural secularisation	Equality = achievement norms notion of citizenship universalistic legal system
			'Rational' government				
'Capabilities' (not included within formal definition of			Capacity of state to maintain order and mobilise resources		Adaptability		Capacity – integrative – innovative – adaptive – responsive
			Political structure necessary for economic development	Political structure necessary for economic development			

TABLE 6.3   Proposed indicators of political development

Level of political		
development (stasis) – capacity		= national government revenue per capita (1965)
	differentiation	
	equality	= degree of polyarchy (1965)
Changes in the level		
of political development		
(process)	Δ capacity	= national government revenue per capita (annual average Δ 1961–70)

cross-national patterns of political instability. It should be re-emphasised immediately, of course, that development, of itself, is not posited as an explicit explanation of any particular phenomenon or set of phenomena: rather, it constitutes a general theoretical framework which seeks to identify the most important features of political change, which can be employed in order to examine specific problems of political change, and from which specific hypotheses can be derived. A large part of the crisis theorists' analysis, for example, is concerned not with building hypotheses but with identifying those mechanisms which hinder the expansion of equality, differentiation and/or capacity, that is to say, which hinder the process of political development itself.

The simplest, but most effectively stated, thesis which links development directly to *instability* is offered by Huntington.[10] Huntington's basic contention is that while a relatively high *level* of development tends to be associated with stability (economically, the resources are available to buy off dissent; politically, the high level of institutionalisation channels dissent into nondisruptive areas), the *process* of development (both economic and political) tends to produce systemic strains and tensions which in turn lead to instability. Specifically, this distinction suggests four hypotheses:

H_1: the level of political instability varies negatively and linearly with the level of political development;

H_2: the level of political instability varies negatively and linearly with the level of socio-economic development;

H_3: the level of political instability varies positively and linearly with changes in the level of political development;

H_4: the level of political instability varies positively and linearly with changes in the level of socio-economic development.

These, then, are the four hypotheses relating to development, which we intend to investigate in our subsequent analysis. As we have intimated, we make no attempt to evaluate the utility of the development framework as a whole – that is well beyond the scope of this study – but are simply concerned with the extent to which the predictive hypotheses relating to instability which that framework generates derive support from our data.

We turn now to examine an alternative framework for analysing political change – that of 'dependency' – which also suggests a number of specific predictions for our data.

PARADIGMS OF POLITICAL CHANGE: 2 DEPENDENCY

While the development approach focuses principally (though not exclusively) upon political change *within* nations, advocates of the 'dependency' thesis emphasise the importance of examining relationships *between* nations in any attempt to explain (or understand) political change. More specifically, the concept of dependency has been adapted and widely used by Marxist analysts as a general explanation for the post-1930 pattern of Latin American politics,[11] and in particular for the chronic political instability which is seen to characterise that region, although the thesis has recently been extended to apply to Third World systems generally.[12] Moreover, many analysts proclaim 'dependency' as a direct analytical alternative to the concept of development. Development, they argue, explains nothing, for two reasons: firstly, change is not a one-dimensional phenomenon, and secondly, the relatively high level of development of the West is functionally related to the relatively low level of development of the Third World.

Given the distinctions which we drew in the preceding section of this chapter, the weaknesses of this so-called critique are readily apparent. On the one hand, the critique ignores the fact that the more sophisticated development theorists see change as a multi-dimensional rather than as a one-dimensional process, and on the other hand, it fails to recognise the dinstiction between economic and political development which most development theorists make. While it does make some sense to identify a functional relationship between the respective *economic* positions of the (economically) developed and (economically) under-developed worlds, I am aware of no theoretical argument (and the proponents of the dependency model certainly do not offer one) which in any functional sense links the relatively high level of *political* development in the western liberal democracies to the relatively low levels of political development in the Third World. Despite the weaknesses inherent in its critique of development, however, the dependency thesis is still worthy of investigation: even though a particular theory fails to make an adequate critique of another, that is not to say that it is without explanatory power. Before we can specify the predictions which the dependency model generates with regard to political instability, and before we can *test* its explanatory power, however, we must examine the model itself in rather more detail.

The dependency thesis is based upon a distinction between 'central' (or metropolitan) and 'peripheral' (or satellite) economies, a distinction derived partly from the Leninist theory of Imperialism, and partly from the twin sociological notions of 'the central value system' (which affirms the legitimacy of established authority) and the 'peripheral value system' (which opposes or contradicts that legitimacy), both of which are considered to exist in all societies.[13] Extending this notion to the international economic system, the dependency model categorises all economic systems as either central or peripheral, upon the basis of their relation to the (non Communist) world market for raw materials, manufactured goods and capital. Given the close relationship between economic and political forces, this categorisation is also regarded as being of fundamental political importance: just as the central value system (in Shils' terms) affirms the legitimacy of and helps to maintain the established political order within a particular society, so the dominant economic and political position of the central economies (in the dependency theorists' terms) assists the maintenance of the present international economic system, a system which itself operates to the considerable advantage of those central economies.

The 'central' economies are defined to be those Western European and North American economies which industrialised in the mid and late-nineteenth century, and which established a dominant political and economic position in the world market, firstly by virtue of their size in terms of their overall share of world trade, and secondly by virtue of their ability to import a wide range of raw materials and to export finished manufactured goods (and more particularly, *capital* goods) to a wide range of countries. The very variety of their current import and export patterns reduces the central economies' dependence upon fluctuations which might occur in any one part of the world commodity or capital goods markets.

The subordinate peripheral economies, on the other hand, are characterised by low levels of capital goods production, and the export of a limited number of types of raw materials to an equally limited number of countries. They

> ... lack the resources to create or choose alternative ways of reponding to the constraints impinging upon them from the international environment. Dependent countries ... are unable to exert substantial influence over the basic decisions affecting their national economies; the issues of what to produce, how to produce and for whom, are all shaped directly or indirectly by international structures and processes.[14]

THE HISTORICAL PATTERN OF DEPENDENCY IN LATIN AMERICA

In providing a descriptive account of the political and economic changes which have taken place in Latin America in the last 200 years or so, the dependency model is reasonably convincing. The description which it offers is self-avowedly complex, but in short the argument is as follows.

(1) Prior to the achievement of independence in the early nineteenth century, the Latin American economies exported food and raw materials to the colonial Iberian powers in exchange for manufactured consumer goods which were reserved exclusively for members of the ruling elite.

(2) From the mid-nineteenth century until 1930, the export of raw materials and food, and the import of consumer durables, continued, but during this period that export/import pattern was increasingly accompanied by the importation of North American

and West European capital, which was channelled (along with most domestic investment resources) directly into the existing export industries (notably mining and agriculture), and into improving the communications network (notably railways). The Latin American economies expanded, therefore, but at the same time they remained highly vulnerable to shifts in the world demand for raw materials.

(3) The world recession of the 1930s, according to the dependency thesis, had a profound effect upon Latin America. The collapse of world demand for Latin American raw material and food exports meant that the necessary foreign exchange was not available for the importation of consumer durables. As a result, a process of 'import substitution' took place: the ruling oligarchy channelled all available domestic capital into the creation of a domestic consumer durable industry.

(4) The effect of import substitution was to prevent the process of industrialisation in Latin America from achieving an economic 'take-off' because the emphasis upon consumption rather than investment prevented the accumulation of capital (and such an accumulation is generally considered to be a prerequisite for 'take-off').

(5) The more important *political* consequence of import substitution, however, was the result of the juxtaposition of this inability to achieve take-off and the particular class structure which characterised the Latin American economies during the 1930s. The dependency theorists argue that the balance of 'social forces' (classes) was such that no *single* class had sufficient political and economic resources to achieve a class hegemony over the others (in the Marxist frame of reference of the dependency theorists, a class hegemony of some sort must, by definition, exist in all societies); and in consequence a class 'alliance' was formed in which the 'modernising' sectors of the land-owning oligarchy, the urban middle class and the working class joined forces under the political banner of populism.

(6) The popular movement (which manifested itself, for example, in the Vargas reforms in Brazil, the Cardenas era in Mexico and Peronism in Argentina) ushered in a period of redistributive economic policies – the price which the modernising oligarchy had to pay for working class co-operation – which in turn had the effect of reinforcing the tendencies away from capital

accumulation which the import substitution process had set in motion.

(7) By the mid 1950s, the redistributive possibilities of import substitution were exhausted, and in consequence the foundation of the populist alliance of social classes was broken. The subsequent attempts of the new coalition of the traditional oligarchy and the educated middle classes to reverse the redistributive process produced a crisis of legitimacy, which in turn, according to the dependency theorists, is the root cause of the high levels of militarism and political instability which prevail in most Latin American systems.

The dependency model, then, provides a set of descriptive statements, which together are considered by its proponents to constitute the definitive explanation of Latin American patterns of political behaviour; and in so far as the concept of dependency has been applied to (other) 'peripheral' systems outside Latin America, the dependency thesis has frequently been posited as a general explanation of militarism and instability in the entire Third World.

But how adequate of these phenomena does the dependency framework, in fact, provide? While it is possible to make *a priori* theoretical criticisms – the Marxist advocates of dependency, for example, see it as the product exclusively of the international capitalist economic system, whereas similar dependency relationships (in terms of trade and capital flows) undoubtedly exist in the Communist world – we intend to test the dependency thesis by examining the adequacy of the predictions which it generates. The central prediction which we investigate is based upon the claim that the dependent status of the Latin American (and of other Third World) countries is the root cause of their instability. Treating dependency as a continuous phenomenon, it follows that the greater the extent of a given country's dependence upon one or more others, the greater its expected level of political instability. Stating this prediction rather more formally, we have the hypothesis that

H_5: the level of political instability varies positively and linearly with the degree of dependency.

In order to operationalise the concept of dependency we use two indicators: the concentration of export commodities, and the concentration of export-receiving countries. The justification for each of these indicators stems from our original characterisation of a peripheral, dependent economy: the relative (trade) dependence of a given system by definition varies in direct proportion to the extent to which that system's economy is unprotected against (1) the seemingly autonomous fluctuations in the level of world demand for its exports – the greater the diversity of its exports (and therefore the lower its concentration of exports), the lower its dependence upon such fluctuations in any one commodity market; and (2) political decisions taken in the export receiving countries – the greater the number of countries which a given system exports to, the less dependent that system is upon adverse political decisions which are taken by any one export-receiving country.

Having specified the hypotheses and operational indicators suggested by the two paradigms of political change which we identified, we turn now to examine some of the *structural characteristics of political systems* which have also been identified as sources of instability in previous analyses: governmental coercion, structured inequality and structured division.

STRUCTURED CHARACTERISTICS: 1 GOVERNMENTAL COERCION

Governmental coercion has been cited as a causal influence upon either the level of instability or the level of political violence in several previous analyses. For many of these analysts – and in particular those who make use of inferred psychological characteristics such as 'relative deprivation' or 'systemic frustration' – the relationship between governmental coercion and mass political violence or instability is the macro or system level equivalent of the punishment-aggression relationship identified by Dollard at the micro or individual psychological level.[15] Essentially, what Dollard suggested was that although aggression *could* be inhibited insofar as punishment was expected, punishment itself could also act as a source of frustration, which could in turn instigate further aggression. In other words, punishment could both inhibit and encourage aggression, the extent of the actual aggressive response being determined by the perceived strength (and the perceived likelihood) of the punishment which was anticipated. Dollard's thesis was refined in the early 1960s by

Buss, who suggested that the impact of the punishment for aggressive behaviours was determined by the actual strength of the punishment.[16] Buss argued that while 'low' levels of punishment did not act as an inhibitor to aggression, the deterrent effects of 'high' levels of punishment were likely to prevent aggression altogether (thereby leading to anxiety and withdrawal). 'Medium' levels of punishment, however, were considered to act fundamentally as frustration-inducing mechanisms which would in turn elicit further aggression, and which would lead consequently to the emergence of a 'circular' aggression → punishment → frustration → aggression sequence.

The extension of this principle (that only medium levels of punishment would effect an aggressive response) to the *macro* level was largely responsible for producing the 'curvilinearity hypothesis', which proposes that in systemic terms, only medium levels of coercion (punishment) are likely to produce high levels of political violence and instability (aggression). The argument can be summarily stated as follows: (1) at 'high' levels of coercion, men cannot be violent because the costs of violence are perceived to be too great; (2) at 'low' levels of coercion, since public order is reinforced by a high level of governmental legitimacy, men neither need nor want to participate in violent challenges to either government or regime; whereas (3) at 'medium' levels of coercion, men are sufficiently motivated towards violence by the frustration which governmental coercion generates, and the punishment expected is not perceived to be sufficiently strong to prevent violence from occurring, that the level of violent challenges varies in direct proportion to the level of governmental coercion. Figure 6.2 describes, the predicted relationship between violence and coercion which this hypothesis suggests.

Now while it may be the case that this direct extension of the frustration-aggression thesis from the micro to the macro level involves the kind of 'ecological fallacy' against which Robinson warned as long ago as 1950, we do not propose to reject that thesis on *a priori* grounds, but rather, in order to determine its utility we intend to subject it to empirical investigation. Before the operational model which we intend to test can be identified, however, several qualifications need to be made.

First, it needs to be recognised that the macro level version of the Dollard–Buss thesis is intended to refer primarily to *violent* political behaviours, and in this sense it could be argued that the

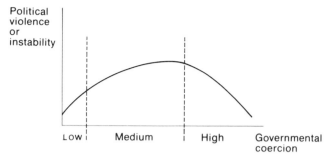

FIGURE 6.2   Diagrammatic representation of the 'curvilinearity
hypothesis'

curvilinear relationship defined by Figure 6.2 is only relevant to
our 'violent challenge' dimension of instability, since it is only that
dimension which explicitly takes account of violent political
behaviours. We would, nonetheless, argue that if governmental
coercion is likely to produce a political response, there is no
necessary reason why that response should take the form of only a
violent (regime or government) challenge; it seems just as likely
on *a priori* theoretical grounds that the political outcome of
coercion-generated frustration could be peaceful challenges to
either the government or the regime, or even (successful or
unsuccessful) attempts to produce a *change* in either government
or regime. The justification for this claim is based on the fact that
in order to explain why coercion-generated violence should be
aimed at the *political* system (rather than at the economic or the
family system, for example), the advocates of the macro level
curvilinearity thesis need to introduce an element of political
rationality into their argument: men presumably seek to vent the
frustration which governmental coercion elicits upon the *political*
system, because they perceive that by *disrupting* the operation of
that system, some kind of policy change will result which will be
more favourable to their own interests. Once the existence of this
element of rationality is acknowledged, it follows that there is
no logical reason why the (aggressive) disruptive response to
coercion-generated frustration should not involve (in addition to
political violence) either attempts to change the government or the
regime, or relatively peaceful, but still disruptive, challenge
behaviours: pacifists are not immune to frustration. In this context,
it seems reasonable to examine the validity of the curvilinearity

hypothesis in relation to each of the four dimensions of instability which were identified in Chapter 3; and this is in fact what we propose to do.

A second qualification which needs to be made relates to the possibility that the relationship between coercion and instability is linear and positive rather than curvilinear. This possibility stems from the results reported by Hibbs, who found evidence of a (reciprocal) positive linear relationship between 'sanctions' (coercion) and 'internal war' (violence).[17] While Hibbs does not explicitly pursue the possibility that the relationship might be curvilinear, the fact that he does find a significant linear relationship means that we need to entertain the possibility that a similar relationship exists in our own data.

The third qualification which needs to be made concerns the distinction between *actual* coercion and *potential* coercion. This distinction is emphasised both by Gurr and by Hibbs, and we make use of it because it reflects the distinction between (1) Dollard's argument that the aggressive response to punishment is determined by the perceived strength and perceived likelihood of the *subsequently anticipated* punishment (that is to say coercive potential is important), and (2) Buss' claim that the aggressive response to punishment varies in direct proportion with the intensity of that punishment (that is to say the actual level of coercion is important).

Given the data which were available for this study, the level of actual coercion is relatively easy to operationalise, since we can use (a temporally aggregated index of) the same 'sanctions' variable which was employed by Hibbs. This variable explicitly measures the extent to which

... action is taken by the authorities ... (in order to) ... neutralise, suppress or eliminate a perceived threat to the government, the regime or the state itself ... The sanctions variable includes ... censorship ... restrictions on political participation ... (and politically motivated) ... arrests ... (It excludes) ... crackdowns against organised crime or drives by the police to reduce crime in the streets.[18]

Following the practice of earlier analyses, we intend to operationalise the level of *coercive potential* by the 'size of the internal security forces' (police) and the 'size of the military', both measured as proportions of the total population. While there are admittedly some weaknesses in this operationalisation – the coercive potential of a government at any given point in time, for example, may be in part a function of that government's prior record of actual coercion – allowing for the fact that in this part of our analysis we are forced by the general paucity of data to use cross-sectional forms of analysis, such limitations are unavoidable.

Given these qualifications, we can now identify the specific hypotheses which we intend to test concerning the impact of governmental coercion upon political instability, although clearly, since some of these hypotheses are mutually contradictory, we cannot expect to find empirical support for all of them.

H_6: The level of political instability varies positively and linearly with the level of actual governmental coercion.

H_7: The level of political instability varies curvilinearly with the level of actual governmental coercion.

H_8: The level of political instability varies positively and linearly with the level of potential governmental coercion.

H_9: The level of political instability varies curvilinearly with the level of potential governmental coercion.

STRUCTURAL CHARACTERISTICS: 2 STRUCTURED INEQUALITY

The possibility that there is a strong relationship between inequality and political disorder or instability has long been recognised. As de Tocqueville suggested,

Remove the secondary causes that have produced the great convulsions of the world and you will almost always find the principle of inequality at the bottom. Either the poor have attempted to plunder the rich, or the rich to enslave the poor. If, then, a state of society can ever be founded in which every man will have something to keep and little to take from others, much will have been done for the peace of the world.[19]

The generalisation, so eloquently stated, and so frequently employed since, seems plausible: inequality of income and wealth is one of the most important factors of those which motivate men to participate in disruptive political activity; remove such inequalities and both the motivation and the disruptive behaviours disappear. (De Tocqueville does not give any clear indication, however, as to what might prevent a few selfish, able and ambitious men – even in a situation where wealth and income are evenly distributed – from coveting and indeed from forcibly securing the wealth and/or income of the less able.) Unless de Tocqueville's generalisation is true by definition (and I am convinced that this is not de Tocqueville's intention), it becomes possible to test that generalisation by examining the empirical relationship between instability and some measure(s) of inequality, since the generalisation (regarded as a causal hypothesis) implies that the greater the level of inequality the greater the level of political disorder. In other words, political instability should vary positively (and linearly) with the level of inequality.

Several analyses have already found some support for this hypothesis, particularly in the context of Latin America.[20] Using our own operational measures of instability, we intend to broaden the sample of countries investigated to include all the systems for which comparable data on inequality exist; although it should be admitted that these data cover only 54 of the 103 countries which we investigate in the rest of our cross-sectional analysis. We, in fact, intend to measure the level of inequality by using the 'Gini' indices of land and sectoral income inequalities provided in the *World Handbook II* collection. While the meaning of the land inequality index is fairly self-evident, it should be noted that the income inequality variable measures the extent to which there is inequality of income between different *sectors* of the economy – between agriculture and manufacturing, between mining and commerce, for example – rather than the extent to which there is inequality of income among households. Using these two variables, we will attempt to evaluate the adequacy of de Tocqueville's thesis by examining the following hypotheses.

H_{10}: The level of political instability varies positively and linearly with the level of land inequality.

H_{11}: The level of political instability varies positively and linearly with the level of sectoral income inequality.

STRUCTURAL CHARACTERISTICS: 3 STRUCTURED DIVISION

Political cleavages of some sort exist in all political systems, and there is a relatively large body of theoretical and empirical literature which seeks, on the one hand, to specify the most important types of cleavage which exist across political systems, and on the other hand, to examine the general political consequences of those cleavages. The existing literature ranges from the formal-mathematical approach of Rae and Taylor to the aggregate comparative approach of Rose and Urwin and the survey-based analyses of Key.[21] With regard to the comparative analysis of political stability and instability, the available evidence seems to suggest that the most important cleavages are those based upon *religion*[22] (at least in Western democracies), and upon (primordial) ethnic-linguistic groups. Recent events in Northern Ireland and in the Lebanon clearly evidence the importance of religious cleavage in the generation of violent political conflict (even if that cleavage is primarily only of symbolic significance), and, as Zolberg has pointed out, deep-rooted ethnic and linguistic divisions inevitably pose considerable problems both for political integration and for the creation and maintenance of a stable political order, particularly when formal political organisations develop along the lines of the ethnic-linguistic cleavage.[23]

Our measures of religious cleavage (religious fractionalisation) and ethnic-linguistic cleavage (ethno-linguistic fractionalisation) are derived from the *World Handbook II* data collection, and the general hypotheses which we intend to test can be formally stated thus:

H_{12}: the level of political instability varies positively and linearly with the level of religious fractionalisation;

H_{13}: the level of political instability varies positively and linearly with the level of ethno-linguistic fractionalisation.

Tables 6.4 and 6.5 respectively summarise (1) the 13 sets of bivariate hypotheses which we have defined in this chapter, and (2) the operational indicators of each of the independent variables specified in those hypotheses, which we propose to employ. Before we can report our findings concerning these hypotheses, however, a final, and important, qualification is necessary.

TABLE 6.4   Hypotheses concerning the possible influences upon the level of political instability, by dimension*

$H_{1.1}$ The level of regime change instability $H_{1.2}$ The level of violent challenge instability $H_{1.3}$ The level of government change instability $H_{1.4}$ The level of peaceful challenge instability	Varies negatively and linearly with the level of political development
$H_{2.1}$ The level of regime change instability $H_{2.2}$ The level of violent challenge instability $H_{2.3}$ The level of government change instability $H_{2.4}$ The level of peaceful challenge instability	Varies negatively and linearly with the level of economic development
$H_{3.1}$ The level of regime change instability $H_{3.2}$ The level of violent challenge instability $H_{3.3}$ The level of government change instability $H_{3.4}$ The level of peaceful challenge instability	Varies positively and linearly with changes in the level of political development
$H_{4.1}$ The level of regime change instability $H_{4.2}$ The level of violent challenge instability $H_{4.3}$ The level of government change instability $H_{4.4}$ The level of peaceful challenge instability	Varies positively and linearly with changes in the level of economic development
$H_{5.1}$ The level of regime change instability $H_{5.2}$ The level of violent challenge instability $H_{5.3}$ The level of government change instability $H_{5.4}$ The level of peaceful challenge instability	Varies positively and linearly with the degree of dependency
$H_{6.1}$ The level of regime change instability $H_{6.2}$ The level of violent challenge instability $H_{6.3}$ The level of government change instability $H_{6.4}$ The level of peaceful challenge instability	Varies positively and linearly with the level of actual government coercion (sanctions)
$H_{7.1}$ The level of regime change instability $H_{7.2}$ The level of violent challenge instability $H_{7.3}$ The level of government change instability $H_{7.4}$ The level of peaceful challenge instability	Varies curvilinearly with the level of actual government coercion
$H_{8.1}$ The level of regime change instability $H_{8.2}$ The level of violent challenge instability $H_{8.3}$ The level of government change instability $H_{8.4}$ The level of peaceful challenge instability	Varies positively and linearly with the level of potential government coercion
$H_{9.1}$ The level of regime change instability $H_{9.2}$ The level of violent challenge instability $H_{9.3}$ The level of government change instability $H_{9.4}$ The level of peaceful challenge instability	Varies curvilinearly with the level of potential government coercion
$H_{10.1}$ The level of regime change instability $H_{10.2}$ The level of violent challenge instability $H_{10.3}$ The level of government change instability $H_{10.4}$ The level of peaceful challenge instability	Varies positively and linearly with the level of land inequality
$H_{11.1}$ The level of regime change instability $H_{11.2}$ The level of violent challenge instability $H_{11.3}$ The level of government change instability $H_{11.4}$ The level of peaceful challenge instability	Varies positively and linearly with the level of sectoral income inequality

TABLE 6.4   continued

$H_{12.1}$ The level of regime change instability $H_{12.2}$ The level of violent challenge instability $H_{12.3}$ The level of government change instability $H_{12.4}$ The level of peaceful challenge instability	Varies positively and linearly with the level of religious fractionalisation
$H_{13.1}$ The level of regime change instability $H_{13.2}$ The level of violent challenge instability $H_{13.3}$ The level of government change instability $H_{13.4}$ The level of peaceful challenge instability	Varies positively and linearly with the level of ethnic fractionalisation

*Dependent variable stated first.

A METHODOLOGICAL QUALIFICATION

It should be noted that we have not attempted to identify any of the possible linkages between the different independent or *exogenous* variables identified in Table 6.4. In this sense, the theoretical framework which we are employing in this chapter corresponds to Kaplan's notion of *concatenated* as opposed to *hierarchical* theory.[24] In the case of the latter, *all* the possible linkages between the variables (or concepts) in the theory need to be specified and evaluated; whereas in the case of 'concatenated' theory, the analyst simply seeks to identify and evaluate the various relationships between the explanandum and each of the explanans.

While in the context of this analysis it is *possible* to hypothesise various causal linkages between the independent variables defined in Table 6.4, we do not consider that the data presently available are suitable for testing such hypotheses in any meaningful way. (It should be pointed out at this stage that the ensuing discussion applies only to variables which measure *levels* of system characteristics, and *not* to variables which measure *changes* in those characteristics: since most of the exogenous variables in Table 6.4 do refer to *levels*, however, the argument which we subsequently present is directly applicable to most of the possible exogenous variable relationships which – for reasons which we will specify – we do not intend to examine.)

In order to justify this claim, we need, initially, to reintroduce a term which we referred to in Chapter 2: the notion of a '*dynamic hypothesis*'. By a 'dynamic' hypothesis, we mean a hypothesis which proposes that a *change* in one variable will elicit a corresponding change in another. The appropriate way of

TABLE 6.5 Summary of the dimensions and indices used for each of the potential exogenous correlates of the level of political instability

(i) *Development*
  (a) level of economic development (stasis)
    – Income
    – Health
    – Education
    – Urbanisation
    – Communication
    – Industrialisation
    – Composite economic development index
  (b) Level of political development (stasis)
    – Capacity = Government revenue + expenditure per capita
    – Degree of polyarchy or 'democratic performance'
  (c) Changes in economic development (process)
    – Income Δ
    – Education Δ
    – Urbanisation Δ
    – Communication Δ
  (d) – Changes in political development (process)
    – Capacity Δ = Δ in government revenue + expenditure per capita

(ii) *Dependency*
    – Concentration of export commodities
    – Concentration of export-receiving countries

(iii) *Government coercion*
  (a) Actual
    – Number of acts of governmental repression 1948–67
      = Sanctions
  (b) Potential
    – Size of internal security forces as a proportion of the total adult population
    – Size of the armed forces as a proportion of the total adult population

(iv) *Structured inequality*
    – Land inequality (Gini index)
    – Sectoral income inequality (Gini index)

(v) *Structured division*
    – Ethno-linguistic fractionalisation (ELF)
    – Religious fractionalisation (RF)

evaluating such a proposition, of course, is to use data which directly measure *changes* in the relevant variables. However, since a regression coefficient calculated from two variables, each of which describes the different *levels* which a number of political systems exhibit on some particular systemic characteristic, by definition measures the predicted change in Y which is produced by a unit increase in X, some analysts have argued that cross-sectional data which describe the *levels* of certain system characteristics can be used in order to test dynamic hypotheses concerning *changes* in those levels. As we will see, this is an argument which requires a strong assumption, which is not always warranted; and as we will attempt to show, that assumption is *not* warranted with regard to (most of) the possible interrelationships between the independent variables specified in Table 6.4 (and this, of course, is one of the main reasons why we do not examine those interrelationships).

Consider then, for example, *the relationship between the level of economic development and the level of political development*, two phenomena which we defined earlier in this chapter. It is possible for us to hypothesise three possible types of *dynamic* relationship between these two variables.

(1) Economic development has a causal influence upon political development. (An increase in the level of economic development is likely to produce an increase in the level of political development.)

(2) Political development has a causal influence upon economic development. (An increase in the level of political development is likely to produce an increase in the level of economic development.)

(3) Economic development and political development influence each other reciprocally. (Increases in political development and economic development are likely to be mutually reinforcing.)

Given that statistical analysis can never establish causality (it is only possible to hypothesise a causal relationship and then see if the data are consistent with that hypothesis), and even assuming that one of the three hypotheses above could be selected (on the basis of purely theoretical considerations) at the expense of the other two, there are two methodological reasons why the kind of cross-sectional data available for this study are inappropriate for evaluating such a hypothesis.

First, suppose that, using cross-sectional data which refer specifically to the *levels* of various system characteristics, we were to try to evaluate the dynamic hypothesis that *economic development has a causal influence upon political development*. We could run the appropriate regression equations and would almost certainly find, as Cutright has in fact found[25] (since countries presently at relatively high levels of economic development also tend to exhibit relatively high levels of political development, and *vice versa*), that there is a strong, positive and significant statistical relationship between economic and political development. In non-technical terms, what such a statistical evaluation would ignore, however, is the *common historical experience* (of gradual and simultaneous development in both the economic and political spheres) of that group of countries which at present exhibit relatively high levels of economic and political development; and that common experience has undoubtedly been a causal factor in the generation of those currently existing 'high' levels of political and economic development. More technically (and more importantly), merely because there is evidence of a high positive correlation between the level of political development and the level of economic development, it does not follow automatically that if a country presently experiencing a 'low' level of economic development does somehow achieve a higher level of economic development, it will necessarily enjoy a concomitant increase in political development. Indeed, there are a good many reasons for expecting that it will not: as both Huntington and Deutsch have pointed out, *changes* in the level of economic development *can* have extremely disruptive effects upon the political system, much to the detriment of the process of political development.

The general point is, that using cross-sectional data relating to *levels*, it is difficult to evaluate *dynamic* hypotheses which describe the interrelationships between the kind of independent variables identified in Table 6.4, because cross-sectional empirical tests ignore the fact that even though the *level* of variable Y may be correlated with the *level* of variable X, it does not follow *necessarily* that an increase in X will automatically elicit an increase in Y. This specific problem is in fact a reflection of the more general methodological problem which we discussed in Chapter 2; that of drawing dynamic causal inferences from cross-sectional data. As we pointed out, given a cross-sectional correlation between the level of X and the level of Y, it is only possible to make a dynamic inference about the impact of X upon Y if we are prepared to assume that an *increase* in the level of X in a country which presently has a *low* level of *X*, will result in conditions which are similar to the conditions obtaining in those countries which currently score highly on *X* (we will refer to this as the *similar conditions assumption*). If it *is* possible to make such an assumption, then we can draw the dynamic causal inference that a *change* in *X*, some time in the future, will elicit a concomitant *change* in *Y* (*ceteris paribus*).

In answer to the question which inevitably follows – 'Under what circumstances can the "similar conditions" assumption be made?' – we would argue that such an assumption is warranted *whenever there are sound* a priori *substantive reasons for expecting that the relevant conditions would be similar*. We would also argue that in the context of the possible interrelationships between the five sets of exogenous variables identified in Table 6.4, there are *no* inescapable *a priori* theoretical considerations which would lead us to believe that, say, an increase in the level of economic development in a country which presently has a low level of economic development will necessarily elicit an increase in the level of political development within that country. In other words, in the context of the possible independent variable interrelationships, there is no justification for making the 'similar conditions' assumption. Indeed, we would contend that the similar conditions assumption is *not* warranted in the context of many of the relationships between variables which measure the *levels* of different system characteristics; relationships which are widely examined in quantitative comparative politics. This is not to say that cross-sectional variables which measure 'levels' are without utility in quantitative comparative research; it simply implies that such data should be used with considerable caution (if at all) if they are to be employed in order to generate or test *dynamic* hypotheses.

The importance of this methodological limitation of cross-sectional 'levels' data, lies in the fact that most of the hypotheses which could be derived in order to link the exogenous variables identified in Table 6.4, are essentially *dynamic* hypotheses, and yet they also involve potential relationships for which the 'similar conditions' assumption is not warranted. As a result, if we were to investigate the possible interrelationships between the various exogenous variables, we could only do so by making an unjustifiable methodological assumption; and in such a situation it seems judicious to avoid making this kind of

unnecessary error, particularly in view of the fact that our
. substantive focus is political *instability*, not the interrelationships
among its exogenous correlates.

As we will see in the next two chapters, whenever we *do*
investigate correlations between 'levels' variables (and we do this
in fact when we examine, for example, the relationship between
the level of political development and the level of political
instability), we shall be concerned *not* to draw dynamic causal
inferences from such correlations.

The second reason for our choice of a 'concatenated' as opposed
to a 'hierarchical' approach relates to the question of *identification*.
Even if we could specify all the possible reciprocal
interrelationships between the various independent variables
specified in Table 6.4 in a series of simultaneous equations (and it
should be emphasised that in terms of *a priori* theoretical
considerations there is no reason to suspect – with the possible
exception of the relationships involving the religious and
ethno-linguistic fractionalisation variables – that each bivariate
relationship would be anything other than reciprocal), and even if
we *were* prepared to make the 'similar conditions' assumption for
these interrelationships, we would not have a sufficient number of
exogenous variables to enable us to *identify* the parameters of the
system of equations. We would not, in short, be able to obtain a
unique (or indeed, sensible) solution to those equations.[26]

To summarise, there are two powerful methodological
considerations which prevent us from examining the
interrelationships between the various exogenous influences upon
instability which we have isolated: (1) the fact that for these
interrelationships the 'similar conditions' assumption is not
warranted; and (2) the impossibility of identifying a system of
simultaneous equations which hypothesises reciprocal causation
between each pair of exogenous variables. We would also argue
that since our analytical focus is political instability, and not
development, dependency, governmental coercion or whatever, this
omission is not particularly serious.

SUMMARY

In this chapter we have outlined a number of testable hypotheses
concerning the possible determinants of political instability which,

either on the basis of *a priori* theoretical reasoning or on the basis of previous empirical research, seem to merit detailed statistical investigation. Clearly, however, since the list of exogenous or independent variables which we have identified represents a compromise between the practical constraints of data availability and our desire to operationalise and evaluate empirically as many suggestive theoretical statements as possible, we would not claim that that list is exhaustive.

We have in fact specified five sets of hypotheses (identified in Table 6.4), two of which are concerned with competing paradigms of political change (development and dependency) and the remainder of which (the level of governmental coercion, structured inequality and structured division) are related to the general structural characteristics of political systems. (i) We intend to examine *development* because of the force of Huntington's elegantly simple thesis that while a high *level* of development (both political and economic) is likely to be associated with relative stability, the *process* of development is likely to produce systemic strains and tensions which will result in instability. (ii) We examine *dependency* because the advocates of that framework strongly contend that the trade and capital dependence of the 'periphery' upon the 'centre' (the satellites upon the metropolis) generates a crisis of legitimacy in the former which acts as a source of instability therein. (iii) We investigate the concept of governmental coercion, because the coercive capabilities of the state have been emphasised by many previous (Marxist and non-Marxist) analysts as a general determinant of political behaviour. (iv) We examine 'inequality' because it has been claimed that the resentment of inequality by the deprived, and the jealous protection of it by the privileged, acts as the single most important source of motivation for attempts to effect political change. And (v) we examine the notions of religious and ethno-linguistic divisions because such structured cleavages have frequently been cited (particularly in relation to the newly independent systems of Black Africa) as sources of a crisis of political integration which in turn tends to produce political instability.

It should be emphasised, however, that the assessments of the development and dependency paradigms (and of the exogenous structural characteristics) which we make in subsequent chapters are not intended as general statistical evaluations of those frameworks or characteristics – such a task would be well beyond the scope of this analysis. Rather, we are concerned with attempting to evaluate the extent to which the concepts of development, dependency, coercion, inequality and/or cleavage are capable of explaining or predicting the level of political instability across different systems. Even if our data suggest that any or all of these concepts fail to effect such an explanation, this will not suggest their general redundancy; it will simply imply their particular irrelevance with regard to the study of political instability.

In addition to outlining the theoretical origins of each of the hypotheses which we intend to examine in subsequent chapters, in this chapter we also reiterated an extremely important methodological problem which we originally discussed in Chapter 2. Broadly, we suggested that in comparative political research there is a considerable danger that empirical correlations which were derived from an examination of the *levels* of two distinct system characteristics (such as political and economic development) may be wrongly employed in order to generate or test *dynamic* hypotheses, which suggest that a *change* in X will produce a corresponding change in Y. We argued that such 'levels' data could only be employed in order to test this kind of dynamic hypothesis if the 'similar conditions' assumption was justified, and suggested that this assumption was only justifiable on the basis of *a priori* theoretical reasoning. We went on to argue that with regard to many of the 'levels' correlations in comparative politics, the 'similar conditions' assumption was not justified. Moreover, since the kind of dynamic hypothesis which we would need to investigate (if we were to examine the interrelationships between each pair of exogenous variables in any meaningful way) *would* require us to make this unwarranted assumption, it was decided to confine our analysis to a (concatenated) examination of the relationships between instability and each of its exogenous correlates. (We also pointed out that even if the similar conditions assumption had been warranted, the problem of *identification* would in any case have prevented us from making an adequate assessment of the possibly reciprocal interrelationships between the various exogenous variables).

In the next two chapters, we attempt to evaluate the various hypotheses identified in Table 6.4. We begin by examining the overall levels of bivariate correlation, and then consider the various regional variations in those levels of correlation. Finally, in Chapter 8, we investigate the consequences of considering the *simultaneous* effects which these exogenous variables have upon each of the dimensions of instability.

7 Exogenous Influences upon Political Instability: Bivariate Levels of Correlation

Our principal objective in the next two chapters is to evaluate the extent to which each of the exogenous variables identified in Chapter 6 is capable of predicting cross-national patterns of political instability. In this chapter, our specific intentions are, on the one hand, to demonstrate the almost overwhelming complexity of the patterns of interrelationship between instability and its exogenous correlates, particularly when regional deviations from the overall, 'global' pattern of correlation are considered; and on the other, to establish which bivariate linkages seem to be worth further empirical investigation. Before we can report our findings in this regard, however, several preliminary qualifications need to be made.

First, it should be noted that in the text of this chapter we will not report the magnitudes of all of the correlation coefficients produced by our analysis of the hypotheses specified in Chapter 6 but rather, we will simply report the *direction* of slope of each relationship and whether or not it is *statistically significant*. The second qualification relates to our use of multiple indicators. It will be recalled that in the previous chapter, in order to operationalise the concept of socio-economic development, for example, we suggested a number of sub-dimensions of development (industrialisation, health, education, urbanisation), each of which was measured by several indicators. Since we constructed an *aggregated* index for each of those sub-dimensions, *and* for the level of socio-economic development as a whole, we were in fact in a position to measure 'level of socio-economic development' on three levels: at the level of the individual indicator, the 'sub-dimension' and the overall 'average'. In reporting our findings in this chapter, we employ the following operating rule: if all the coefficients relating to, say, the level of socio-economic development are of a similar status with regard to significance and direction of slope, we will simply report the *overall* pattern rather than comment in detail upon the significance and slope of each coefficient. In Table 7.1, therefore, since all of our measures of socio-economic development are related to regime instability in more or less the same way, we summarise our findings on the bivariate relationship between regime instability and the level of socio-economic development by a single negative sign $(-)$, which indicates that the relationship is significant and negative.

Finally, it is necessary to point out that in this chapter we intend to examine only the *bivariate* relationships between instability and its exogenous correlates. We will begin by examining the overall

TABLE 7.1   Summary of global levels of bivariate correlation ($N = 103$)

Hypo-thesis **	Independent variable	Pre-dicted rela-tion	$R\Delta$	VC	$G\Delta$	PC
H_1	Level of political development					
	– democratic performance	–	–	0	0	0
	– capacity	–	–	0	0	0
H_2	Level of socio-economic development	–	–	0	+	–
H_3	Changes in political development	+	0	0	0	0
H_4	Changes in socio-economic development	+	0	–	–	0
H_5	Level of trade dependency	+	0	–	0	0
H_6	Level of actual coercion (linear)	+	0	0	0	0
H_7	Level of actual coercion (curvilinear)	*	0	*	0	0
H_8	Level of potential government coercion (linear)	+	0	0	0	0
H_9	Level of potential government coercion (curvilinear)	*	0	0	0	0
H_{10}	Level of structured inequality	+	0	0	0	0
H_{12}	Level of structured division	+	0	+	0	0

* denotes significant curvilinear relationship.
+ denotes significant positive relationship.
– denotes significant negative relationship.
0 denotes no relationship.

**Throughout this chapter 'H_{10}' will be used as a shorthand for both H_{10} and H_{11}; 'H_{12}' will be used for both H_{12} and H_{13}

level of correlation and discuss the implications of these correlations for each of the hypotheses identified in Chapter 6. We will then investigate the nature and significance of *variations* in the levels of bivariate correlation, on a region by region basis.

PATTERNS OF BIVARIATE RELATIONSHIP: GLOBAL LEVELS OF CORRELATION

Table 7.1 summarises our findings in relation to the global levels of correlation between each dimension of instability and the exogenous predictor variables which were defined in Chapter 6.[1] A plus sign (+) indicates a significant positive linear relationship, a minus sign (−) indicates a negative linear relationship and an asterisk (*), a significant curvilinear relationship. A zero denotes 'no relationship': *it defines all those instances where a hypothesis is to be rejected.*

Several conclusions are immediately evident from the table, not least of which is the general observation that out of 72 predicted relationships, only 20 are statistically significant, and only 13 are in the predicted direction: *the majority of the hypotheses which we specified in the previous chapter do not derive much support from the data.* More specifically, the following general tendencies are apparent.

(i) It would appear to be the case that the level of *political development* is directly (and negatively) related only to the *regime change* dimensions of instability, and not to governmental change or to violent or peaceful challenge behaviours. Huntington's generalisation that a high level of political development should be associated with a low level of instability, therefore, would seem only to apply to regime change instability. We will not at this stage speculate as to the possible mechanisms which might be generating these empirical tendencies (this is a theme which we take up in the next chapter): it is sufficient to note here that neither the level of political development (H_1) nor *changes* in that level (H_3) appear to be particularly satisfactory predictors of the level of political instability.

(ii) The apparent role of *socio-economic development* (H_2), however, is not quite so disappointing. As predicted, the probability of both regime change (RΔ) and peaceful challenge (PC) instability decreases at higher levels of economic development, although somewhat surprisingly, governmental change (GΔ) and economic development are *positively* rather than negatively related,[2] while contrary to the findings of several previous analyses, violent challenges (VC) do not appear to be directly related to the level of economic development at all. The impact of *socio-economic change*, however, contradicts the predicted relationships specified in H_4 in relation to each of the four types of instability: the social mobilisation/systematic frustration thesis which we have outlined in earlier chapters would seem to derive very little support from our data.

(iii) A similar conclusion must also be drawn with regard to the predicted role of *dependency*. The three zero coefficients for H_5 in Table 7.1 clearly indicate that in general the level of instability does *not* increase in proportion to the degree of dependency; and, indeed, the significant negative coefficient for VC suggests that dependency may actually serve to *decrease* the level of violent challenge instability.

(iv) *Governmental coercion* – either actual or potential, considered linearly or curvilinearly – also consistently fails to be related to instability. The only exception to this tendency is the (curvilinear) 'actual coercion' – violent challenge relationship, for which the data suggest that almost 10 per cent of the variance in VC instability can be explained by acts of governmental repression (actual coercion).[3]

(v) The impact of *structured inequality* (H_{10}) and *structured division* (H_{12}) upon the level of instability also appears to be negligible. Again, the data suggest that with the exception of the structured division–violent challenge linkage, there is no general relationship either between instability and inequality or between instability and ethnic-linguistic or religious fractionalisation.

Clearly, then, the overall patterns of intercorrelation between instability and the potential exogenous influences upon it which are described in Table 7.1, suggest that the generalisations which we advanced in Chapter 6 are of somewhat limited value. Indeed, purely on the basis of the global patterns of intercorrelation (bearing in mind particularly that all of these correlations are in fact below $r = \pm 0.3$), we would be forced to conclude that despite the strong theoretical arguments presented in the previous chapter, development, dependency, governmental coercion, inequality and cleavage do not have any consistent influence upon the level of political instability. Such a conclusion, however, ignores two important considerations: (1) the problem of measurement, and (2) the possibility that global correlations may hide more than they reveal.

The measurement problem (which we discussed in Chapter 2) consists in the possible disparty between theoretical concepts and the indicators which are employed in order to operationalise them. While it could be argued that the comparative dearth of 'positive findings' in Table 7.1 is simply a reflection of the inadequate mensurative capabilities of the operational referents used, we will in fact retain the assumption advanced in Chapter 6 that this disparity is *not* great, particularly in view of the fact that the indicators which we have employed are the best available given the present general paucity of accurate cross-national data.

While the measurement problem can only be resolved by assumption, the 'possibility that global correlations may hide more than they reveal' is a problem which can be approached in a far more direct manner – through rigorous empirical analysis. Indeed this is precisely what we propose to do in the remainder of this chapter. Rather than conclude, on the basis of the global correlations, that our five sets of exogenous variables are without explanatory value, we will in fact re-examine the hypotheses specified in Table 7.1 on a region by region basis. Our purpose in this exercise is clear: even though there may be no *general* relationship, for example between dependency and regime change (see Table 7.1), it is possible that in, say, Latin America (and not elsewhere) such a relationship does exist. To examine only the overall correlation may reveal nothing, simply because of the fact that the lack of a relationship between regime change and dependency *outside* Latin America renders the overall correlation non-significant. In short, as we noted in Chapter 5, the relationship between any pair of variables may vary across different regions and across different types of political system.

REGIONAL VARIATIONS

Before we report the regional breakdown of the patterns of intercorrelation between instability and our series of exogeneous variables it is necessary to provide a brief indication of the theoretical relevance of the concept of region itself. There are two principal reasons why these posssible regional variations are worthy of consideration. The first is simply a reflection of the empirical findings which we presented in Chapter 5, where it was demonstrated that there are considerable regional variations in the linkages between our dimensions of instability: given these differential regional patterns it seems reasonable to expect that similar variations may well exist in the relationship between instability and its exogenous correlates.

The second reason is perhaps of greater substantive import: we would argue that region, and we employ a similar operational definition of region as we did in Chapter 5 (North America/ Europe, Far East, Mid East and North Africa, Sub-Saharan Africa and Latin America), constitutes an indirect surrogate not only for the general level of economic development but also *for historical experience*, a variable which is frequently ignored in quantitative cross-national research, largely because it is not amenable to precise quantitative operationalisation. While we would not wish to argue that to know a country's region is also to know its specific history and culture, we would contend that such knowledge does give a *general* picture of that country's likely historical experience over the last 200 years or so. In short, while there are admittedly a number of ambiguously placed countries – South Africa in Sub-Saharan Africa, and Australia and New Zealand in Far East are among the more obvious candidates for such a characterisation – geographical region is an extremely valuable classificatory tool in any comparative analysis of political systems.

In the ensuing description of the pattern of regional variations, we will not in the text make explicit reference to *all* of the generalisations which our data suggest, since these generalisations are in effect embodied in the tables which we present. Rather, our comments in the text will simply attempt to identify the most important differences and similarities between, on the one hand, the *overall* patterns of interrelationships between instability and its exogenous correlates which we specified in the preceeding section, and on the other hand, each of the specific regional patterns of interrelationship which we report. *Moreover, at this stage we will not speculate as to the substantive implications of these various empirical tendencies, because as we will see in the next chapter, the significance of some of these tendencies is dissipated when their simultaneous effects are considered in a series of single equation multiple regression models. We intend to examine the more important theoretical implications of our consistently significant findings in Chapter 8.*

(a) Europe/North America variations (Table 7.2)

It should be recognised immediately that in examining Europe/North America as a distinct group of countries, we are, to a certain extent, violating our claim that to control for region enables us to make allowance for 'historical experience', since this particular regional grouping includes both the NATO and the Warsaw Pact countries. (It will be recalled that in our earlier time-series analysis Eastern Europe was regarded as a separate region.) This amalgamation was forced upon us by the fact that if we had attempted to analyse Eastern Europe as a separate sub-set, we would have had only nine cases to investigate, a number which does not permit sufficient degrees of freedom for meaningful correlative procedures to be undertaken. Nonetheless, an analysis of the patterns of interrelationship between instability and its exogenous correlates in this merged Eastern Europe-Western

TABLE 7.2   Patterns of bivariate correlations in Europe/North America ($N = 30$)

		$R\Delta$	VC	$G\Delta$	PC
H_1	Level of political development				
	– democratic performance	–	0	0	0
	– capacity	–	0	0	0
H_2	Level of socio-economic				
	development	–	–	+	+
H_3	Changes in political development	0	0	0	0
H_4	Changes in socio-economic				
	development	+	0	–	0
H_5	Dependency	0	–	–	+
H_6	Actual coercion (linear)	+	+	0	+
H_7	Actual coercion (curve)	0	*	0	0
H_8	Potential coercion (linear)	0	+	0	–
H_9	Potential coercion (curve)	*	0	0	0
H_{10}	Structured inequality	–	+	0	0
H_{12}	Structured division	0	+	+	0

* denotes significant curvilinear relationship.
+ denotes significant positive relationship.
– denotes significant negative relationship.
0 denotes no relationship.

Europe/North America sub-set does mean that we are examining the predominantly *economically developed industrialised countries* in order to see if the patterns of interrelationship therein differ significantly from the overall pattern.

As a comparison between Table 7.1 and Table 7.2 indicates, there are some important similarities between the Europe/North America pattern and the overall pattern. In both cases, *the level of political development is likely to have a reductive effect upon the level of regime change instability* (significant negative coefficient), *but is unrelated to governmental change, violent challenges and peaceful challenges* (zero coefficients). In other words, in Europe/North America, as is the case generally, it would appear that development only inhibits the most severe form of instability – regime change – and has no direct effect at all upon the other three types of instability which we have identified.

A comparison between Table 7.1 and Table 7.2 also indicates that this similarity between the Europe/North America and overall patterns is paralleled in the (lack of) relationships between instability and *changes* in political development (H_3); between instability and actual coercion (curvilinear, H_7); and between instability and structured division (H_{12}).

Significant *differences* between these patterns, however, do exist. (1) The level of *dependency* (H_5), which overall only has an impact upon the level of violent challenges, in Europe/North America assumes a much more important role, influencing all forms of instability except for regime change. Similarly, (2) in Europe/North America, the influence of *governmental coercion* (H_6, H_8 and H_9) upon instability is much more marked than the overall pattern might lead us to believe. Finally (3), while *structured inequality* (H_{10}) in global terms appears to have no effect upon instability, as Table 7.2 indicates, in Europe/North America such inequalities serve to *increase* the probability of violent challenges and to *reduce* the probability of regime change.

There are, then, specific differences between the overall and the Europe/North America patterns. As we have suggested, however, before we attempt to draw detailed theoretical inferences from these differential regional patterns we need to see if they also occur under the more rigorous conditions of the multiple regression models which we investigate in Chapter 8: at this stage we will limit our discussion to the reporting of observed empirical tendencies.

(b)   Middle East/North Africa variations (Table 7.3)

The Middle East/North Africa pattern of interrelationship between instability and its exogenous correlates also varies from the global pattern, although (as a comparison between Table 7.1 and Table 7.3 shows) there are two notable similarities: the lack of relationship (1) between instability and coercive potential (four zero coefficients for H_9), and (2) between instability and inequality (four zero coefficients for H_{10}). These similarities apart, however, there are several distinct 'Middle East' tendencies.

(i) The most important of these is the tendency both for *economic development* (H_2) and for the democratic performance dimension of *political development* (H_1) to correlate *negatively* with *regime change*, but to correlate *positively* with each of the other instability dimensions. While the negative coefficient for regime change is, of course, in the direction predicted in the previous chapter, the two positive coefficients clearly contradict those predictions: in the Middle East/North Africa it would appear to be

TABLE 7.3   Patterns of bivariate correlations in Middle East/North Africa
($N = 12$)

		RΔ	VC	GΔ	PC
H_1	Level of political development				
	– democratic performance	–	+	+	+
	– capacity	–	0	+	0
H_2	Level of socio-economic				
	development	–	+	+	+
H_3	Changes in political development	+	+	+	0
H_4	Changes in socio-economic				
	development	–	–	+	+
H_5	Dependency	–	–	+	–
H_6	Actual coercion (linear)	+	0	–	0
H_7	Actual coercion (curvilinear)	0	0	0	0
H_8	Potential coercion (linear)	0	+	+	+
H_9	Potential coercion (curvilinear)	0	0	0	0
H_{10}	Structured inequality	0	0	0	0
H_{12}	Structured division				
	– religious fractionalisation	0	+	–	–
	– ethnic fractionalisation	0	–	–	+

+ denotes significant positive relationship.
– denotes significant negative relationship.
0 denotes no relationship.

the case that higher levels of economic and political development increase the probability of most forms of instability rather than reduce it.

(ii) This tendency also applies, firstly, to changes in the level of *political development*, and secondly, to *changes in the level of socio-economic development* (both of which yield significant positive coefficients in Table 7.3): in Middle East/North Africa at least, therefore, Huntington's thesis that political and socio-economic *change* tend to generate instability appears to receive substantial support.

(iii) The dependency thesis (H_5), however, is strongly contradicted by the data: dependency (three negative coefficients) would appear to *reduce* the probability of instability rather than to increase it.[4]

(iv) It is finally worth noting that *structured division* (H_{12}) plays a particularly ambivalent role in Middle East/North Africa, the only consistent tendency being that *both ethno-linguistic and religious fractionalisation tend to reduce the probability of government change instability.* This apart, it would seem to be the case that while ethno-linguistic divisions reduce the likelihood of *violent* challenges (negative coefficient, Table 7.3) and religious divisions encourage them (positive coefficient), religious fractionalisation inhibits *peaceful* challenges (negative coefficient) and ethno-linguistic fractionalisation renders such challenges more likely (positive coefficient). In short, the role of structured division in Middle East/North Africa is highly ambiguous.

(c) Latin America variations (Table 7.4)

The ambiguous role of structured division in Middle East/North Africa also extends to Latin America. As Table 7.4 indicates, such divisions have a positive effect upon regime change, a negative effect upon violent challenges and governmental change, and no effect upon peaceful challenges; a configuration which deviates considerably from the overall global pattern of Table 7.1. There are, none the less, some similarities between the Latin American and the American global patterns, in relation to the 'capacity' dimension of political development (H_1), actual coercion (H_6) and potential coercion (H_9).

The most significant differences between the two patterns, however, can be seen in relation to *dependency* (H_5), the

TABLE 7.4   Patterns of bivariate correlations in Latin America ($N = 20$)

		$R\Delta$	VC	$G\Delta$	PC
H_1	Level of political development				
	– democratic performance	+	–	+	+
	– capacity	–	0	0	0
H_2	Level of socio-economic				
	development	–	+	0	+
H_3	Changes in political development	+	–	0	0
H_4	Changes in socio-economic				
	development	+	–	+	+
H_5	Dependency	+	+	+	–
H_6	Actual coercion (linear)	0	0	0	0
H_7	Actual coercion (curvilinear)	0	0	0	0
H_8	Potential coercion (linear)	–	+	0	–
H_9	Potential coercion (curvilinear)	0	0	0	0
H_{10}	Structured inequality	0	0	0	+
H_{12}	Structured division	+	–	–	0

+ denotes significant positive relationship.
– denotes significant negative relationship.
0 denotes no relationship.

'democratic performance' aspect of *political development* (H_1), and *socio-economic change* (H_4).

(i) *Dependency.* As we pointed out in the previous chapter, the dependency thesis was originally advanced in order to explain Latin American patterns of political behaviour. It is perhaps not surprising, therefore, that despite the absence of any consistent *global* relationship between dependency and instability, in Latin America itself there is a consistent tendency for dependency to be related to instability. As Table 7.4 indicates, while dependency may *reduce* the probability of peaceful challenges (negative coefficient), in accordance with the predictions of the dependency theorists, it is *positively* correlated with the three other instability dimensions.

(ii) *Democratic performance.* The thesis that higher levels of *political development* reduce the probability of instability, however, is strongly contradicted by the data for Latin America: the three positive coefficients for H_1 in Table 7.4 indicate that the prevailing tendency is for instability to be associated with a *higher* rather than a lower level of democratic performance.

(iii) *Socio-economic change.* While the social mobilisation thesis embodied in H_4 receives very little support from the global correlations which we reported in Table 7.1, it is clear from the coefficients presented in Table 7.4 that in Latin America, socio-economic change *does* have the contributory impact upon instability (with the exception of violent challenges) which H_4 predicts: in Latin America at least, a high rate of social change does increase the probability of peaceful challenge, regime change and government change instability.

(d)   Sub-Saharan Africa variations (Table 7.5)

Table 7.5 reports the pattern of interrelationships between instability and its exogenous correlates for Sub-Saharan Africa, and, in common with the other regions which we have examined, several departures from the global pattern of Table 7.1 are in evidence. The overriding tendency is for each of the exogenous variables to behave in more or less the same way with each of the instability dimensions – democratic performance, for example, consistently varies positively with each instability dimension – and

TABLE 7.5   Patterns of bivariate correlations in Sub-Saharan Africa
($N = 23$)

		RΔ	VC	GΔ	PC
H_1	Level of political development				
	– democratic performance	+	+	+	+
	– capacity	0	0	0	0
H_2	Level of socio-economic				
	development	+	+	+	0
H_3	Changes in political development	0	0	0	0
H_4	Changes in socio-economic				
	development	–	–	–	–
H_5	Dependency	–	0	–	–
H_6	Actual coercion (linear)	+	+	+	+
H_7	Actual coercion (curve)	0	0	0	0
H_8	Potential coercion (linear)	–	0	0	–
H_9	Potential coercion (curvilinear)	0	0	0	0
H_{10}	Structured inequality	0	0	0	0
H_{12}	Structured division	+	+	0	0

+ denotes significant positive relationship.
– denotes significant negative relationship.
0 denotes no relationship.

there are in fact only three exceptions to this tendency H_5, H_8 and H_{12}.

More specifically, however, it is clear from Table 7.5, firstly that the level of *governmental coercion* (either 'potential' or 'actual', considered linearly or curvilinearly) in Sub-Saharan Africa has only a very limited impact upon the level of political instability. Secondly, as is also generally the case in Middle East/North Africa, the levels of *economic development* and (the democratic performance dimension of) the level of *political development* vary *positively* with instability, rather than *negatively*, as H_1 and H_2 predict. Thirdly (and this again contradicts the prediction which was made in the previous chapter), the rate of *socio-economic change* (H_4) consistently varies *negatively* with instability rather than positively. In other words, in Sub-Saharan Africa, the roles of level of socio-economic development and socio-economic change are the complete reverse of what was anticipated in Chapter 6. Finally, Table 7.5 indicates that the level of *dependency* (H_5) is negatively correlated with regime change, governmental change and peaceful challenge (and unrelated to the level of violent challenge): it would appear to be the case, therefore, that the applicability of the 'dependency thesis' – though it may be well suited to Latin America – does not extend to Sub-Saharan Africa, as some writers have contended;[5] and that if dependency has any role at all in the latter region, it is to *reduce* the probability of instability occurring.[6]

(e)   Far East variations (Table 7.6)

Table 7.6 reports our bivariate findings on each of our eleven hypotheses, for the Far East region. The most notable similarity between the Far East pattern and global pattern of Table 7.1 is the behaviour of the democratic performance dimension of political development: in both cases, democratic performance varies negatively with regime change and yet is unrelated to the other forms of instability.

The most distinctive Far East tendency, however, concerns the role of *governmental repression*. It is clear from Table 7.6 that only 'actual' governmental coercion (H_6) is important as a correlate of political instability, and indeed it correlates positively and significantly with all forms of instability: the other coercion functions which we estimated (the zero coefficients in H_7, H_8 and

TABLE 7.6   Patterns of bivariate correlations in the Far East ($N = 22$)

		$R\Delta$	VC	$G\Delta$	PC
H_1	Level of political development				
	– democratic performance	–	0	0	0
	– capacity	0	–	+	+
H_2	Level of socio-economic	–	–	+	+
	development				
H_3	Changes in political development	0	+	+	0
H_4	Changes in socio-economic	+	+	+	–
	development				
H_5	Dependency	+	0	0	+
H_6	Actual coercion (linear)	+	+	+	+
H_7	Actual coercion (curvilinear)	0	0	0	0
H_8	Potential coercion (linear)	0	0	0	0
H_9	Potential coercion (curvilinear)	0	0	0	0
H_{10}	Structured inequality	0	0	0	–
H_{12}	Structured division	0	0	0	0

+ denotes significant positive relationship.
– denotes significant negative relationship.
0 denotes no relationship.

H_9) were of no explanatory value in predicting the level of political instability. It is also interesting to note from Table 7.6 that *changes* in both *socio-economic* (H_4) and *political development* (H_3) are, as predicted, *positively* correlated with two of the instability dimensions. This contrasts sharply with the patterns observed above (i) for Sub-Saharan Africa (where socio-economic change, for example, consistently has a *reductive* impact upon instability), and (ii) for Latin America (where, as we saw earlier, socio-economic change appears to have a distinctly ambivalent role in the genesis of instability). Finally, it is necessary to point to the ambivalent role of *dependency* (H_5) in the Far East: as Table 7.6 indicates, although dependency has no direct influence upon violent challenges or governmental changes (both have zero coefficients in H_5), it does (as predicted) have a contributory impact upon regime change and peaceful challenges.

There are, then, numerous specifically 'regional' tendencies in the pattern of interrelationships between instability and its exogenous correlates which the overall global correlations did not reveal. As we intimated earlier, while in the foregoing *text* we have only made reference to (what appear to be) the most significant tendencies in each of the regions, strictly speaking the *detailed findings reported in Tables 7.2 to 7.6* represent the specific bivariate generalisations which we wish to make about the regional variations in the correlates of political instability (bearing in mind that a zero coefficient in any of those tables denotes a hypothesis rejected). As we also suggested earlier, however, *since the significance of a number of these bivariate relationships in fact (as we shall see) disappears when appropriate statistical controls are made, we do not attempt at this stage to draw any detailed theoretical inferences about the sources of instability beyond the general statements of empirical tendency which we have already made.* None the less, some sort of synthesis – or, at least, simplification – of the complex pattern of interrelationship which we have just described would be of considerable value.

Of course, the principal problem involved in attempting to effect such a synthesis or simplification is that the very complexity and ambiguity of the overall pattern almost defies any attempt to reduce that complexity to a number of more basic processes or mechanisms: an exogenous variable such as political development, for example, appears to have a largely positive impact upon instability in the Middle East/North Africa, and in Sub-Saharan Africa, but a mainly negative role in Europe/North America; a negative impact upon regime change, but little or no effect upon violent challenge. While it is possible to concoct some kind of 'explanation' for many of these tendencies individually, it is extremely difficult to conceive of one particular mechanism – or even a set of mechanisms – which would be capable of providing a satisfactory 'theoretical' explanation of their *simultaneous* occurrence.

However, even though it is perhaps not possible to provide a *theoretical* simplification of the diversity which we have described in Tables 7.1 to 7.6, a number of simplifying *empirical* generalisations can be offered which attempt to describe the most significant cross-regional tendencies.

(i) While there appears to be no *general* relationship between instability and development, in accordance with Huntington's prediction about the role of development, *regime change instability does appear to be negatively related to both the level of socio-economic development and the level of political development.*

(ii) *The level of 'potential government coercion' consistently fails to offer any suitable regional basis for predicting the level of instability*, except in the Europe/North America region where a curvilinear function explains some 20 per cent of the variance in regime challenge.

(iii) While the rate of socio-economic change appears to have no consistent impact either upon regime or government change or upon the level of peaceful challenge, with the exception of the Europe/North America region (where there is no relationship) *the level of violent challenge instability consistently correlates negatively with the rate of socio-economic change* (H_4). This entirely contradicts the theoretical predictions of the social mobilisation thesis which we outlined in the previous chapter. That is to say, there would seem to be no evidence whatsoever to support the hypothesis that a high rate of socio-economic change is likely to produce social dislocations and frustrations which lead to political violence: on the contrary, the data suggest that a high rate of socio-economic change is perhaps more likely either to *satisfy* expectations (thereby preventing 'frustrations', and hence violence) or else to lead to a depoliticising form of alienation which in turn leads to a relatively low level of violent challenge instability.

(iv) With regard to the remaining bivariate relationships, it can only be re-emphasised that considerable ambiguities and inconsistencies exist. Although there are certain specific regional tendencies, identified above, it would appear to be the case that few immutable global tendencies are in evidence which would provide a suitable basis for predicting cross-national levels of political instability. In short, most of the exogenous variables which we have isolated as influences upon political instability perform a *double edged* function: in some circumstances they can serve to increase the level of (a particular type of) instability whereas in others they serve to reduce it.

As a postscript to our discussion of regional variations, it is worth noting that on a purely numerical basis, some of our eleven hypotheses, perhaps not surprisingly, were more consistently corroborated than others. As Table 7.7 indicates, *actual government coercion* (H_6 – linear) furnished a significant coefficient with the correct sign far more frequently than any of the other hypotheses (12 out of 24), while *structured inequality* (H_{10}) and the two *curvilinear coercion functions* (H_7 and H_9) provided such a coefficient *least* frequently. Table 7.7, therefore, in effect provides a sort of *rank ordering* of our eleven hypotheses in terms of the

TABLE 7.7 Summary of the number of times each hypothesis correctly predicts the observed correlation in Tables 7.1–7.6 (possible total of predictions = 24 : 6 tables, 4 instability dimensions per table)

		Number of correct predictions Tables 7.1—7.6	Total number of predictions Tables 7.1—7.6
H_6	Actual government coercion (linear)	12	24
H_2	Level of socio-economic development	8	24
H_{12}	Structured division	8	24
H_4	Socio-economic change	7	24
H_8	Potential governmental coercion (linear)	7	24
H_1	Political development		
	– democratic performance	6	24
	– capacity	6	24
H_3	Changes in political development	5	24
H_5	Dependency	5	24
H_{10}	Structured inequality	2	24
H_7	Actual governmental coercion (curvilinear)	2	24
H_9	Potential governmental coercion (curvilinear)	1	24

extent to which they isolate consistent empirical tendencies both globally and across particular regions, and clearly, the sheer number of 'incorrect predictions' can only serve to emphasis our earlier conclusion that in general, none of the hypotheses which we have examined consistently derives support from the data.

A similar conclusion must also be drawn from Table 7.8, which reports the number of times each instability dimension was correctly predicted in Tables 7.1 to 7.6. Again the table effectively provides an ordinal scale of 'predictability' with regime change representing the 'most predictable' (though still relatively 'unpredictable') form of instability, and peaceful challenge the 'least predictable'. As we will see in the next chapter, when we develop a single equation predictive model for each of these instability dimensions, the rank ordering of the dimensions of instability in Table 7.8 directly parallels the respective levels of explained variance which we achieve for each instability dimension in these predictive models: our model for regime change, for example, furnishes an R^2 of 0.53 whereas the R^2 for peaceful

TABLE 7.8 Number of times each instability dimension is correctly predicted by H_1 to H_{12} in Tables 7.1–7.6

Instability dimensions	Number of times correctly predicted by $H_1 - H_{12}$	Total number of predictions
Regime change	27	72
Violent challenge	18	72
Government change	11	72
Peaceful changes	10	72

challenge is only $R^2 = 0.22$. It would seem, therefore, that certain types of instability are inherently more difficult to predict than others, and, indeed, this is a theme to which we will return later.

SUMMARY AND CONCLUSIONS

In this chapter we have undertaken a bivariate examination of the applicability of a series of general hypotheses (outlined in Chapter 6) which purport to isolate the main determinants of political instability. These general hypotheses were investigated at two levels. We began by examining the overall 'global' level of correlation between each instability dimension and each exogenous variable. Our results in this context however, were somewhat disappointing: most of our hypotheses, even stated only as probabilistic tendencies, derived very little support from the data, yielding either non-significant parameters or else parameters with incorrect signs.

Rather than conclude that this lack of global correlation evidenced the total inadequacy of our stated hypotheses, we then proceeded to examine the possible *regional* variations in the patterns of intercorrelation. This part of the analysis enabled us to isolate a number of distinct regional tendencies, which demonstrated that some of our original hypotheses did in fact derive a limited amount of support: firstly, in relation to certain regions (for example, the dependency thesis was broadly corroborated in the context of Latin America), and secondly, in relation to certain instability dimensions (regime change, for example, consistently varied negatively with the level of political development). Nonetheless, the main conclusion which our regional analysis suggested was that the pattern of interrelationship between instability and its exogenous correlates (or non-correlates) is extremely complex and not easily susceptible to simplifying generalisations.

What then, if anything, are the implications of the numerous findings which we have reported in this chapter? As we have intimated, we shall be better able to provide a reasonably precise answer to this question during the course of the *next* chapter, when we consider a number of multivariate models which seek to evaluate the *simultaneous* effects of the various exogenous influences upon each dimension of instability.

At this stage, however, we can conclude with some certainty (1) that we are in a position to *reject* a large number of bivariate hypotheses (it will be recalled that a zero coefficient observed in Tables 7.1–7.6 represents a hypothesis rejected), and (2) that we have at the same time identified many statistically significant bivariate relationships (which are signified in Tables 7.1–7.6 and largely summarised in Table 7.7) which merit further empirical investigation and possible subsequent theoretical interpretation.

In the next chapter, this 'further empirical investigation' takes the form of a series of multiple regression equations. As we will see, the complexity which we have described here is in fact reducible to the operation of a much smaller number of statistically significant empirical tendencies. Once these tendencies have been isolated we will then be in a position to undertake a realistic evaluation, firstly, of the utility and scope of each of our initial hypotheses, and secondly, of the general possibilities for predicting cross-national patterns of political instability.

8 Four Predictive Models of Political Instability

In Chapter 6 we introduced a series of bivariate hypotheses which sought to identify the principal influences upon the level of political instability. In Chapter 7 we attempted to demonstrate that, considered as bivariate propositions, these hypotheses derive varying degrees of support, both in relation to the different types of instability, and in relation to different regional groupings.

In this chapter, using multivariate techniques, we have three (interrelated) objectives. The first is to reduce the complex pattern of interrelationship between instability and its exogenous correlates to a smaller number of empirical tendencies, which are more easily capable of substantive theoretical interpretation than the mass of bivariate findings which we reported in Chapter 7. Our second objective is to assess the adequacy and scope (in terms of the regions to which they are most applicable) of each of the hypotheses which we advanced in Chapter 6. Finally, we attempt to develop a series of *predictive models of instability* (one for each instability dimension) which attempt to evaluate the extent to which cross-national levels of instability can be predicted, at least using the sort of data currently available for empirical research. We will begin this chapter, however, by reviewing two methodological techniques which we intend to use in our subsequent analysis; we then turn to examine each of our predictive models of instability in detail.

SOME METHODOLOGICAL CONSIDERATIONS: 'BEST
MODEL' PROCEDURE AND REGIONAL INTERACTIONS

In order to achieve the three objectives cited above, we intend to employ a series of statistical operations based upon the multiple regression model, because by the use of that model it is possible, simultaneously: (1) to establish which of a large number of independent or exogenous variables have the most significant impact upon any specified dependent variable (our first objective: reducing complexity); (2) to evaluate the significance (or otherwise) of specific hypotheses which link a particular dependent variable to a number of independent or predictor variables (our second objective: evaluating particular hypotheses); and (3) for any given dependent variable, to develop a predictive linear additive equation (our third objective), which describes the effect of each independent or predictor variable within that equation upon the dependent variable, whilst simultaneously controlling for the effects of all the other predictors in the equation.[1] In this chapter we will attempt to show how the multiple regression model can be employed to establish which of our exogenous variables, considered in linear combination rather than individually, have statistically significant effects upon the level of political instability, and which do not.

Our intention, in other words, is not only to identify the most important predictors of political instability, but also to *broaden the range of hypotheses concerning its determinants which require rejection, because the relatively large number of statistically significant bivariate correlations which we reported in the last chapter means that there is a large group of probabilistic hypotheses concerning the exogenous influences upon instability which cannot be rejected.* What we attempt to demonstrate here is that when a multivariate (as opposed to a series of bivariate) model(s) is considered, the significance of many of these bivariate relationships is drastically reduced, which in turn implies that (in the Popperian tradition) we are in a position to reject a greater number of hypotheses.

In order to establish precisely what we mean by 'hypothesis rejection', however, we need to provide an outline of the 'series of operations' which we will refer to as our 'best fitting equation' or 'best model' procedure. Given the sophisticated and complex nature of the multiple regression model itself, of course, the question as to what might constitute the 'best fitting equation' is somewhat problematic, particularly in view of the fact that in order to secure a 'good' regression model, trade-offs often need to be made between explained variance, the avoidance of collinear predictors or independent variables (multicollinearity), and the maintenance of parameter significance. The criteria which we employ here are, firstly, the maximisation of R^2 with all parameters significant at the 0.01 level (as evidenced by the magnitude of the relevant t statistic);[2] and secondly, the avoidance of intercorrelations between predictor variables greater than $r = 0.6$.[3]

Using these criteria, our 'best model' procedure is somewhat analogous to the 'stepwise regression' programme which SPSS provides. For each instability dimension, a *data bank* of *theoretically relevant* independent variables was established. Each of these data banks contained two sets of variables: (1) all of the exogenous variables which we defined in our eleven bivariate hypotheses in Chapter 6, and (2) a series of *interaction* variables, defined below, which were constructed as a result of the findings which we reported in Chapter 7. The bivariate correlations between the dependent instability dimension and each of the independent variables in the 'bank' were then examined, and the predictor variable or set of non-collinear predictor variables which explained most of the variance in the dependent variable was (were) identified. A regression equation incorporating that (those) variable(s) was then estimated and if any of the predictors furnished non-significant parameters then the offending predictor was dropped from the model and the equation re-estimated: if all the parameters were then found to be significant at the 0.01 level, the residuals from that equation were correlated against all the remaining potential predictors in the data bank. The predictor (or non-collinear predictors) which explained most of the variance in the residuals was (were) then added to the original independent variables and the equation re-estimated. If all the parameters proved significant, the 'new' predictor(s) was (were) retained ... and so on. If the addition of a predictor rendered one of the preceding independent variables nonsignificant, but that additional predictor retained its significance, the preceding predictor was dropped from the subsequent equation.

The end result of this best model procedure is a predictive equation for each instability dimension which (1) maximises explained variance while ensuring that each of the coefficients in each equation is statistically significant, and (2) provides an optimal linear additive combination of the independent variables defined by the relevant data bank. The procedure consequently enables the identification of the most important influences upon each of our instability dimensions, and therefore enables us to assess which of our original hypotheses have the most explanatory power. Simultaneously, however, the direct implication of our definition of 'best' is that the inclusion of additional predictor variables from the 'data bank', either singly or in combination, furnishes non-significant parameters for those additional variables. Throughout this chapter, therefore, our method of 'hypothesis rejection' consists in identifying variables which do *not* appear in our 'best' predictive equations. Indeed, for any 'best' equation, the potential independent variables *excluded* from it can be interpreted as having no additional predictive power (and, therefore, no effect) over and above that of the independent variables *included* within it. The reason for this simple. The rejection of the model

$$Y = \hat{\alpha} + \hat{\beta}_1 X_1 + \hat{\beta}_2 X_2 + E$$

on the grounds that $\hat{\beta}_2$ is non-significant entails the simultaneous rejection of the hypothesis that 'controlling for X_1, Y is influenced by X_2'. Not accepting a model in terms of our 'best model' procedure, therefore, is in this sense the same as rejecting a hypothesis: each time we eliminate a particular predictor, that is to say, each time we reject a model, we reject a hypothesis.

Regional interactions

We suggested in the preceding section, then, that our predictive 'best models' are derived from a systematic examination of a number of variables contained within a defined 'data bank'. While we mentioned that some of these variables were simply the exogenous correlates of instability which we specified in Chapter 6, we were not in a position to identify the remaining independent variables. These variables are in fact regional *intercept shift* and *slope shift interaction* terms, and it is their nature and significance which we now examine.

As we saw in Chapter 7, there are a number of specific regional variations in the patterns of interrelationship between instability and its exogenous correlates. Given these variations, it might seem that the ideal way in which to establish a predictive model of any given instability dimension would in fact be to our 'best model' procedure in order to generate a *series* of predictive equations – one for each regional grouping. In relation to regime change instability, for example, this would entail the construction of a 'best model' for Latin America, a 'best model' for Europe/North America, and so on. There are two principal methodological reasons why this course of action was rejected. Firstly, such an approach makes no allowance for the fact that *some* regional variations may in fact be at least partly explained by the action of some more general tendency which operates across all (or most) regions. Secondly, this kind of disjointed approach provides a very limited number of observations (and consequently degrees of freedom) for each of the regional subsets. While the restricted number of observations for each subset is not particularly serious for the analysis of *bivariate* relationships, when *multiple* regression models are being considered, the problems of parameter significance, and particularly of parameter stability, are enormous. For these two reasons, then, we chose to develop predictive models for each instability dimension which are globally applicable, but which at the same time enable specific regional variations to be taken into account, and it is to this end that we make use of intercept shift, and more particularly, of slope shift interaction terms.

The nature of these terms is best introduced by reference to a two-dimensional space, although the principles involved in the following exposition are generalisable to the n-dimensional case. Consider a scattergram as in Figure 8.1, in which the slope of the relationship between Y and X for the Latin American cases or countries is different from the slope for the rest of the cases (the 'minimum position').

It can be shown that if the equation $Y = a + b_1X + b_2X(\text{LA}) + E$ is estimated [where Y and X have obvious interpretations, and where $X(\text{LA})$ is an artificially

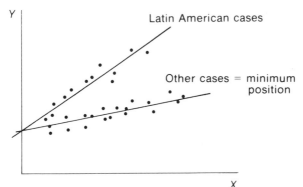

FIGURE 8.1 Hypothetical relationship between Y and X showing differential slopes for different groups of cases

constructed variable, which is the actual value of X if a country is in Latin America and zero otherwise], b_1 provides an estimate for the slope of the relationship between Y and X for *non*-Latin American countries (the minimum position), and b_2 provides a measure of the *shift* in slope for the Latin American countries away from the minimum position. $X(LA)$, therefore, is a 'slope shift interaction term'.

Using this principle, it is not only possible to estimate *intercept* shifts (as in Figure 8.2) and multiple slope shifts (as in Figure 8.3) from the 'minimum position', but also to estimate such slope and intercept shifts in a multi-dimensional space, while simultaneously controlling for the effects of a number of other independent variables. It is also possible (using an independent variable such as $X(LA)$ on its own) to estimate the slope between Y and X for only one region or group of countries, while constraining the slope for the rest of the cases to be zero (as in Figure 8.4).

Figures 8.1 to 8.4, and the definitions beneath each of them, then, describe the way in which the various non-linear

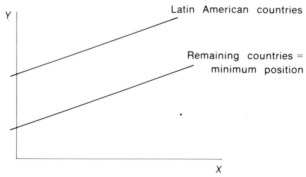

Estimated equation: $Y = a + b_1X + b_2D + E$

where E is a series of random errors;
      Y and X are two continuous, independently defined variables;
      D is a dichotomous variable which is 1 if a country is in Latin America and zero otherwise;
      b_1 estimates the slope for both groups of countries;
      b_2 estimates the (intercept) shift along the Y axis for the Latin American countries;
      a is the point where subspace for minimum position countries intersects Y axis.

FIGURE 8.2   Intercept shift model for the regression of Y on X

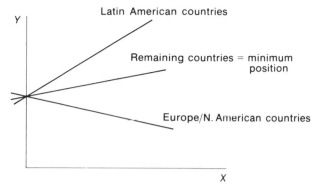

Estimated equation: $Y = a + b_1 X + b_2 X(LA) + b_3 X(EUR) + E$

where E is a series of random errors;
   Y and X are two continuous independently defined variables;
   $X(LA)$ is a constructed variable which is the actual value of X if a country is in Latin America and zero otherwise;
   $X(EUR)$ is a constructed variable which is the actual value of X if a country is in Europe/North America and zero otherwise;
   a is the point where the three subspaces intersect the Y axis;
   b_1 estimates the slope of Y on X for the minimum position countries;
   b_2 estimates the shift in slope for the Latin American countries away from the minimum position slope;
   b_3 estimates the slope of Y on X for the Europe/North America countries away from the minimum position slope.

FIGURE 8.3   Multiple slope shift model for the regression of Y on X

modifications to the simple bivariate (and by implication, multivariate) regression model can be operationalised. Moreover, the constructed variables which the figures describe are precisely the sort of intercept shift and slope shift interaction terms which go to form part of the 'data banks' to which we referred earlier. [The four 'banks' of independent variables (one bank for each instability dimension) which were subjected to our 'best model' procedure are in fact presented in Appendix 3.]

The decision as to whether or not a particular slope or intercept shift term should be included within each of these banks was made on the basis of the findings which we reported in Chapter 7, Tables 7.2 to 7.6. Wherever a significant bivariate regional relation-

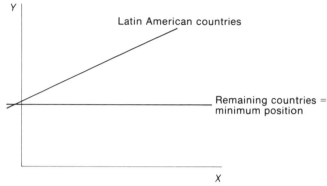

Estimated equation: $Y = a + bX(\text{LA}) + E$

where E is a series of random errors;

 $X(\text{LA})$ is a constructed variable which is the actual value of X if a country is in Latin America and zero otherwise;

 a is the estimated point where the Latin America line intersects the Y axis;

 b is the estimated shift in slope for Latin American countries away from the minimum position. Since the slope for the minimum position countries is zero, this shift in slope is equal to the estimated slope for Latin American countries.

FIGURE 8.4 Slope shift model for Y on X, Latin American countries only (slope for remaining countries constrained to be zero)

ship was found to exist in those tables, an appropriate slope shift interaction term and an appropriate intercept shift dummy variable were constructed. This means, for example, that (on the basis of Table 7.2) for the 'governmental change' data bank, Europe/North America intercept shift and slope shift interaction terms were constructed (1) for level of socio-economic development (H_2, significant positive coefficient), (2) for socio-economic change (H_4, significant negative coefficient), (3) for dependency (H_5, significant negative coefficient), and (4) for structured division (H_{12}, significant positive coefficient). What is of fundamental importance, however, is that the inclusion of these various interaction terms in each of the four data-banks enables us to assess (via our best model procedure) how far the *additional* information about regional variations (in the patterns of interrelationship between instability and its exogenous correlates), which we obtained in the previous chapter, is capable of improving any predictions which we might wish to make about the level of instability in different systems, over and above the effects of those exogenous variables which are of *general* significance.

Having established the nature and implications of our 'best model' procedure, and having identified the general origins of the source exogenous variables contained within the four data-banks upon which that procedure operates, we turn now to examine each of the predictive models of instability which the procedure suggests. As we will see, while many of the bivariate regional variations which we identified in the previous chapter lose their significance when the simultaneous effects of other independent variables are controlled for, some of the regional interaction terms do in fact retain their significance.

FOUR PREDICTIVE MODELS OF INSTABILITY

We suggested in the previous section, then, that the 'data bank' of potential predictors for each instability dimension was composed of (1) the exogenous variables defined by each of the eleven hypotheses which we presented in Chapter 6, and (2) a series of regional interaction terms derived from the findings which we reported in Chapter 7. Before we can present our predictive models, however, we need to mention briefly three additional predictor variables[4] which were also included in each of the data-banks, not because previous analyses have in any systematic way attempted to show that any of them has a direct and consistent impact upon the level of political instability, but because each of them *may* be of predictive value in certain circumstances: 'press freedom', 'changes in the level of exports', and 'communist status'.

(a) **Press freedom**

This variable was included for the simple reason that, while it might not be expected that there would be any *general* relationship between instability and press freedom (indeed the bivariate correlations between press freedom and each instability dimension are all close to zero), it is possible that in certain systems (for example, those where political institutions are relatively weak), press freedom may in fact serve to exacerbate political divisions and conflicts, and encourage criticism of the encumbent regime, thereby increasing the likelihood of political instability. Moreover, as we will see later, when used in conjunction with other variables which *do* have a general impact upon the level of instability, the explanatory power of press freedom is considerable.

(b)   Changes in the level of exports (1960–65)

One of the most marked features of the international economic system since 1945 has been the general expansion of world trade. For any given country, however, the impact of this expansion has been uncertain. The inclusion of the 'export change' variable into each of the exogenous variable data banks, therefore, is designed to establish the general role which such economic changes might play in relation to political stability: does the expansion of trade produce economic dislocations which in turn lead to (certain types of) political instability, or does it represent an improvement in economic performance which in turn might be expected to reduce the probability of political disruption?

(c)   Communist status

This dummy variable (1 = communist, 0 = not) was included in order to examine the simple proposition that communist systems tend, on the whole, to be more stable than non-communist systems: as we will see, although this is certainly the case in relation to regime change instability, such a conclusion is not merited with regard to the other instability dimensions.

Tables 8.1 to 8.4 summarise our four 'best' predictive models of

TABLE 8.1   Predictive model of peaceful challenge instability

Independent variable	Standardised regression coefficient
Level of transport communication development	−0.27
Population size	0.22
Latin America urbanisation change interaction term	0.34
Latin America dependency interaction term	0.21
Sub-Saharan Africa press freedom interaction term	0.23

$N = 103$, $R^2 = 0.22$.
All estimates significant at 0.01 level.

TABLE 8.2   Predictive model of violent challenge instability

Independent variable	Standardised regression coefficient
Population size	0.23
Religious cleavage	0.19
Level of urbanisation	−0.32
Sub-Saharan Africa communications change interaction term	−0.40
Far East changes in income per capita interaction term	0.40

$N = 103$, $R^2 = 0.48$.
All estimates significant at 0.01 level.

instability. As we suggested earlier, the direct implication of our definition of 'best' is that, for any given instability dimension, the variables contained within the appropriate data-bank presented in Appendix 3 which are *excluded* from the tables, have no additional predictive power over and above that of the variables *included* within that table (without introducing an unacceptable degree of multicollinearity or loss of parameter significance into the relevant model). In other words, the data suggest that *the independent variables included in each of the 'best models' are the only ones which have a direct and consistently significant impact upon the level of political instability: when these variables are controlled for, the significance of all the other variables contained in the relevant data-bank disappears.*

Peaceful challenge instability

As Table 8.1 shows, cross-national levels of peaceful challenge instability are extremely difficult to predict: despite the large 'bank' of potential predictors, our 'best model' predictors together only explain 22 per cent of the variance in peaceful challenge instability ($R^2 = 0.22$). Clearly, with such a comparatively low level of statistical explanation, this model is not particularly valuable for predictive, or indeed explanatory, purposes of any sort. All that it really demonstrates is (1) that despite the numerous hypotheses which purport to explain cross-national levels of (peaceful challenge) instability, peaceful challenge behaviours in fact remain inherently difficult to predict, and (2) that only five of the potential exogenous correlates of peaceful challenge instability in fact play a significant role in its genesis:

the level of communications development
population size[5]
(in Latin America) the level of trade dependence
(in Latin America) changes in the level of urbanisation
(in Sub-Saharan Africa) the degree of press freedom.

Given the general inadequacy of the 'peaceful challenge' model, we do not intend to make any further detailed comment about it, beyond the general observation that it provides corroborative evidence for only a very limited number of our original hypotheses, and disconfirmation for most of them: even considered in combination, and making full allowance for regional variations, the exogenous variables defined by the eleven hypotheses which we proposed in Chapter 6 quite simply do not provide a satisfactory explanation of peaceful challenge instability.

Violent challenge instability

A similar conclusion must also be drawn with regard to the level of violent challenge instability. In contrast to earlier analyses which have purported to achieve levels of statistical explanation in excess of 60 per cent (Gurr, for example, achieves an R^2 of 0.64 for his 'Total Magnitude of Civil Strife Index'),[6] as Table 8.2 shows, our 'best model' in fact furnishes an R^2 of less than 50 per cent. Again, on the basis of such a highly stochastic model, it is difficult to draw firm conclusions as to precisely why some countries experience a higher level of violent challenge instability than others. What is clear from Table 8.2 is that, apart from population size (which is again included for 'control' purposes), the only variables which have a consistent *general* impact upon violent challenge behaviours are *religious fractionalisation*, one of our indices of 'structured division' (which, as H_{12} predicts, has a positive effect, $B = 0.23$), and *urbanisation*, an indicator of socio-economic development (which, as H_2 predicts, has a negative effect, $B = -0.32$).

The scope of the remaining propositions which receive partial support, however, is limited to particular regions: the evidence presented in Table 8.2 suggests that the level of violent challenge instability is significantly influenced: negatively by changes in the level of communications development *in Sub-Saharan Africa* ($B = -0.40$); positively by changes in GNP per capita *in the Far East* ($B = 0.40$). In other words, it would seem to be the case that socio-economic change plays a distinctly double-edged role in the genesis of violent challenge instability. On the one hand, in the Far East, the data would appear to support the frustration/expectations thesis, that socio-economic change produces structural distortions and raised aspirations, which in turn lead to violence. On the other hand, the evidence for Sub-Saharan Africa seems to indicate that such changes – since they imply higher material standards of living at least among the influential bourgeois sectors – perhaps produce a greater degree of satisfaction with the encumbent regime, which in turn reduces the probability of violent challenge instability.

Apart from the small number of significant tendencies which we have just outlined, therefore, the hypotheses which we put forward in Chapter 6 clearly derive no support from the data. Moreover (as we suggested with regard to our 'best model' of peaceful challenge instability), the low level of statistical explanation which is associated with our violent challenge best model makes it very difficult to establish any firm generalisations about the sources of political violence, beyond the statements of empirical tendency which we have already made. Specifically, the most important conclusions which can be drawn are as follows. Firstly, socio-economic change (if it has any effect upon political violence at all) does not of itself appear necessarily to generate the kind of systemic strains and tensions which the 'frustration' theorists claim lead to violence and instability. Indeed, in certain contexts, such changes can instead serve to reduce instability. Secondly, it would seem to be the case that the only *general* influences upon the level of violent challenge instability are religious division and urbanisation. While these are not particularly stimulating conclusions, they again serve to demonstrate the inherent difficulty of predicting cross-national levels of (violent) political instability, given the data which are presently available, and given the kinds of hypotheses which have so far been advanced to explain those levels.

Government change instability

As Table 8.3 indicates, the level of statistical explanation which our best model procedure achieves for governmental change

TABLE 8.3   Predictive model of governmental change instability

Independent variable	Standardised regression coefficient
Ethnic-linguistic cleavage	−0.16
Population size	0.32
Changes in the level of transport development (socio-economic change)	−0.16
Dependency	0.32
Europe/North America dependency interaction term	−0.24
Latin America ethnic-linguistic cleavage interaction term	−0.27
Latin America religious cleavage interaction term	−0.32
Latin America press freedom interaction term	0.25
Europe/North America religious fractionalisation interaction term	0.35
Sub-Saharan Africa press freedom interaction term	0.44
Sub-Saharan Africa dependency interaction term	−0.34

$N = 103$, $R^2 = 0.46$.
All estimates significant at 0.01 level.

instability $(R^2 = 0.46)$ is some improvement upon the level achieved for peaceful challenge instability. Again, however, only a limited number of our exogenous variables are of *general* significance: ethno-linguistic fractionalisation (H_{12}), socio-economic changes (H_4), trade dependence (H_5) and population size (again included as a control). While the standardised coefficient for dependency $(B = 0.32)$ is positive, as predicted by H_5, the coefficients for fractionalisation and for socio-economic change are in the *opposite* direction to that which was predicted. In other words, although fractionalisation and socio-economic change do have an impact upon governmental change instability, the effect is to *reduce* the level of instability, not to increase it, as H_{10} and H_4 respectively predict.

Apart from these general relationships, Table 8.3 also indicates that there are several significant *regional* influences upon the level of governmental instability. In Latin America, both *religious* $(B = -0.32$ for religious fractionalisation) and *ethnic divisions* $(B = -0.27$ for ethnolinguistic fractionalisation) further reduce the probability of governmental change instability. In Latin America and in Sub-Saharan Africa, a higher level of *press freedom* increases the probability of instability $(B = 0.25$ and $B = 0.44$

respectively), suggesting perhaps that in (Third World) systems where political institutions are relatively weak, a free press is likely to have a disruptive effect on governmental stability. Finally, Table 8.3 indicates that in Europe/North America, *religious fractionalisation* has a significant and positive impact upon governmental change instability ($B = 0.35$).

An additional feature of the governmental change 'best model', however, is the *negative* coefficients which Table 8.3 reports for the Sub-Saharan Africa and Europe/North America *dependency* interaction terms. Given (as we saw earlier) that these coefficients identify the *change* in slope away away from the minimum position for the regions to which they refer, it is clear that in Europe/North America,[7] and in Sub-Saharan Africa,[8] dependency has virtually *no* effect upon the level of governmental change instability. Combined with the conclusions which we drew earlier concerning the incorrect direction of slope of the fractionalisation and socio-economic change coefficients, therefore, the implication of these interaction term coefficients is that none of the possible influences upon governmental change instability which our original hypotheses specified, in fact has the *general* effect which was predicted. In other words, although some of our original hypotheses derive a limited amount of support in relation to certain regions, their *general* ability to predict cross-national levels of governmental instability is extremely weak.

It would seem to be the case, then, that with regard to the exogenous sources of peaceful challenge, violent challenge and governmental change instability, generalisation is extremely difficult. This difficulty is not quite so marked, however, in relation to regime change instability: as we will see, not only is the level of statistical explanation which our 'best model' procedure achieves, a considerable improvement upon the three previous models, but the regime change best model itself also provides several *general* mechanisms which appear to operate across all systems quite independently of regional type. It is for these two reasons that we will devote rather more attention to our predictive equation for regime change than we have accorded to the three other equations.

Regime change instability

As Table 8.4 indicates, the exogenous variables in our regime change best model jointly explain some 53 per cent of the variance

TABLE 8.4   Predictive model of regime change instability

Independent variable	Standardised regression coefficient
Press freedom	0.45
Democratic performance	−0.71
Actual government coercion	0.18
Level of economic development	−0.25
Changes in the level of political development	0.22
Changes in the level of exports ⎫	−0.23
Changes in the level of education ⎬ Performance	
(socio-economic change) ⎭	−0.26
Communist status	−0.29
Europe/North America changes in communication inter- action term	0.42
Latin America ethnic-linguistic cleavage interaction term	0.23
Sub-Saharan Africa press freedom interaction term	0.22
Far East changes in exports interaction term	0.27

$N = 103$, $R^2 = 0.531$.
All estimates significant at the 0.01 level.

in regime change instability, and, given the general absence of previous quantitative attempts aimed at predicting changes in regime, this relatively high level of statistical explanation is almost satisfactory. The model also implies corroboration for a much wider range of general propositions than any of the three previous 'best models'. As Table 8.4 shows, significant coefficients (in the predicted direction) were obtained for democratic perform- ance $(H_1:B = -0.71)$, for actual governmental repression $(H_6:B = 0.18)$, for the level of socio-economic development $(H_2:B = -0.25)$, for changes in political development $(H_3:B = 0.22)$, and for the communist/non-communist dummy variable $(B = -0.29)$. Significant coefficients were also obtained (1) for socio-economic change (for which the slope was opposite to that predicted, $B = -0.26$), and (2) for press freedom $(B = 0.45)$ and changes in exports $(B = -0.23)$, for which no slope predictions were made.

It is also clear from Table 8.4 that there are several additional (significant) *regional* tendencies. Before we comment upon these, however, it is necessary to examine the *general* tendencies which we have just identified in rather more detail.

Some of the findings reported in Table 8.4 are not at all surprising: the significant negative coefficient for socio-economic development, for example, simply suggests that a relatively high level of socio-economic development is likely to inhibit regime change instability. Similarly, the coefficients for the communist/ non-communist dummy and for democratic performance suggest that regime change is less likely to occur in communist systems or in countries which have achieved a relatively high level of democratic performance. On the other hand, a high level of governmental repression ($B = 0.18$) or a marked increase in the extent to which the state has penetrated society and economy (change in the level of political development, $B = 0.22$), tends to be associated with a comparatively high level of regime change instability.

The tendencies evident in Table 8.4 which have less obvious interpretations, however, are the coefficients for (1) socio-economic change, (2) changes in exports, and (3) press freedom. It is the implications of these coefficients which we now examine.

The negative coefficients for socio-economic change and for changes in exports, imply that such changes do *not* (falsely) raise expectations, thereby generating frustration and instability as Huntington suggests. Rather, since these kinds of change in fact reduce the probability of instability occurring, it would appear to be the case that increases in the level of socio-economic development and increases in the level of exports per capita instead, perhaps, represent an improvement in the economic *performance* of the system as a whole, which in turn tends to improve the regime's potentiality for survival.[9]

One of the most important features of Table 8.4, however, is the positive coefficient for the press freedom index ($B = 0.45$): a high level of press freedom (controlling for all the other exogenous variables included in the regime change 'best model') is likely to result in a comparatively high level of regime change instability. A more detailed examination of the relationship between regime change, press freedom and *democratic performance*, however, reveals that *the effects of press freedom and democratic performance upon regime change instability cannot be divorced from each other*. When the regime index is regressed *separately*, firstly, on press freedom, and secondly, on democratic performance (in two separate bivariate models), neither of these independent variables has any real effect upon the level of instability:[10] it is only when they are considered in linear *combination* that their joint impact upon regime change instability is so marked. In short, the *simultaneous additive effect* of democratic performance and press freedom upon regime change instability is greater than the sum of the individual effects of each of those independent variables when considered in isolation. Given that democratic performance has a *negative* and press freedom a *positive* impact upon regime change instability for any particular system, the following conclusions can be drawn.

1. If the levels of democratic performance and press freedom are broadly equivalent – that is to say, if they are both relatively high or both relatively low – then their joint effect upon the level of instability will be negligible, since the positive effects of press freedom will more or less cancel out the negative effects of democratic performance.

2. If the level of press freedom is relatively high and the level of democratic performance is relatively low, the positive effect of press freedom will strongly outweigh the negative effects of democratic performance, thereby resulting in a relatively high level of regime change instability.

3. If the level of democratic performance is relatively high and the level of press freedom is relatively low, the negative effects of democratic performance will strongly outweigh the positive effects of press freedom, thereby resulting in a relatively low level of regime change instability.

Clearly, therefore, *for any given political system, the probability of regime instability is only influenced if the levels of democratic performance and of press freedom are imbalanced:* where democratic performance and press freedom are in equilibrium, the likelihood of regime instability is unaffected.

In addition to these *general* sources of regime change instability, Table 8.4 also reports a number of significant *regional* tendencies which need to be briefly mentioned.

1. While the general influence of socio-economic change upon regime change instability (as we saw above) seems to be a negative one ($B = -0.26$), the coefficient for the 'communications change' index in Europe/North America ($B = 0.42$) suggests that, in that region, rapid changes in communications development can actually serve to increase the probability of RΔ instability: it is interesting to note that two of the three countries in the Europe/North

America region which experienced the highest levels of regime change instability during the period 1948–67 (Greece and Hungary) also experienced the most rapid expansion of communication networks.

2. A comparable 'deviation' from the general overall pattern is the positive coefficient for trade expansion in the Far East ($B = 0.27$). Bearing in mind that this coefficient measures the shift in slope away from the minimum position, this implies that while trade expansion in countries *outside* the Far East tends to *reduce* the probability of RΔ instability, in the Far East itself, trade expansion has no effect upon RΔ instability ($0.27 - 0.23 = 0.04$).

3. In Latin America, on the other hand, the only significant interaction term is for the ethno-linguistic fractionalisation variable ($B = 0.23$). Again, it is instructive to note that of the four Latin American systems which experienced the most RΔ instability during the period 1947–68, three (Bolivia, Guatemala and Peru) also exhibit the highest scores (for Latin America) on the ethno-linguistic fractionalisation index.

4. The final regional interaction term in the regime change best model which Table 8.4 identifies is the positive coefficient for press freedom in Sub-Saharan Africa ($B = 0.22$): in this region, therefore, a relatively free press would appear to have an even more disruptive effect upon regime stability ($B = 0.45 + 0.22 = 0.67$) than is the case generally ($B = 0.45$).

The general and regional tendencies which we have outlined above (and specifically, the 'best models' which we have identified), then, constitute the generalisations which we wish to make about the cross-national sources of (each of our dimensions of) political instability. While these generalisations also constitute our conclusions as to the scope and applicability of each of the hypotheses which we originally proposed, and while they simultaneously provide a considerable simplification of the findings which we reported in Chapter 7 by isolating the *most important* empirical tendencies which are evident within our data, a number of ambiguities still remain. Why, for example, does democratic performance inhibit regime change instability, but not governmental change or violent challenge instability? Why does ethno-linguistic fractionalisation in Latin America inhibit governmental change instability, but encourage regime change instability? Clearly, given the data available for this study, it is only possible to *speculate* as to the sort of mechanisms which might be capable of generating these tendencies; and, equally clearly, further research is necessary if such speculations are to be adequately evaluated. Nonetheless, the questions themselves are extremely important ones, and it is for this reason that in the final section of this chapter we attempt not only to summarise the most important features of the findings we have reported, but also to resolve, by speculation, some of the more significant empirical ambiguities and inconsistencies which are apparent in those findings.

SUMMARY AND CONCLUSIONS

How satisfactory, then, are each of the original hypotheses which we advanced earlier? How great is the explanatory power of the various exogenous correlates of instability which we have identified? On the basis of the foregoing multivariate analysis, the following conclusions can be drawn.

(a)   Level of political development (H_1)

The level of political development, defined in terms of the degree of *'democratic performance'* and the degree of state penetration into society and economy (or *'capacity'*), has a reductive impact only upon the *regime change* dimension of political instability: it has no significant effect (when appropriate multivariate controls are made) upon either violent or peaceful challenges or upon the level of governmental change instability. In other words, it would appear to be the case that while countries at relatively high levels of political development tend to experience lower levels of regime change instability than comparatively (politically) underdeveloped systems, both developed and underdeveloped countries experience broadly equivalent levels of governmental change and of violent and peaceful challenge instability.

In order to provide some kind of explanation for these differential tendencies, it needs to be recognised that for any given system a high level of political development (*ceteris paribus*) involves two things: (1) it provides the *governing élite* with political and economic *resources* ('capacity') which can be employed if necessary to *prevent dissent* and/or to prevent dissent from having 'serious' consequences; (2) by virtue of the greater individual freedom which a comparatively high level of *'democratic performance'* entails, it provides the *non-élite* members of the political system with *opportunities to rebel* and/or to demonstrate their dissent with the current government.

This double-edged implication of a comparatively high level of political development provides a possible reason for the discrepancy between the regime change-political development relationship and the government change-, peaceful challenge- and violent challenge-political development relationships. It is perhaps the case that in (politically) developed systems, the ruling *élite* permits the masses and/or rival *élites* to use the liberty which development provides – to rebel, to express their discontent – *only in so far as the survival of the regime itself* (the system of rules which govern the way in which political conflicts shall be resolved) *is not directly threatened*. In consequence (as the non-significant linkages in our data imply), a comparatively high level of political development would not be expected to act as an insulation either against governmental change or against violent or peaceful challenges, since these behaviours (as we saw in Chapter 5) do not of themselves either constitute or necessarily lead to regime change instability. When, for whatever reason, regime survival is seriously threatened in developed systems, however, the fact that (political) development *does* reduce the probability of regime change instability suggests that the governing elite can and will use its political and economic resources – the resources which are at its disposal precisely because of the system's relatively high level of development – in order to prevent a change in regime from taking place.[11] Conversely, of course, the data imply that in (plitically) underdeveloped systems the governing elite simply does not have the necessary resources to prevent regime change instability from occurring.[12] While we would not argue that this is the only interpretation which can be derived from the empirical tendencies identified above, we would contend that it is the least unconvincing account of those tendencies which can be offered. Nonetheless, it is clear that there is no simple relationship between development and political instability, and that further research into the complex (possibly reciprocal) linkages between development and the *different types* of instability is required.

(b)   Level of socio-economic development (H_2)

As was the case in relation to political development, the level of socio-economic development has a reductive effect upon regime change instability but *no* significant impact upon the three other instability dimensions. What this perhaps implies is that the material benefit which advanced economic development bestows upon a nation can itself serve to inhibit radical regime change, because the mass of the population (whatever other changes they might seek to procure) recognise that they have a vested interest in preserving the existing system of economic distribution. In economically developed countries it may be generally perceived that this source of economic payoff can only be successfully defended and maintained if regime change instability is avoided.

(c)   Changes in the level of political development (H_3)

It would appear from our data that changes in political development (capacity) have a significant and positive impact upon RΔ instability, but are unrelated to GΔ, VC and PC instability: *the systemic strains and tensions which changes in capacity appear to encourage only the most severe form of instability, regime change.* There seems to be no obvious mechanism in operation here which might explain why increases in the intrusiveness of the state should encourage *only* RΔ instability and in consequence we intend to regard this finding simply as a statement of empirical tendency.

(d)   Changes in the level of socio-economic development (H_4).

At least one socio-economic change variable appears in each of our four best models. The role of socio-economic change, however, as we implied in Chapter 7, is distinctly double-edged. In some circumstances (see the *positive* coefficients for urbanisation change in Latin America in the peaceful challenge best model, and for communication change in Europe/North America in the regime change best model), socio-economic change is *positively* related to instability, thereby lending support to the expectations – social mobilisation thesis which we outlined in Chapter 6. In other circumstances, however (see the *negative* coefficients for socio-economic change in the RΔ best model; for communications change in Sub-Saharan Africa in the violent challenge best model; and for socio-economic change in the RΔ best model), a high rate of socio-economic change actually *reduces* the probability of instability. This empirical tendency in turn suggests either (1) that socio-economic change, rather than 'galvanising' men into disruptive political action as Huntington suggests, can serve instead to disorientate them to such an extent that concerted and united political opposition to the incumbent government or regime is impossible, or (2) that socio-economic changes – particularly changes in income, education and consumption – in fact represent the (partial) achievement of material economic goals, which in turn might be expected to reduce the likelihood of dissatisfaction with the incumbent regime, and consequently also to reduce the probability of political instability. Clearly, our data cannot reveal which of these two mechanisms is dominant in the genesis of the positive relationship between instability and socio-economic change – this, again, is a matter for future research. What is important, however, is that in certain (regional and instability dimension) contexts, defined above, socio-economic change has a *contributory* impact upon the level of political instability, whereas in other contexts (also defined above) its effects are essentially *reductive*.

(e) Dependency (H_5)

Given that the dependency thesis originates from the analysis of Latin American political behaviour, it is perhaps not surprising that dependency in Latin America (as predicted) has a significant positive impact at least upon peaceful challenge instability. Dependency has only a *general* impact (that is to say, outside Latin America), however, upon the level of governmental change instability, and does not feature at all in the regime change 'best model'. In other words, although dependency does appear to play a significant role in a limited number of situations, it does not feature significantly in the generation of the most severe form of (regime change) instability, and certainly does not have the general, all-pervading impact upon instability which its protagonists claim: in so far as a choice has to be made between the supposedly competing paradigms of development and dependency (and I am not at all convinced that the two are in fact necessarily mutually exclusive), the development paradigm would appear to be of far greater value in explaining cross-national levels of (particularly regime change) political instability.

(f) Governmental coercion (H_6, H_7, H_8, H_9)

The level of (actual) governmental coercion features significantly (and in fact, linearly) only in the regime change best model, and by implication, therefore, has no direct impact upon the three other dimensions of instability. (The level of *potential* government coercion has no direct effect upon any of the dimensions of instability.) While a high level of actual governmental repression increases the probability of regime change instability, therefore, it neither increases nor reduces the probability of violent challenge, peaceful challenge or governmental change.

(g)   Structured division (H_{12}, H_{13})

The role of structured division is not as restricted as that of governmental coercion, but it is rather more ambiguous. *Religious fractionalisation* has a *positive* (general) impact upon the level of violent challenge instability and a positive effect upon governmental change in Europe/North America; tendencies which require little interpretation, since they are entirely consistent both with previous findings and with our original hypotheses.[13]

Ethno-linguistic fractionalisation, on the other hand, has a (general) *reductive* effect upon governmental change, which suggests that for any given system, governmental stability can be preserved if the governing *élite* is able to exploit the ethnic divisions which exist within that system. The position is further complicated by the fact that in Latin America, ethnic divisions have an even greater *reductive* effect upon the level of *governmental* instability than is the case generally (witness the significant slope shift interaction term for ethno-linguistic fractionalisation in Latin America in the governmental change best model), yet at the same time these same (Latin American) ethnic divisions have a *contributory* impact upon the level of *regime* change instability. To summarise, in Latin America, (a) ethnic-linguistic divisions encourage regime change instability and (b) ethnic-linguistic divisions inhibit governmental change instability.

If only the second of these tendencies, (b), had been observed, using a quasi-Marxist interpretation of the data, we could have inferred that the negative association between governmental change and ethnic cleavage was a result of the fact that in Latin American systems which exhibit relatively high levels of ethno-linguistic fractionalisation, the ruling *élite* is able to exploit those divisions (on the 'divide and rule' principle) and to use its hegemonic economic and political position in order to maintain the stability of the incumbent *government* which, by definition, acts primarily in the interests of that ruling *élite*. But if this argument did indeed provide a satisfactory 'explanation' of the observed empirical tendency, then it could presumably be expected that the ruling *élite* would also be able (again by virtue of its dominant economic and political position) to exploit those ethnic divisions in order to preserve the existing normative political structure – *the regime* – which enables it to maintain that dominant position. Moreover, this extension of the quasi-Marxist argument would generate an empirical (cross-nationally applicable) prediction: we would also expect ethno-linguistic fractionalisation to be negatively correlated with the level of *regime change* instability as well as with the level of governmental change instability.

As we saw earlier, however, this prediction is *not* corroborated: ethno-linguistic fractionalisation in Latin America *encourages*, rather than inhibits, regime change instability. Given that one of the best ways of evaluating a theoretical proposition is to examine the accuracy of the empirical predictions which it generates, we would then be forced to conclude that our original quasi-Marxist theoretical interpretation of the observations was somewhat inadequate.

If the quasi-Marxist interpretation is found to be unsatisfactory, however, what sort of explanation of the empirical regularities described in (a) and (b) above can be offered in replacement? We would contend that these empirical tendencies in fact suggest the rather simple conclusion that, while the ruling elite in most Latin American countries may be sufficiently strong to prevent ethnic divisions from leading to the untimely downfall of governments (hence the *negative* association between ethnic-linguistic fractionalisation and *Government* change instability), that *élite* is *not* sufficiently powerful to prevent such divisions from leading to the unexpected overthrow of regimes (hence the *positive* association between ethnic fractionalisation and *regime* change instability): in other words, the data point to the fundamental *weakness* of the so-called 'ruling *élite*' in Latin America, not its hegemonic dominance.

(h) Structured inequality (H_{10}, H_{11})

Neither of our measures of inequality (land inequality and sectoral income inequality) appear in any of our four instability 'best models'. While the superficial implications of these findings are obvious, it is necessary to recognise that data on these two indicators were available for only 53 out of the 103 countries over which our cross-sectional analysis was conducted, and that the 'missing data' countries were predominantly located in the Third World. Strictly speaking, therefore, all we can really conclude from the non-significant coefficients observed in relation to our two inequality indicators is that there is at present no evidence to support the proposition that 'inequality' constitutes an important source of political instability, at least with regard to those systems for which data are currently available.

(i) Press freedom

The press freedom index furnished significant (and consistently positive) coefficients in three of our four 'best models' of instability. As we discussed earlier, press freedom is of considerable importance (particularly in combination with the level of democratic performance) as a *general* source of regime change instability, but it is also important in Sub-Saharan Africa as a source of peaceful challenges, and in Sub-Saharan Africa and Latin America as a source of governmental change instability. Indeed, perhaps the most notable feature of the behaviour of the press freedom index is its absence from the violent challenge 'best model' – a relatively free press is *not* likely to either increase or decrease the probability of violent challenge instability. In other words, while a relatively free press may encourage peaceful dissent and/or governmental or even regime change (particularly where political institutions are comparatively weak as is the case in Sub-Saharan Africa), it is *not* likely to encourage *violent* political challenge: a free press is less irresponsible, perhaps, in fomenting political grievances than it sometimes might appear.

We have sought, then, to establish how far, and in which contexts, our various exogenous variables are capable of predicting (or, more correctly, postdicting) cross-national patterns of political instability. Apart from the specific observations which we have just made, however, the complexity of our findings demands that we now attempt to draw a limited number of general conclusions.

To begin with, it is necessary to re-emphasise that all the empirical regularities which we isolated in the foregoing analysis are essentially stochastic, probabilistic *tendencies*, as opposed to deterministic, invariant laws or rules. Since we did not expect to find (and indeed did not find) that any single exogenous predictor of instability would exhibit outstanding explanatory power, we have consistently attempted to avoid close adherence to any single theoretical position and have instead adopted a fundamentally eclectic approach to the problem of identifying and evaluating the possible cross-national sources of political instability.

In consequence, we have drawn hypotheses from Marxist theorists (dependency), from supposedly 'common sense' assumptions about the role of certain variables (for example, the level of socio-economic development), from contemporary 'bourgeois' political theorists (political development, structured cleavage), and from nineteenth century classical theorists (de Tocqueville on the role of structured inequality). Moreover, we have established (and this is particularly important) that (1) none of these phenomena, considered in isolation, is capable of providing an adequate explanation of political instability, and (2) that there are many contexts in which several of them have no direct impact upon instability whatsoever.

The second general conclusion which the foregoing analysis suggests is that a limited number of the exogenous variables which we have investigated play a decidedly *double-edged* role in the genesis of political instability. One of the most notable of these 'double-edged' variables is socio-economic change, which (for example) inhibits violent challenge instability in the Far East and yet encourages peaceful challenge in Latin America. On the basis of these ambiguous tendencies, we did not conclude that all current theoretical speculations as to the general relationship between instability and socio-economic change are broadly incorrect, but rather we argued that different theoretical speculations deserve support in relation to different groups of countries, that is to say, that different mechanisms are brought into operation in different contexts. This may seem a trivial conclusion to draw, but it is a vitally important one: as we suggested in Chapter 7, even though there may be no *general* relationship between any two variables, the attendant global 'non-relationship' may in fact be composed of a number of mutually cancelling, *partial* (regional) relationships. In this and in the previous chapter, we have demonstrated that this kind of phenomenon is indeed comparatively common, and that it needs to be fully taken into account in any analysis of cross-national levels of political instability.

The final general conclusion which needs to be made concerns the overall difficulty of achieving a satisfactory predictive model of dimension of instability. The highest R^2 achieved was $R^2 = 0.53$ (for our regime change equation) and the lowest only $R^2 = 0.22$ (for the peaceful challenge equation). The comparatively large amount of error in each of the four 'best models' inevitably suggests that each of those models fails to identify a number of unmeasured variables which undoubtedly have important effects upon the level of political instability. The nature and precise role of those unmeasured variables – whether they are related to such 'immeasurables' as ideology, culture, leadership factors, foreign intervention or whatever – is of course a matter for further empirical research. Within the context of those phenomena which currently *can* be operationalised, however, what we have demonstrated here is that, firstly, only a comparatively small number of exogenous variables have a direct and consistent impact upon each dimension of political instability, and secondly, that even acting simultaneously, those variables achieve what can at best be regarded as only moderately high levels of statistical explanation. At worst – and this applies principally to peaceful and violent challenge behaviours – cross-national levels of political instability remain largely unexplained.

9 Conclusions and Prospects

Throughout this investigation we have been concerned with two principal research problems: what is meant by 'political instability' and why are some political systems more unstable than others? In order to resolve the first of these problems, we suggested that several subsidiary *theoretical* questions need to be answered; in an attempt to resolve the second, we undertook a systematic *empirical* analysis of the patterns of political instability across some 103 nations over the period 1948–67.

In this concluding chapter, we will review the major arguments which have been developed in this study and the main implications of the empirical findings which we have reported. We will not, however, make detailed references to the various substantive inferences which we have drawn, since these conclusions have already been outlined in the 'Summary and Conclusions' sections of each of our earlier chapters. As we will see, while a reasonably satisfactory *definition* of political instability has been provided, our attempts to *explain* the cross-national incidence of instability have not been particularly successful: although our predictive model of *regime change* instability is reasonably satisfactory, the patterns of government change, violent challenge and peaceful challenge instability have (to varying degrees) tended to elude quantitative explanation.

WHAT IS POLITICAL INSTABILITY?

The first 'subsidiary' problem which requires resolution, if the concept of instability is to be adequately defined, concerns the *range of behaviours* which are to be regarded as constituting 'destabilising' political action. Following the practice of earlier analyses of 'domestic conflict behaviour', these behaviours were defined to include *coups d'état*, attempted (but unsuccessful) *coups d'état*, acts of guerrilla warfare, riots, demonstrations, political strikes, deaths from political violence, assassinations, changes in the chief executive, and cabinet changes, together with changes in type of normative structure, changes in party system and change in civilian-military status.[1]

The question which immediately follows from the identification of these behaviours, of course, is how they are to be organised: are they all to be regarded as indicators of some 'general' notion of instability, or can some of the behaviours be grouped together to denote different *types* of instability? Most analysts, with the notable exception of Lipset, have in fact argued that there are several different types of instability or 'domestic conflict behaviour'. As we saw in Chapter 2, however, the widespread use of a largely inappropriate statistical technique (factor analysis) in order to identify the principal dimensions of such domestic conflict behaviour has led to somewhat unconvincing, and indeed mutually contradictory, theoretical inferences being drawn as to the *nature* of those dimensions. In consequence, we concluded that the most satisfactory method of differentiating between different types of instability is to use essentially theoretical, as opposed to pseudo-empirical criteria. What we argued was that, since our unit of analysis is the 'political system', it makes sense to employ two of the conceptual dimensions of political systems which were originally advanced by Easton: 'government' (or 'political authorities') and 'regime'.

Having identified these two dimensions, we then suggested that the *instability* of governments or of regimes is manifested either (1) in the form of *changes* in the government or regime, or (2) in the form of *challenges* (violent or non-violent) to either the government or regime. Figure 9.1 summarises our typology of political instability and the indicators of each dimension which were employed in our attempt to operationalise it.

Even when the constituent behaviours of instability have been identified and schematised, however, a second 'subsidiary' problem persists. This problem, broadly one of 'cultural relativity',[2] concerns the question as to whether equivalent or identical *frequency* scores on any given instability dimension can, in different system contexts, be regarded as constituting equivalent *levels* of instability. In other words (for example), do ten riots in country *A* during a given time period represent the same 'amount' of instability as ten riots in country *B* during the same period, even

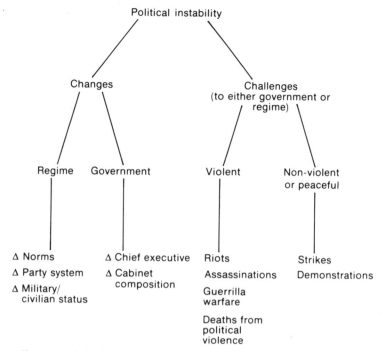

FIGURE 9.1   Dimensions and indicators of political instability

though country *A* has a long history of frequent and intense rioting while country *B* has not experienced such violent political outbursts for twenty years or more? Our answer to this question was an unqualified 'no'. We concluded that the destabilising impact of any given political event needs to be considered in the *context* of the system *and* of the time period in which it occurs; that it needs to be considered in terms of the extent to which it constitutes a *deviation* from the previous system pattern. It is for this reason that in our formal definition of instability in Chapter 5 we argued that

the extent to which a political system may be characterised as 'unstable' at any given point in time varies in direct proportion to the extent to which the occurrence or non-occurrence of changes in and challenges to the government, . . . (or) . . . regime . . . deviate from the previous system specific 'normal' pattern of regime/government changes or challenges; a pattern which will itself vary over time.

Now, of course, the meaning of the term 'normal' in this formal definition is by no means self evident. We suggested, however, that for any given system and for any given change or challenge event a reasonably objective, *statistically defined* assessment of 'normality' can be achieved by reference to the *regularities* in the occurrences of that event which are observed over time. In so far as a series of observations on a specific event variable exhibits regularity, it is possible to use (some postdictive function of) time itself to describe that regularity. What we argued, therefore, is that the appropriate function of time, since it describes what is 'regular', also describes what is 'normal'; and the extent to which the *i*th occurrence of the event series in fact deviates from this function (that is to say, the extent to which it deviates from 'normality') determines its instability score.

Since the pattern of 'regularity' (and therefore, what is 'normal') will vary from system to system, the definition of political instability which we have proposed is essentially a *system specific* one. It is a definition which does *not* accord identical instability intensities to similar political events regardless of system context, but instead measures the destabilising impact of any given political event in terms of the extent to which it deviates from the specific 'normal' pattern of the system in which it occurs.

An additional problem related to the nature of political instability concerns the possible interrelationships between its component dimensions. As we suggested in Chapter 5, at least two scenarios purport to describe these interrelationships: the instability 'syndrome' thesis (which suggests that all types of instability should be highly intercorrelated), and the 'safety valve' thesis (which argues that peaceful protest – or as we have termed it, peaceful 'challenge' – serves to *inhibit* other forms of political instability, and therefore that it should be *negatively* correlated with those other types of instability). Our empirical analysis in Chapter 5, however, produced very little support for either of these models. Rather, our principal conclusion was that in the Third World regions of Latin America, Sub-Saharan Africa, Middle East and Far East, there was a general tendency for relatively mild forms of instability (peaceful challenge and governmental change) to develop an internal dynamic of their own and to escalate into more disruptive forms of political behaviour (violent challenge and regime change instability); a tendency which we attributed to the relatively low levels of *institutionalisation* which are evident within most Third World systems. Specifically, however, we identified a number of essentially regional tendencies:

(i) In the Atlantic Area	peaceful challenges tend to precede regime changes
	violent challenges tend to precede governmental changes
(ii) In the Middle East	peaceful challenges tend to precede governmental changes
(iii) In Eastern Europe	governmental changes tend to precede peaceful challenges
(iv) In the Far East	peaceful challenges tend to precede violent challenges
	violent challenges tend to precede regime changes
	governmental changes tend to precede regime changes
(v) In Sub-Saharan Africa	violent challenges tend to precede regime changes
(vi) In Latin America	peaceful challenges tend to precede violent challenges
	violent challenges tend to precede governmental changes

It would appear to be the case, therefore, that there is no consistent *general* relationship among the different types of political instability, but rather, simply a series of differential regional effects. Thus, although these differential effects are unified by the fact that some kind of escalatory process does seem to operate across *all* regions, the *form* of that process (as the tendencies described immediately above indicate) in fact varies from region to region, a tendency which suggests the overall redundancy of any *universal* empirical generalisations which attempt to specify the interrelationships between the various types of instability.

This pattern of regional variation continued, moreover, when we attempted to answer the second of our two major research questions. (What are the principal determinants of cross-national patterns of political instability, that is to say, why are some political systems more unstable than others?) Indeed, given the numerous regional effects which are evident with the patterns of interrelationship between instability and its exogenous correlates, our attempts to generalise about the sources of instability necessarily had to take full account of the confounding role of region. As we saw in Chapter 8, regional interaction terms figured very significantly in each of our predictive models of instability.

Why are Some Political Systems more Unstable than Others?

Our attempts to provide an answer to this question have been essentially and unashamedly *empirical*. It is important to note that the basic principle underlying this approach is not to be confused with the accusatory label of 'empiricism' which Althusser and his fellow Marxists[3] so frequently (and almost equally frequently, unjustifiably) try to pin on any non-Marxist study which attempts to subject theories to empirical test. The 'empiricism' which Althusser condemns as being superficial and theoretically spurious (on the grounds that it is only concerned with observation and inductive generalisation) corresponds not to the actual procedures which non-Marxist political scientists follow in order to explain a given set of political phenomena, but rather, corresponds to the 'narrow' inductivist view of scientific enquiry which Hempel has so convincingly demolished and to which no respectable (bourgeois) practitioner of social science any longer subscribes.

> (The inductivist account of explanation) ... distinguishes four stages in an ideal scientific enquiry: (1) observation and recording of all facts; (2) analysis and classification of these facts; (3) inductive derivation of generalisations from them; (4) further testing of the generalisations. The first two of these stages are specifically assumed not to make use of any guesses or hypotheses as to how the observed facts might be interconnected; this restriction seems to have been imposed in the belief that such preconceived ideas would introduce a bias and would jeopardise the scientific objectivity of the investigation.
>
> But ... (this) ... view is untenable for several reasons ... Firstly, a scientific investigation as envisaged here could never get off the ground. Even its first phase would never be carried out, for a collection of *all* the facts would have to await the end of the world, so to speak; and even all the facts *up to now* cannot be collected, since there are an infinite number and

variety of them. Are we to examine, for example, all the grains of sand in all the deserts and on all the beaches, and are we to record their shapes, their weights, their chemical composition, their distances from each other, their constantly changing temperature, and their equally changing distance from the centre of the moon? Are we to record the floating thoughts that cross our minds in the tedious process? The shapes of the clouds overhead, the changing colour of the sky? The construction and the trade name of our writing equipment? All these, and untold other things, are, after all, among 'all the facts up to now' . . . (It is obviously the case that) . . . *empirical 'facts'* . . . *can be qualified as logically relevant only in reference to a given hypothesis.*[4]

This study, then, has been empirical in the sense that we have attempted to confront theories or hypotheses (which purport to explain why some political systems are more unstable than others) not with *other* theories (as Althusser would have us do), but with *observations*: in short, we have attempted to test theoretical propositions *by examining the adequacy of the predictions* (or more correctly in this case, 'postdictions') *which they generate*.

Before we summarise the results of our empirical analysis, however, it is necessary to reiterate the principal conclusion which emerged from our discussion of *previous* studies of political instability, which we reviewed in Chapters 1 and 2. In brief, we argued that with the exception of Hibbs' analysis of 'mass political violence', most of these previous attempts to isolate the major determinants of political instability have, for a variety of methodological reasons, been largely inadequate. Some have used an inappropriate definition of instability (notably the factor analytically based studies); some have employed highly questionable techniques of parameter estimation (notably, the Schneiders and Hurwitz), some have virtually rendered their theoretical propositions true by definition (notably Gurr); and all (with the notable exception of Hibbs) have made somewhat questionable assumptions in order to link theoretical concepts to indicators. The main point, then, is that Hibbs' findings constitute the only satisfactory conclusions which can be drawn as to the sources of cross-national patterns of political violence and *coups d'état*, despite a wealth of empirical research. Even Hibbs' conclusions, however, are, for two reasons, of doubtful relevance in the analysis of political instability. Firstly, as we pointed out in Chapter 2, at least one study has shown that the core propositions of Hibbs' final block-recursive model, which concern the interrelationships between 'internal war', 'collective protest', 'sanctions' and *'coups d'état'*, simply do not stand up to rigorous time-series analysis: his assessment of the 'average' relationship between these four variables masks the fact that these are in fact several distinct and conflicting *regional* patterns of interrelationship, conflicting patterns which inevitably undermine the utility of identifying only one 'average', general pattern.

The second reason why Hibbs' findings are not entirely relevant to an understanding of the genesis of political instability is that despite the fact that Hibbs occasionally uses the terms (political) violence and instability synonymously, his fundamental concern, as the title of his book suggests, is *political violence*. In consequence, since he is trying to explain why some countries are more politically *violent* than others, his dependent variable is, not surprisingly, the observed 'level of *political violence*'. In contrast to our definition of *instability*, therefore, which attempts to assess the destabilising impact of any given violent (or indeed, non-violent) event by reference to the prevailing system 'normality', Hibbs' definition of the level of political violence is what, in Chapter 3, we termed a *frequency*-oriented definition. It neither aspires nor needs to set each violent event in the system context in which it occurs; but instead simply assumes that raw frequency denotes the total magnitude of political violence. Given Hibbs' objectives, this emphasis on frequency is of no consequence. What it does imply, however, is that *Hibbs' empirical generalisations concerning the exogenous correlates of mass political violence cannot be extended to cover generalisations about political instability*, at least in the sense in which we have defined that term. As a result, the empirical findings which we reported in Chapters 5, 7 and 8 and which (for Chapters 7 and 8) are summarised below, represent an original contribution (if a limited one) to our understanding of the mechanics and the genesis of political instability.

EMPIRICAL FINDINGS: AN OVERVIEW

Whereas our investigation of the interrelationships *between* the dimensions of instability [which we discussed in the section above] was largely undertaken using time-series data, our analysis of the potential causal influences upon each of instability dimensions was entirely cross-sectional. In order to convert the monthly time-series instability scores (which were derived from the operational method described in Chapter 4) into a suitable cross-sectional form, it was necessary, *for each country and for each instability dimensions*, to *additively aggregate* those monthly scores to form a single *twenty-year* instability measure. Taken over all countries, these measures defined an instability index for each dimension. Our hypothesis testing procedure then consisted in correlating[5] each twenty-year instability index with five sets of exogenous predictor variables – (economic and political) *development*, *dependency*, *governmental coercion*, *structured cleavage*, and *structured inequality* – most of which were measured for the year *1965*. Strictly speaking, therefore, our analysis attempts to see how far data relating to various exogenous system characteristics which were collected for 1965 are capable of predicting (or 'postdicting') aggregate levels of instability over the period 1948–67.[6]

We would contend that this apparent anomaly can be justified on the following grounds. Firstly, the aggregated instability scores provide, by dimension, a *composite* indication of the relative magnitudes of instability for each of the 103 nations in our sample. In short, they give us the least inaccurate means of specifying which systems were the most stable and which the least stable (as well as the various gradations in between) over almost the entire post-war period up to 1967. Our twenty-year aggregates, therefore, clearly provide information which is of considerable substantive interest. Secondly, and perhaps more importantly, we would argue that the data (relating to the exogenous correlates of instability) collected for 1965 in a sense constitute a good *representative sample of the effects of the general long term processes and mechanisms* which appear to have been in operation during the post-war period; processes and mechanisms *which our operational measures of development, dependency, coercion, cleavage and inequality attempt to tap*. Moreover, it is probable that, for any given system, *several of our exogenous variables have hardly varied at all during the post-war period*: phenomena such as ethnic and religious cleavage, levels of inequality, and, in particular, region (which, it will be recalled, we use as a control variable), clearly tend to remain constant in the long term. In the context of these variables, at least, therefore, it is certainly the case that data for

1965 constitute a 'representative' sample, since data from any other post-war date would undoubtedly provide identical scores.

To summarise, then, the underlying principle of our analysis of the exogenous correlates of political instability has been to use a representative sample of exogenous predictor variables in order to evaluate how far *general* processes or system characteristics (which each of those predictors attempts to describe) are capable of explaining why certain political systems have been more unstable than others during the post-war period. The specific conclusions which we have arrived at, however, have been many and varied, and highly probabilistic. In Chapter 7 we emphasised the extreme complexity of the patterns of interrelationship between each instability dimension and the potential exogenous influences upon it, particularly when controls for region were made. We also suggested that, in so far as these patterns of interrelationship were considered in terms only of bivariate correlation coefficients, it was impossible to subject them to simplifying generalisation. It was for this reason that, in Chapter 8, we presented the main empirical findings derived from the operation of our (multiple regression) 'best model procedure', since that procedure enabled us to identify the most significant influences upon each type of instability.

The general results of our four predictive models of instability, however, were somewhat disappointing: the 'best' equations for governmental change, violent challenge and peaceful challenge all produced R^2 values of less than 0.50. Nonetheless, the 'best' model for regime change achieved an R^2 of 0.53, which is perhaps a passable level of explained variance, given that previous published quantitative research has not focussed explicitly upon regime change instability at all.

The specific conclusions which are suggested by our predictive models are summarised in Table 9.1. Since we have already discussed these conclusions in considerable detail in Chapter 8, however, we will not make further reference to them here. Nonetheless, the findings reported in Table 9.1 do suggest one *general* conclusion which is sufficiently important to warrant reiteration: it is clear from the different exogenous variables which appear in that table that if cross-national patterns of political instability are to be satisfactorily explained, then a fundamentally *eclectic* theoretical approach needs to be adopted. As we pointed out in Chapter 8, the hypotheses and exogenous variables which we examined were drawn '. . . from Marxist theorists . . . from

TABLE 9.1 Summary of final predictive models of each dimension of instability

Regime Change Instability
$(R^2 = 0.53)$

Varies positively with
(1) press freedom
(2) acts of government coercion
(3) increases in the level of political development
(4) (in Europe/North America only) increases in the level of communications development
(5) (in Latin America only) ethnic-linguistic cleavage
(6) (in Far East only) growth of exports

Varies negatively with
(1) democratic performance
(2) economic development
(3) growth of exports
(4) expansion of education
(5) communist status

Peaceful Challenge Instability
$(R^2 = 0.22)$

Varies positively with
(1) population size
(2) (in Latin America only) socio-economic change
(3) (in Latin America only) dependency
(4) (in Sub-Saharan Africa on press freedom.

Varies negatively with
(1) communications development

Violent Challenge Instability
$(R^2 = 0.48)$

Varies positively with
(1) population size
(2) religious cleavage
(3) (in Far East only) changes in income per capita

Varies negatively with
(1) level of urbanisation
(2) (in Sub-Saharan Africa only) changes in communications development

Government Change Instability
$(R^2 = 0.49)$

Varies positively with
(1) population size
(2) (in Middle East, Far East and Latin America only) dependency
(3) (in Latin America and Sub-Saharan Africa only) press freedom
(4) (in Europe/North America only) religious cleavage

Varies negatively with
(1) ethnic-linguistic cleavage
(2) socio-economic change
(3) (in Latin America only) religious cleavage

supposedly "common sense" assumptions about the behaviour of certain variables ... from contemporary "bourgeois" theorists ... and from nineteenth century classical theorists ...'. What we have established is that considered in isolation, none of the phenomena which the various authors cite is capable of providing an adequate explanation of political instability. Rather, it would appear to be the case that they need to be considered *in combination* if a remotely acceptable level of statistical explanation is to be achieved. Moreover, there are numerous contexts in which several of these exogenous variables have no direct impact whatsoever upon instability.

SOME PROSPECTS FOR FUTURE RESEARCH

Even when the five sets of exogenous predictors of instability are considered in combination, however (and taking full account of the numerous regional effects which we isolated in Table 9.1), it needs to be recognised that the exogenous variables which we have investigated at best only explain some 53 per cent of the variance in (regime change) instability. In what way, it must be asked, can the 'unexplained variance' in each of our predictive models of instability be accounted for? While in the context of this study we can only speculate as to the additional factors which may provide a somewhat fuller explanation of the genesis of political instability, the lesson of the comparatively low levels of statistical explanation which have been obtained throughout this investigation is clear. Given the kinds of data which are currently available for cross-national political research, quantitative analyses of political violence and instability (including this study) have tended to ignore certain variables which, on an *a priori* theoretical basis, might be expected to have a direct impact upon the level of instability. Two possible variables which seem particularly important in this regard are (1) the susceptibility of populations to the attractions of revolutionary ideologies, together with the conditions which determine these susceptibilities, and (2) the potential role of leaders as mobilisers of mass support – either as incumbent office holders who are intent on preserving the dominance of the established *élite*, or as opponents of the existing structure of authority who are prepared and able to use their charisma and/or leadership skills as a means of undermining established authority.

The kinds of general explanations of cross-national patterns of political instability which have to date been proposed and empirically investigated have largely ignored these factors, and have instead concentrated upon rather more tangible (and perhaps more easily observable) political and economic processes and conditions. As we have intimated, this is partly the result of the constraints of data availability, but it is also partly the consequence of the *theoretical* positions adopted by many of the leading contemporary political thinkers whose indirect influence upon the research strategies of others has been considerable. Huntington, for example, always a persuasive and convincing writer, implicitly denies that such peripheral phenomena as ideology or leadership have any significant impact upon political instability. This is not to say that Huntington argues that these phenomena have no role to play whatsoever, but simply that for him their impact is insignificant in comparison with (and is indeed dependent upon) the operation of the far more fundamental processes of 'social mobilisation', 'economic development', 'political participation' and 'institutionalisation': the operation of these processes overrides any role which 'revolutionary' ideologies or 'leadership' might have in the genesis of political instability.

What the empirical findings reported in this study demonstrate is that a satisfactory answer to the question 'Why are some political systems more unstable than others?' *cannot* be achieved given the sort of exogenous concepts which have been employed in this analysis. Explanations of political instability which concentrate upon system characteristics and macro-level political and economic processes can, as we have seen, account for up to 53 per cent of the variance in cross-national levels of instability. Perhaps the *residual* variance can only be explained by reference to such less tangible phenomena as ideology and leadership. Needless to say, adequate data are eagerly awaited.

Of course, one interpretation which could be made of the somewhat 'negative' findings reported in this investigation is that the aggregated instability indices which have been employed simply do not measure what is 'conventionally' understood by instability. To be sure, the dependent variable measures which have been used *are* different from the kind of scoring systems adopted in other analyses, and deliberately so. What I would contend is that the theoretical arguments advanced in Chapters 3 and 4, which suggested that the destabilising impact of any political event needs to be *contextualised* on the basis of some *system specific normality*, are sufficiently compelling to require a new approach to the measurement and analysis of political instability. This is what the present study has attempted to offer. In doing so, I hope to have demonstrated that the patterns of interrelationships, on the one hand among the different dimensions of instability, and on the other between each of those dimensions and its exogenous correlates, are extremely complex: perhaps the most important message of this entire study is that linear, global generalisations simply cannot adequately explain the variety, the inconsistencies and the ambiguities which characterise cross-national patterns of political instability.

Appendices

APPENDIX 1: TWENTY-YEAR AGGREGATE INSTABILITY SCORES FOR EACH COUNTRY IN THE CROSS-SECTIONAL ANALYSIS, BY DIMENSION

Country	Regime change instability	Aggregate instability score 1948–67 Government change instability	Violent challenge instability	Peaceful challenge instability
Albania	−24.23	−5.52	36.07	−18.74
Argentina	51.48	−6.62	−16.86	17.72
Australia	−68.04	−5.34	0.0	−2.19
Belgium	−26.5	−22.79	−5.58	−1.88
Bolivia	81.15	−21.9	−16.98	−15.40
Brazil	30.13	24.48	−20.64	10.68
Bulgaria	−24.23	18.17	1.90	−0.57
Burma	67.10	−5.3	−73.95	−2.19
Cambodia	−16.3	−5.3	7.9	−2.19
Canada	−26.5	42.0	15.12	12.72
Central African Republic	2.76	−14.5	−29.18	−5.02
Sri Lanka (Ceylon)	−68.04	−5.3	115.47	−2.19
Chad	−13.2	−14.5	−29.18	−5.02
Chile	−95.3	−17.18	−0.02	0.106
China	−47.3	33.20	30.43	22.65
Colombia	49.93	11.00	53.14	−13.11
Congo	−28.18	11.77	12.35	−5.02
Costa Rica	−95.3	10.59	−14.3	13.5
Cuba	9.67	−8.04	4.41	−19.4
Cyprus	234.3	−10.36	−2.72	−4.10
Czechoslovakia	65.4	−2.23	10.0	18.6
Dahomey (Benin)	67.85	6.95	23.0	9.19
Denmark	−26.5	−0.6	−31.7	−0.50
Dominican Republic	58.8	43.3	85.1	−4.71
Ecuador	201.95	−8.4	−12.4	31.4
Egypt	52.54	−11.37	−1.69	−4.82
El Salvador	73.76	16.7	4.79	−22.6
Ethiopia	−50.5	−1.2	−19.1	−5.02
Finland	−26.5	−3.4	10.91	−1.73
France	−26.5	1.6	48.3	−23.0

211

APPENDIX 1: *continued*

| Country | Regime change instability | Aggregate instability score 1948–67 | | |
		Government change instability	Violent challenge instability	Peaceful challenge instability
Gabon	−13.2	−14.57	−29.18	−5.02
German Democratic Republic	−6.3	12.4	1.05	39.6
German Federal Republic	−5.9	32.86	58.0	7.96
Ghana	125.5	11.62	15.3	−2.5
Greece	254.7	−3.41	10.9	−1.73
Guatemala	109.8	−27.08	−3.64	−12.7
Haiti	−1.49	−26.4	8.53	14.6
Honduras	85.49	6.5	19.8	−3.64
Iceland	−26.5	−35.37	−26.9	11.2
India	−68.04	37.13	91.69	16.8
Indonesia	62.05	−5.3	42.78	−2.19
Iran	−35.29	−1.7	−34.7	6.97
Iraq	29.5	−9.44	−21.4	−5.04
Ireland	−26.5	18.21	−11.51	14.8
Israel	−75.2	7.05	17.9	9.75
Italy	−26.5	−11.5	8.79	46.6
Ivory Coast	−36.04	−14.57	−29.1	−5.02
Japan	−68.0	−5.3	0.0	−2.19
Jordan	−35.2	−8.0	4.26	4.37
Kenya	−13.2	41.28	18.6	25.5
Korea, North	−68.04	−5.3	66.88	−2.1
Korea, South	247.6	20.44	39.68	−2.1
Laos	47.99	−5.3	46.49	−2.1
Lebanon	−61.7	−15.31	8.00	−23.9
Liberia	−50.5	−31.1	−29.1	−21.62
Libya	−83.0	14.6	−10.1	−11.39
Luxembourg	−26.5	−7.6	−20.2	−36.0
Malagasy	−50.5	−14.57	−29.1	−5.02
Malaysia	−68.0	−5.3	104.93	−2.19
Mali	−36.0	−14.57	−29.1	−5.02
Mauritania	−36.0	−14.57	−29.1	−5.02
Mexico	−95.3	−11.97	−4.37	24.5
Mongolia	−68.04	−5.3	0.0	−2.19
Morocco	−83.0	−9.4	−21.4	−5.04
Nepal	−13.7	−5.3	75.89	−2.19
Netherlands	−26.5	25.3	−1.55	12.85
New Zealand	−68.04	−0.53	0.0	−2.19
Nicaragua	−95.3	12.1	45.39	−10.1
Niger	−36.0	25.27	−7.67	−22.3

APPENDIX 1: *continued*

Country	Regime change instability	Aggregate instability score 1948-67 Government change instability	Violent challenge instability	Peaceful challenge instability
Nigeria	84.6	42.19	116.1	5.12
Norway	−26.5	−2.99	−28.1	−17.93
Pakistan	108.8	−5.3	93.88	−2.19
Paraguay	−61.3	−15.9	−5.00	5.62
Peru	127.3	−0.37	12.38	3.97
Philippines	−68.04	−5.34	127.7	−2.19
Poland	−24.2	−2.12	−23.75	−1.21
Portugal	−26.5	21.47	50.58	−3.83
Rumania	−24.2	−17.2	−49.7	−21.0
Saudi Arabia	−88.2	−2.6	−21.4	−5.04
Senegal	−36.04	−12.57	−14.69	3.92
Somali Republic	−36.04	−19.1	−66.3	−5.02
South Africa	57.9	−14.5	−29.18	−5.02
Spain	−26.5	−27.8	6.89	19.62
Sudan	223.3	52.6	54.61	31.35
Sweden	−26.5	−3.4	−30.71	−17.5
Switzerland	−26.5	−3.6	−19.8	−36.0
Syria	435.4	−9.4	43.1	−12.0
Thailand	114.8	−5.34	−15.17	−2.19
Togo	48.44	−14.57	−29.1	−5.02
Tunisia	−83.0	4.57	−17.65	−16.1
Turkey	65.6	2.81	13.97	22.86
UK	−26.5	−5.08	−36.7	−13.8
USA	−26.5	22.2	33.7	40.5
USSR	−24.2	13.43	0.83	−16.7
Upper Volta	25.6	−14.57	−29.1	−5.02
Uruguay	−95.3	−5.93	−21.0	4.18
Venezuela	36.4	0.61	24.0	11.71
Vietnam, North	−59.7	−5.34	23.07	−2.19
Vietnam, South	101.2	−5.34	185.57	−2.19
Yugoslavia	−24.2	−14.46	13.5	−18.5
Zaire	130.2	1.67	71.3	9.67

APPENDIX 2:   SCORING SYSTEM EMPLOYED IN THE
              CONSTRUCTION OF THE REGIME CHANGE
              INDEX (see chapter 4)

Three variables taken from Blondel's 'Time-series Data' (unpublished Data Collection, University of Essex) were used in order to construct the regime change index: (1) change in regime norms; (2) change in party system; and (3) change in military-civilian status. Appropriate definitions of all terms are provided in J. Blondel, *Introduction to Comparative Government* (London: Weidenfeld and Nicholson, 1968).

(i) Blondel's regime norm variable

As we pointed out in Chapter 3, Blondel argues that, empirically, there are seven major types of regime, defined by their respective positions within the three-dimensional regime norm space: a *change* from one normative type to another involves movement along one or more axes of the space. As we also suggested in Chapter 3, however, Blondel's regime norm model has not been developed sufficiently to enable any kind of interval or quasi-interval level assessment to be made of the *extent* to which 'movement' occurs along the dimensions of the regime norm space. All that can be done, therefore, is to assume that if Blondel has coded a particular country differently at t_1 and t_2, then 'significant movement' must have occurred along certain axes of the space between those two time points. Given the additional assumption that all three axes are of equal importance, we assume finally that 'significant movement' along any one axis will produce a (numerical) 'norms change score' of unity, while no 'significant movement' will score zero. Similarly, 'significant movement' along two axes will produce a norms change score of two; three axes, a score of three. It follows, therefore, that a change from liberal democratic to authoritarian conservative norms, for example, involves significant movement along all *three* axes: such a change would involve a regime becoming

(a) more authoritarian (movement along the (means) liberal-authoritarian axis),
(b) more conservative (movement along the (goals) radical-conservative axis), and
(c) more oligarchic (movement along the (participation) democratic-oligarchic axis).

Grouping the three types of populist system into one category, it can be shown that the numbers defined in Table A2.1 describe the

TABLE A2.1 The number of dimensions through which a polity moves when it experiences a change in regime type

		RA	LD	TC	AC	Pop
Radical Authoritarian	(RA)	0				
Liberal Democratic	(LD)	2	0			
Traditional Conservative	(TC)	3	2	0		
Authoritarian Conservative	(AC)	2	3	1	0	
Populist	(Pop)	1	2	2	1	0

number of dimensions along which significant movement takes place in order to effect a change from one regime type to another. As we saw in Chapter 4, the change from LD to AC (Liberal Democratic to Authoritarian Conservative) involves a change in means, goals and degree of participation, and since this requires movement along three dimensions of the space, this yields a regime change score of three. Similarly, a shift from populist to radical authoritarian, for example, involves movement only along the *goals* (radical-conservative) axis, implying (because there is movement along only one dimension of the space) a regime change score of one. The principle employed here is, I think, self-evident on the basis of these two examples.

(ii) Blondel's party system variable

Blondel proposes an eight-category (ordinal level) typology of party system type. For the sake of simplicity, however, in this study several of the Blondel categories were grouped together to produce a trichotomous typology: 'competitive party systems' (two-party, two-and-a-half-party, multi-party with a single dominant party, multi-party); 'non-competitive party systems' (single-party, forced coalition under the aegis of a single-party, dominant single-party); and 'no-party' systems. *Changes* in authority structure, from one type of party system to another, were scored as indicated in Table A2.2.

The justification for this scoring system is simple. As Figure A2.1 indicates, the scores assume the existence of a quasi-interval level 'complexity of party system' scale in which the transition from a no-party system to a one-party system (or *vice versa*) and the

TABLE A2.2 Scoring system for changes in party system variable

no-party to non-competitive	=	1
no-party to competitive	=	2
non-competitive to competitive	=	1
competitive to non-competitive	=	1
competitive to no-party	=	2

transition from a one-party to a competitive party system (or *vice versa*) denote 'changes in party system' of equal magnitude (unity). It follows, therefore, that the transition from a no party to a competitive party system entails a 'change in party system' score of twice unity, i.e. 2.

(iii) Blondel's military/civilian status variable

Blondel's codings of this variable permit the identification of three types of authority structure change: military takeovers from civilian authorities (*coups*), the civilianisation of military regimes, and military takeovers from existing military authorities. While it is obvious that the first two types of change affect the overall 'authority structure' of the system, it does not follow that a military takeover from some existing military authority constitutes any real change in the structure of authority. Rather, *coups* against the military are of two types: they are either perpetrated with the intention of effecting a fairly rapid return to civilian rule, or they are not. ('Fairly rapid' is defined, in this context, to mean 'within one year'. I choose this figure somewhat arbitrarily – but given the psychological impact of anniversaries it is a time period frequently chosen by the leaders of 'liberalising' *coups*.) *Coups* against the military, when rapid civilianisation does occur, can reasonably be

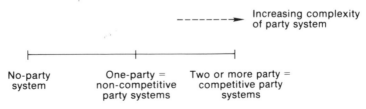

FIGURE A2.1   Quasi-interval scale underlying 'changes in party system' scores

regarded as producing a limited amount of change in the authority structure: *coups* which effect no such civilianisation cannot. In relation to the military-civilian status variable, then, we have three types of changes in authority structure which were scored as follows:

(a) military takeover from the military, with civilianisation
    following within 12 months   = 1
(b) military takeover from civilian government   = 2
(c) military handovers of government to civilian
    authorities excluding all cases of (a)   = 2.

The total regime change score for the ith country in the jth month was defined as a weighted sum[1] of the scores on the three Blondel variables:

Regime change ij = (change in norms × 2) + changes in party
         system + changes in military/civilian status

which produces a theoretical maximum regime change score of 10 for any given country month and minimum value of zero.

APPENDIX 3: 'DATA-BANKS' FOR EACH INSTABILITY
             DIMENSION USED IN BEST MODEL
             PROCEDURE (see Chapter 8)

(i) Variables common to all four data-banks

GNP per capita
calories per capita
infant mortality as proportion of
   live births
physicians per capita
composite health index
education expenditure as
   percentage of GNP
primary and secondary pupils as
   percentage of eligible children
university enrolment per capita
   percentage literature
composite education index

composite urbanisation index
newspapers per capita
telegrams per capita
telephones per capita
mail per capita
radios per capita
televisions per capita
highway vehicles per capita
rail passenger miles
rail ton miles
composite communications
   index
energy production per capita

energy consumption per capita
electricity consumption per
    capita
steel production per capita
percentage workforce in
    industry
composite industrialisation
    index
composite economic
    development index
government revenue and
    expenditure per capita
democratic performance index
changes in GNP per capita
changes in primary and
    secondary school enrolment
changes in urbanisation
changes in telephones per
    capita
changes in highway vehicles per
    capita

changes in government revenue
    and expenditure per capita
concentration of export
    commodities
concentration of
    export-receiving countries
acts of governmental coercion
internal security forces as
    percentage of adult population
armed forces as percentage of
    adult population
land inequality (Gini index)
sectoral income inequality (Gini
    index)
ethno-linguistic fractionalisation
religious fractionalisation
press freedom
communist status
exports per capita
changes in exports per capita
population size

(ii) **Additional regional interaction variables included for
      Europe/North America countries***

Regime change data-bank
government revenue and
    expenditure per capita
education expenditures as
    percentage of GNP
percentage literate
newspaper circulation per capita
television per capita
GNP per capita
composite economic
    development index
urbanisation changes
telephone changes

school enrolment changes
acts of governmental repression
land inequality

Violent challenge data-bank
exports per capita
concentration of exports
internal security forces as
    percentage of adult population
percentage literature
newspaper circulation
calories per capita
religious fractionalisation

*Intercept shift and slope shift interaction terms were constructed
for each of the variables in these lists.

acts of governmental repression
income inequality

Governmental change data-bank
concentration of exports
university enrolment per capita
radio ownership per capita
mail per capita
urbanisation
energy consumption per capita
composite economic
   development index
religious fractionalisation
urbanisation changes
highway vehicles changes
telephone changes

concentration of export
receiving countries

Peaceful challenge data-bank
urbanisation
armed forces as percentage of
   adult population
primary and secondary
   education as percentage of
   eligible school age children
radio ownership per capita
rail passenger miles
energy consumption
acts of governmental repression
concentration of export-
   receiving countries

(iii)   Additional regional interaction variables included for Middle East/North Africa countries*

Regime change data-bank
government revenue and
   expenditure per capita
exports per capita
composite education index
GNP per capita
democratic performance
press freedom
changes in government revenue
   per capita
highway vehicle changes
acts of governmental repression
concentration of exports
concentration of export-
   receiving countries

Violent challenge data-bank
urbanisation
concentration of exports

armed forces as percentage of
   adult population
composite economic
   development index
ethno-linguistic fractionalisation
religious fractionalisation
democratic performance
changes in government
   revenue per capita
changes in primary and
   secondary education
concentration of export-
   receiving countries

Government change data-bank
government revenue and
   expenditure per capita
exports per capita
concentration of exports

*Intercept shift and slope shift interaction terms were constructed for each of the variables in these lists.

internal security forces as
percentage of population
composite industrialisation
index
composite communications
index
GNP per capita
religious fractionalisation
democratic performance
urbanisation changes
government revenue per capita
changes
highway vehicle changes
telephones changes
GNP per capita changes
acts of governmental repression

concentration of export-
receiving countries

Peaceful challenge data-bank
urbanisation
armed forces as percentage of
adult population
composite industrialisation
index
ethno-linguistic fractionalisation
religious fractionalisation
democratic performance
highway vehicle changes
concentration of export-
receiving countries

(iv)   Additional regional interaction variables included for Latin American countries*

Regime change data-bank
government revenue and
expenditure per capita
concentration of exports
internal security forces as
percentage of population
composite economic
development index
ethno-linguistic fractionalisation
religious fractionalisation
democratic performance
press freedom
urbanisation change
government revenue per capita
change
concentration of export-
receiving countries

Violent challenge data-bank
composite economic
development index
internal security forces as
percentage of population
democratic performance
press freedom
government revenue per capita
change
GNP per capita change
concentration of export-
receiving countries

Government change data-bank
composite health index
composite education index
ethnolinguistic fractionalisation

*Intercept shift and slope shift interaction terms were constructed
for each of the variables on these lists.

religious fractionalisation
press freedom
exports per capita changes
changes in school enrolment
concentration of exports

Peaceful challenge data-bank
concentration of exports
armed forces as percentage of

adult population
university enrolment per capita
composite industrialisation
   index
democratic performance
urbanisation change
export per capita change
land inequality

(v)   Additional regional interaction variables included for Sub-Saharan African countries*

Regime change data-bank
armed forces as percentage of
   adult population
composite economic
   development index
ethno-linguistic fractionalisation
press freedom
highway vehicle changes
telephone changes
school enrolment changes
acts of governmental repression
concentration of export-
   receiving countries

Violent challenge data-bank
composite economic
   development index
ethno-linguistic fractionalisation
religious fractionalisation
press freedom
highway vehicle changes
telephone changes
school enrolment changes
GNP per capita changes
acts of governmental repression

Government change data-bank
exports per capita
composite industrialisation
   index
press freedom
highway vehicle changes
school enrolment changes
acts of governmental repression
concentration of export-
   receiving countries
GNP per capita changes

Peaceful challenge data-bank
exports per capita
internal security forces as
   percentage of adult population
calories per capita
press freedom
highway vehicle changes
school enrolment changes
GNP per capita changes
acts of governmental repression
concentration of export-
   receiving countries

*Intercept shift and slope shift interaction terms were constructed for each of the variables in these lists.

(vi)   Additional regional interaction variables included for Far East countries*

Regime change data-bank
government revenue and
    expenditure per capita
exports per capita
armed forces as percentage of
    adult population
composite economic
    development index
religious fractionalisation
democratic performance
exports per capita changes
GNP per capita changes
acts of governmental repression

Violent challenge data-bank
concentration of exports
radio ownership per capita
religious fractionalisation
GNP per capita changes
acts of governmental repression
land inequality
concentration of export-
    receiving countries

Government change data-bank
government revenue and

expenditure per capita
exports per capita
concentration of exports
internal security forces as
    percentage of adult population
composite industrialisation
    index
calories per capita
exports per capita changes
GNP per capita changes
acts of governmental repression
land inequality

Peaceful challenge data-bank
concentration of exports
internal security forces as
    percentage of adult population
radio ownership per capita
religious fractionalisation
press freedom
government revenue per capita
    changes
GNP per capita changes
acts of governmental repression
concentration of export-
    receiving countries

*Intercept shift and slope shift interaction terms were constructed for each of the variables on these lists.

APPENDIX 4:   COUNTRIES INCLUDED IN EACH OF THE
REGIONAL SUBSETS

(i) *Europe/North America*
    subset (N = 30)
        Austria
        Belgium
        Canada
        Cyprus
        Denmark
        Finland
        France
        Germany, Federal
        Greece
        Iceland
        Ireland
        Italy
        Luxembourg
        Netherlands
        Norway
        Portugal
        Spain
        Sweden
        Switzerland
        United Kingdom
        United States

Eastern
Europe
subset in
Chapter 5
{
        Albania
        Bulgaria
        Czechoslovakia
        German Democratic
            Republic
        Hungary
        Poland
        Rumania
        USSR
        Yugoslavia
}

(ii) *Middle East/North Africa*
     subset (N = 12)
        Egypt
        Iran

        Iraq
        Israel
        Jordan
        Lebanon
        Libya
        Morocco
        Saudi Arabia
        Syria
        Tunisia
        Turkey

(iii) *Latin American subset*
      (N = 20)
        Argentina
        Bolivia
        Brazil
        Chile
        Colombia
        Costa Rica
        Cuba
        Dominican
            Republic
        Ecuador
        El Salvador
        Guatemala
        Haiti
        Honduras
        Mexico
        Nicaragua
        Panama
        Paraguay
        Peru
        Uruguay
        Venezuela

(iv) *Sub-Saharan Africa subset*
     (N = 23)
        Central African
            Republic

Chad
Congo
Dahomey
Ethiopia
Gabon
Ghana
Guinea
Ivory Coast
Kenya
Liberia
Malagasy
Mali
Mauritania
Niger
Nigeria
Senegal
Somali Republic
South Africa
Sudan
Togo
Upper Volta
Zaire

(v) *Far East subset (N = 22)*
Afganistan
Australia
Burma
Cambodia
Ceylon
China
India
Indonesia
Japan
Korea, North
Korea, South
Laos
Malaysia
Mongolia
Nepal
New Zealand
Pakistan
Philippines
Taiwan
Thailand
Vietnam, North
Vietnam, South

Notes

NOTES TO THE INTRODUCTION

1. T. Gurr, *Polimetrics* (Englewood Cliffs, N.J.: Prentice-Hall, 1972); D. Hibbs, *Mass Political Violence: A Cross-national Causal Analysis* (New York: Wiley, 1973); J. Blondel, *An Introduction to Comparative Government* (London: Weidenfeld & Nicolson, 1968).
2. A. Przeworski and M. Teune, *The Logic of Comparative Social Inquiry* (New York: Wiley, 1970) esp. pp. 32–4.
3. The author is grateful to the SSRC Survey Archive, University of Essex, for supplying the *World Handbook II* Aggregate, Annual Events and Daily Events data-sets (ICPSR study numbers 5027, 5028, 5215).

NOTES TO CHAPTER ONE

1. W. Bagehot, *The English Constitution* (London: Chapman & Hall, 1867).
2. See, for example, D. Hibbs, op. cit.; D. Snyder and C. Tilly, 'Hardship and Collective Violence in France 1830–1960', *American Sociological Review*, vol. 37 (1972) pp. 520–32; R. Rummel, 'Dimensions of Conflict Behaviour within and between Nations', *General Systems Yearbook*, vol. 8 (1963) pp. 1–50. For a detailed review of existing studies of political violence, see E. Zimmerman, *Political Violence, Crises and Revolution* (London and Beverley Hills: Sage, forthcoming).
3. See, for example, S. P. Huntington, *Political Order in Changing Societies* (New Haven, Conn.: Yale University Press, 1968); L. M. Terrell, 'Societal Stress, Political Instability and Levels of Military Effort', *Journal of Conflict Resolution*, vol. 15 (1971) pp. 329–46; D. Bwy, 'Political Instability in Latin America: The Crosscultural Test of a Causal Model', *Latin American Research Review*, vol. 3, no. 2 (Spring 1968) pp. 17–66; I. Feierabend and R. Feierabend, 'Systemic Conditions of Political Aggression: An Application of Frustration–Aggression Theory', in I. Feierabend, R. Feierabend and T. Gurr (eds), *Anger, Violence and Politics* (Englewood Cliffs, N.J.: Prentice-Hall, 1972) pp. 136–83; A. Schneider and P. Schneider, 'Social Mobilisation, Political Institutionalisation and Political Violence', *Comparative Political Studies*, vol. 4 (1971–2) pp. 69–90.
4. M. Janowitz, *The Military in the Political Development of New Nations* (Chicago, Ill.: Chicago University Press, 1964). See also M. Janowitz

and J. Van Doorn (eds), *On Military Intervention* (Rotterdam: Rotterdam University Press, 1971); D. Hibbs, op. cit., pp. 81–112; E. Fossum, 'Factors Influencing the Occurrence of Military *Coups d'Etat* in Latin America', *Journal of Peace Research*, vol. 4 (1967) pp. 228–51.

5. S. M. Lipset, *Political Man* (New York: Doubleday, 1963); F. Castles, *Political Stability* (Milton Keynes: Open University Press, 1974); G. Field, *Comparative Political Development* (London: Routledge Kegan Paul, 1967).

6. M. Taylor and V. Herman, 'Party Systems and Government Stability', *American Political Science Review*, vol. 65 (1971) pp. 28–37; L. Hurwitz, 'Democratic Political Stability: Some Traditional Hypotheses Re-examined', *Comparative Political Studies*, vol. 4 (1971–2) pp. 476–80; L. Dodd, 'Party Coalitions in Multi-party Parliaments: A Game Theoretic Analysis', *American Political Science Review*, vol. 67 (1973) pp. 453–69.

7. Lipset, op. cit.

8. Two of the most important mechanisms cited in this regard are (1) a strong belief in the efficacy of democratic political institutions on behalf of political activists, and (2) 'overlapping cleavages'.

9. Op. cit., p. 48.

10. See D. Easton, *The Political System* (New York: Knopf, 1953).

11. G. Almond and S. Verba, *The Civic Culture* (Boston, Mass.: Little, Brown, 1965); D. Neubauer, 'Some Conditions of Democracy', *American Political Science Review*, vol. 61, no. 4 (Dec. 1967) pp. 1002–9; P. Cutright, 'National Political Development: Measurement and Analysis', *American Sociological Review*, vol. 28 (Apr. 1963) pp. 253–64.

12. C. Cnudde and D. McCrone, 'Toward a Communications Theory of Democratic Political Development', *American Political Science Review*, vol. 61, no. 1 (Mar. 1967) pp. 72–9; D. Lerner, 'Toward a Communication Theory of Modernisation: A Set of Considerations', in L. Pye (ed.), *Communications and Political Development* (Princeton, N.J.: Princeton University Press, 1963); R. Tanter, 'Toward a Theory of Political Development', *Midwest Journal of Political Science*, vol. 11 (1967) pp. 145–72.

13. Feierabend and Feierabend, op. cit; Hibbs, op. cit.

14. I. Budge, *Agreement and the Stability of Democracy* (Chicago, Ill.: Markham, 1970); R. Dahl, *Polyarchy* (New Haven, Conn.: Yale University Press, 1974); A. Lijphart, *The Political of Accommodation* (Berkeley, Calif.: University of California Press, 1968).

15. See R. Dahl, op. cit.

16. See Binder *et al., Crises and Sequences in Political Development* (Princeton, N.J.: Princeton University Press, 1971).

17. H. Eckstein (ed.), *Internal War* (New York: Free Press, 1964).

18. A. Janos, 'Authority and Violence: The Political Framework of Internal War' in H. Eckstein, ibid., p. 130. Eckstein himself offers a slightly different definition of internal war: 'The attempt to change, using violence or the threat of it, policies, rulers or organisations'.

19. A. Feldman, 'Violence and Volatility: The Likelihood of Revolution', in Eckstein, ibid.

20. Among the most important methodological pieces were K. Deutsch, 'Toward an Inventory of Basic Trends and Patterns in Comparative and International Politics', *American Political Science Review*, vol. 64 (Mar. 1960) pp. 34–57; H. Alker, 'Causal Inference and Political Analysis', in J. Bernd (ed.), *Mathematical Applications in Political Science*, vol. II (Dallas, Texas: Southern Methodist University Press, 1966) pp. 7–43; R. Merritt and S. Rokkan, *Comparing Nations: The Uses of Data in Cross-National Quantitative Research* (New Haven, Conn.: Yale University Press, 1966).

21. A. Banks and R. Texter, *A. Cross Polity Survey* (Cambridge, Mass.: MIT Press, 1963); A. Banks, *Cross Polity Timeseries Data* (Cambridge, Mass.: MIT Press, 1971), supplied as a card-image dataset by the Centre for Comparative Political Research, State University of New York at Binghampton; C. Taylor and M. Hudson, *World Handbook of Social and Political Indicators*, 2nd edn (New Haven, Conn.: Yale University Press, 1972), supplied as a card image dataset by ICPSR, University of Michigan, Ann Arbor, and referred to here as *World Handbook II*; B. Russett *et al.*, *World Handbook of Social and Political Indicators* (New Haven, Conn: Yale University Press, 1964); R. Rummel, 'Dimensions of Conflict Behaviour within Nations 1946–59', *Journal of Conflict Resolution*, vol. 10 (Mar. 1966) 65–74.

22. R. Rummel, 'Dimensions . . . Within and Between . . .', op. cit., and 'Dimensions . . . Within . . .', op. cit.; R. Tanter, 'Dimensions of Conflict Behaviour within and between Nations, 1958–60', *Journal of Conflict Resolution*, vol. 10 (1966) pp. 41–64.

23. I. Feierabend and R. Feierabend, op. cit., pp. 136–43.

24. F. Hoole, 'Political Stability and Instability Within Nations: A Crossnational Study', unpublished M.A. thesis, San Diego State College, 1964 (cited in *Ibid.*)

25. D. Hibbs, op. cit.

26. D. Morrisson and H. Stevenson, 'Political Instability in Independent Black Africa', *Journal of Conflict Resolution*, vol. 15 (1971) pp. 347–68.

27. J. Dollard *et al.*, *Frustration and Aggression* (New Haven, Conn.: Yale University Press, 1939).

28. T. Gurr, 'Psychological Factors in Civil Violence', *World Politics*, vol. 20 (Jan. 1968) pp. 245–78; T. Gurr, 'A Causal Model of Civil Strife . . .', *American Political Science Review*, vol. 62 (Dec. 1968) pp. 1104–24; T. Gurr, *Why Men Rebel* (Princeton, N.J.: Princeton University Press, 1970); T. Gurr, 'Persistence and Change in Political Systems, 1800–1971', *American Political Science Review*, vol. 68, no. 4 (1974) pp. 1482–1504; T. Gurr and V. Bishop, 'Violent Nations, and Others', *Journal of Conflict Resolution*, vol. 20, no. 1 (1976) pp. 79–110; I. Feierabend and R. Feierabend, op. cit.; I. Feierabend, R. Feierabend and B. Nesvold, 'Social Change and Political Violence; Cross-national Patterns', in Feierabend, Feierabend

and Gurr (eds), op. cit., pp. 107–18; S. Huntington, op. cit.; D. Bwy, op.cit.; B. Nesvold, 'Scalogram Analysis of Political Violence', *Comparative Political Studies*, vol. 2 (1969–70) pp. 172–94; N. Smelser, *Theory of Collective Behaviour* (New York: Free Press, 1963); J. Davies, 'Toward a Theory of Revolution', *American Sociological Review*, vol. 27, no. 1 (Mar. 1962) pp. 5–19; H. Eckstein, *Internal War*, op. cit.; P. Lupsha, 'Explanations of Political Violence: Some Psychological Theories Versus Indigation', unpublished manuscript, Department of Political Science, Yale Univeristy, 1970; A. Schneider and P. Schneider, op. cit.; D. Schwartz, 'On the Ecology of Political Violence: the Long Hot Summer as a Hypothesis', *American Behavioural Scientist*, vol. 11 (July/Aug. 1968) pp. 24–36; H. Whitt and C. Gordon, 'Religion, Economic Development and Aggression', *American Sociological Review*, vol. 37 (1972) pp. 193–201; R. Williamson, 'Toward a theory of Political Violence: The Case of Rural Colombia', *Western Political Quarterly*, vol. 18 (Mar. 1965) pp. 35–44.

29. For definitions of all these terms see Gurr, 'A Causal Model of Civil Strife . . .', op. cit., pp. 1104–9.

30. For an attempt to operationalise Huntington's thesis, see D. Sanders, 'An Empirical Investigation of Huntington's Gap Hypothesis', unpublished manuscript, University of Essex, 1974. See also M. Ruhl, 'Social Mobilisation and Political Instability in Latin America: A Test of Huntington's Theory', *Inter American Economic Affairs*, vol. 29, no. 2 (1975) pp. 3–21.

31. S. Huntington, op. cit., chs 1 and 2, esp. the symbolic equations on p. 53.

32. For the definitions of these terms and a summary statement of Huntington's thesis, see Sanders, op. cit., part I.

33. C. McPhail, 'Civil Disorder Participation: A Critical Examination of Recent Research', *American Sociological Review*, vol. 36 (1971) pp. 1058–71; R. Fogelson and R. Hill, 'Who Riots? A Study of Participation in the 1967 Riots', in *Supplemental Studies for the National Advisory Commission on Civil Disobedience* (no named editor) (Washington, D.C.: Government Printing Office, 1968) pp. 221–48; D. Sears and J. McConahay, *The Politics of Violence: The New Urban Blacks and the Watts Riot* (Boston, Mass.: Houghton Mifflin, 1973); J. Paige, 'Political Orientation and Riot Participation', *American Sociological Review*, vol. 36 (1971) pp. 810–20.

34. Paige, op. cit., p. 820.

35. D. Sears and J. McConahay, op. cit., p. 199.

36. C. Cnudde and D. McCrone, op. cit.; J. Nye, 'Corruption and Political Development: A Cost-Benefit Analysis', *American Political Science Review*, vol. 71 (1967) pp. 417–23; R. Chilcote and J. Edelstein (eds), *Latin America: the Struggle with Dependency and Beyond* (Cambridge, Mass: Schenkman, 1974); A. Madian, 'Review Article: Latin American Developments: Recent Literature', *Political Quarterly* (1968) pp. 229–32.

37. D. Snyder and C. Tilly, op. cit.; R. Flanigan and E. Fogelman, 'Patterns of Political Violence in Comparative Historical Perspective',

Comparative Politics, vol. 3, no. 1 (Oct. 1970) pp. 1–20: D. Hibbs, op. cit.

38. R. Putnam, 'Toward Explaining Military Intervention in Latin America', *World Politics*, vol. 20 (Oct. 1967) pp. 83–110; M. Janowitz, op. cit.
39. M. Taylor and V. Herman, op. cit.; L. Hurwitz, op. cit.; D. Sanders and V. Herman, 'The Stability and Survival of Governments in Western Democracies', *Acta Politica*, vol. 12 (July 1977) pp. 346–77.
40. I use the word 'types' loosely in this context since 'instability in general' is meant to cover violence, coups and governmental instability.
41. A. Madian, op. cit.
42. A. Passos, 'Development Tension and Political Instability: Testing some Hypotheses concerning Latin America', *Journal of Peace Research*, vol. 7 (1968) pp. 79–86.
43. R. S. Weinert, 'Violence in Pre-Industrial Societies: Rural Colombia', *American Political Science Review*, vol. 60, no. 2 (1966) pp. 340–7. See also J. Booth, 'Rural Violence in Columbia, 1943–63', *Western Political Quarterly*, vol. 27, no. 4 (1974) pp. 657–79.
44. I. L. Horowitz, 'Political Legitimacy and the Institutionalisation of Crises in Latin America', *Comparative Political Studies*, vol. 1 (1968–9) pp. 45–70; E. N. Miller, 'Correlates and Consequences of Beliefs in the Legitimacy of Regime Structures', *Midwest Journal of Political Science*, vol. 14 (1970) pp. 392–9.
45. J. Cockcroft, A. Frank and D. Johnson, *Dependence and Underdevelopment Latin America's Political Economy* (New York: Anchor Books, 1972).
46. R. Flanigan and E. Fogelman, op. cit.; M. Olson, 'Rapid Growth as a Destabilising Force', *Journal of Economic History*, vol. 23 (Dec. 1963) pp. 529–52.
47. I. Feierabend and R. Feierabend, op. cit., pp. 145–148; D. Lerner, op. cit.; C. Cnudde and D. McCrone, op. cit.
48. J. Stycos and J. Arias (eds), *Population Dilemma in Latin America* (Washington, D.C.: Potomac Books, 1966).
49. R. Chilcote and J. Edelstein (eds), *Latin America: The Struggle with Dependency and Beyond* (Cambridge, Mass.: Schenkman, 1974).
50. M. Kling, 'Toward a Theory of Power and Instability in Latin America', *Western Political Quarterly*, vol. 9 (Mar. 1956) pp. 21–35.
51. M. Gluckman, *Custom and Conflict in Africa* (Oxford: Blackwell, 1956).
52. B. Crozier, *The Rebels: A Study of Postwar Insurrections* (London: Chatto & Windus, 1960).
53. J. C. Davies, 'Political Stability and Instability', *Journal of Conflict Resolution*, vol. 16 (1969) pp. 1–12.
54. B. Nesvold, op. cit., pp. 172–94.
55. B. Russett, 'Inequality and Instability: The Relation of Land Tenure to Politics', *World Politics*, vol. 16 (1964) pp. 442–54.
56. R. O'Kane, 'A predictive model of *coups d'état*', unpublished M.A. thesis, University of Essex, 1972.
57. It should be admitted immediately, however, that we do not intend to

examine the role of 'corruption' in our empirical analysis: given the covert nature of this phenomenon, the necessary cross-national data are simply not available to make such an exercise feasible.

58. R. Flanigan and E. Fogelman, op. cit.; D. Snyder and C. Tilly, op. cit.; D. Hibbs, op. cit.

59. D. Snyder and C. Tilly, op. cit.

NOTES TO CHAPTER TWO

1. Hibbs, op. cit., for example, uses '0.60 or the highest shown' (pp. 12–13), whereas Feierabend and Feierabend, op. cit., use 0.500.

2. See for example A. J. Ayer, *Logical Positivism* (Glencoe, Ill.: Free Press, 1959); K. Popper, *The Logic of Scientific Discovery* (London: Hutchinson, 1959).

3. An example of a correlation which even a factor analyst would find difficult to describe as a 'definitional' relationship occurs in Table 2.1, which we discussed earlier: 'Mass arrests of insignificant persons' (variable 19) loads significantly on the Feierabends' 'riots' factor ($r = 0.54$). Participating in a riot and arresting 'insignificant persons' seem to me to be behavioural manifestations which can in no sense be regarded as part of the same 'underlying' phenomenon: the latter is, by definition, undertaken by governments and the former, by definition, is not. What the empirical correlation suggests to me is that mass arrests of 'insignificant persons' probably tend to be the result of 'insignificant persons participating in riots': in short, there is in all probability a *causal* relationship between the two variables, not a definitional one as the factor analysts assume. For a further critique of the factor analytic technique, see E. Zimmerman, 'Factor Analyses of Conflicts Within and Between Nations: A Critical Evaluation', *Quality and Quantity*, vol. 10, no. 4 (1976) pp. 267–96.

4. H. Schadee, unpublished manuscript, University of Essex, 1973.

5. Feierabend and Feierabend, op. cit.

6. T. Gurr, *Why Men Rebel*, (Princeton, N.J.: Princeton University Press, 1970); 'Psychological Factors in Civil Violence', World Politics, vol. 20 (Jan. 1968) pp. 245–78. For an excellent review of the 'relative deprivation' literature, see A. Marsh, *Protest and Political Consciousness* (Beverley Hills and London: Sage Publications, 1976) chapter 6.

7. T. Gurr, 'Sources of Rebellion in Western Democracies', in J. Short and M. Wolfgang (eds), *Collective Violence* (New York: Aldine, 1972).

8. T. Gurr, *Why Men Rebel*, op. cit., p. 210.

9. W. H. Riker, 'Bargaining in a Three Person Game', *American Political Science Review*, vol. 61 (1967) pp. 642–6; G. Markus and R. Tanter, 'A Conflict Model for Strategists and Managers', *American Behavioural Scientist* (1971–2) pp. 809–36; A. Oberschall, 'Group Violence: Some Hypotheses and Empirical Uniformities', paper to the

American Sociological Association, San Francisco, Sep. 1969. See also A. Oberschall, 'Rising Expectations and Political Turmoil' *Journal of Development Studies*, vol. 6, no. 1 (1969) pp. 5–22.

10. D. Sears and J. McConohay, *op. cit.*

11. This criticism does *not* apply to Huntington's analysis, which we also included in our 'psychologically oriented approaches' category in Chapter 1. Huntington in fact, attempts to explain the politicisation of 'social frustration' or discontent through the concept of 'mobility opportunities'. The frustration generated by the 'gap' between the rate of social mobilisation and the level of economic development will only lead to 'political participation' and thence to 'instability', in so far as opportunities for social mobility are closed; in so far as opportunities for social mobility exist, frustration will *not* lead to participation and instability. See Huntington, op. cit., ch. I, and D. Sanders, op. cit.

12. W. S. Robinson, 'Ecological Correlations and the Behavior of Individuals', *American Sociological Review*, vol. 45 (1950) pp. 351–7.

13. Although Gurr and the Feierabends, in a vain attempt to pre-empt criticism, make reference to relative deprivation and societal frustration as 'social' phenomena, the actual frustration/deprivation → violence thesis originates and is developed fundamentally at the level of the individual.

14. Our discussion in the text is confined to an examination of the disparity between the central 'psychological' concept of the frustration/deprivation theorists and the operational referents of those concepts. The problem of disparity, however, in fact extends to several of the 'non-psychological' correlates of violence and instability which are cited by the frustration/deprivation theorists. Gurr's 'social-structural facilitation', and 'legitimacy' are particularly strong candidates in this regard.

15. Feierabend and Feierabend, op. cit., p. 145.

16. For definitions of these various terms see Gurr, 'A Causal Model of Civil Strife' in Feierabend, Feierabend and Gurr, op. cit., pp. 191–5.

17. Ibid., p. 191 (my emphasis).

18. See, for example, A. Schneider and P. Schneider, 'Social Mobilisation, Political Institutions and Political Violence', *Comparative Political Studies*, vol. 4 (1971–2) pp. 69–74; D. Hibbs, *Mass Political Violence*, op. cit.; Huntington, op. cit.

19. K. Deutsch, 'Social Mobilisation and Political Development', *American Political Science Review*, vol. 55 (1961) pp. 494–512.

20. A. Schneider and P. Schneider, op. cit.;, L. Hurwitz, 'Democratic Political Stability: Some Traditional Hypotheses Re-examined', *Comparative Political Studies*, vol. 4 (1971–2) pp. 476–90.

21. See R. Wonnacott and T. Wonnacott, *Econometrics* (New York: Wiley, 1970) pp. 67–9.

22. For a detailed exposition of this problem, see M. Ezekiel and K. Fox, *Methods of Correlation Analysis* (New York: Wiley, 1959).

23. See the references to Bwy, Morrisson and Stevenson, Flanigan and Fogelman, Snyder and Tilly, in chapter 1.

24. D. Hibbs, 'Problems of Statistical Estimation and Causal Inference in

Time Series Regression Models', in H. Costner (ed.), *Sociological Methodology 1973–1974* (London: Jossey-Bass, 1974).
25. D. Hibbs, *Mass Political Violence*, op. cit.
26. D. Sanders, 'Away from a General Model of Mass Political Violence: Evaluating Hibbs', *Quality and Quantity*, vol. 12 (1978) pp. 103–29.
27. It should be emphasised that the ensuing remarks are *not* intended as a direct critique of Hibbs' entire model but only of his analysis of the relationships between the (endogenous) core political event variables of the model which are outlined immediately below. However, the discussion does perhaps cast *some* doubts on the relationships which Hibbs specifies between each endogenous core event variable and its exogenous correlates or determinants, in the sense that the estimation of these exogenous linkages is undertaken simultaneously with the estimation of the endogenous relationships. If the coefficients for the core linkages are mis-specified, therefore, it is possible that the coefficients for the exogenous variable → endogenous variable linkages are also distorted. This is a matter which can only be resolved empirically, however, and constraints of time and space preclude the possibility of their investigation here.

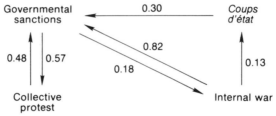

28. Strictly, Hibbs uses 'block recursive' models, a sub-species of non-recursive models.
29. In this context, I use correlation coefficient as a shorthand for any measure of strength or form of relationship.
30. For definitions of these terms see Hibbs, *Mass Political Violence*, op. cit. ch. 10.
31. Ibid., pp. 201–2.
32. By 'region' in this context we mean 'region of the world'. The specific areas delineated in this study are Western Europe/North America, Eastern Europe, Far East, Middle East, Sub-Saharan Africa, Latin America.
33. A *dynamic* interpretation of Fig. 2.4 would be 'an increase in the rate of urbanisation will produce a concommitant increase in the level of political instability'.

NOTES TO CHAPTER THREE

1. See G. Almond and S. Verba, *The Civic Culture* (London: Little, Brown, 1965).
2. G. Field, op. cit.; F. Castles, op. cit. For Castles, a stable regime should also avoid 'serious challenge in recent years' (p. 47).

3. These studies were investigated in detail in ch. 2. The specific authors to which the term refers include Rummel, Tanter, Gurr, the Feierabends, Morrisson and Stevenson, Bwy and Hibbs.

4. There is, of course, the additional danger in this context of the 'self-fulfilling prophecy': journalistic speculations as to the imminent resignation of a government can, of themselves, undermine its position.

5. To some extent the idea of instability as uncertainty corresponds to Mazrui's notion of 'imminent instability', which characterises many African systems. See A. Mazrui, *Africa's International Relations* (London: Heinemann, 1977) pp. 11–17.

6. See J. Blondel, *Introduction to Comparative Government* (London: Weidenfeld & Nicolson, 1968) chs 3–8.

7. Needless to say, there are numerous other typologies of political systems. See, for example, A. Lijphart, 'Typologies of Democratic Systems', paper presented to the IPSA 7th World Congress, Brussels 1967.

8. See, for example, E. J. Meehan, *Contemporary Political Thought: a Critical Study* (Homewood, Ill.: Dorsey Press, 1967).

9. Anecdotal evidence perhaps offers the best demonstration of this point. In the BBC World Service programme *Twenty Four Hours* on 29 September 1976, Richard Harris (the Asian correspondent of *The Times*) predicted that Hua Kuo Feng would be the next chairman of the Chinese Communist Party. This prediction was made 3 weeks after Mao's death and several days before the wall poster campaign which unofficially signified the victory of the Hua faction in the post-Mao leadership struggle. The basis of Harris' prediction was that in the week before Mao died the official *China Newsagency* released a photograph of Hua in which he was not accompanied by any other (Chinese or foreign) leader. Apart from Mao, no other Chinese leader since 1949 had received such symbolic acclaim.

10. D. Easton, *A Systems Analysis of Political Life* (New York: Wiley, 1965) p. 21.

11. Ibid., p. 177.

12. L. Hurwitz, 'An Index of Democratic Political Stability: A Methodological Note', *Comparative Political Studies*, vol. 4 (1971) p. 43.

13. For the definition of this term, see Taylor and Hudson, op. cit., pp. 82–3.

14. Easton, *A Systems Analysis*, op. cit., p. 179.

15. Hibbs concludes that guerrilla attacks, assassinations, and deaths from political violence constitute 'internal war', and that riots, political strikes and protest demonstrations constitute 'collective protest'. See D. Hibbs, *Mass Political Violence*, op. cit., p. 179.

16. As far as data availability permits, these suggested indicators are incorporated into the operational definition of instability which is outlined in the next chapter, where appropriate definitions are also provided.

NOTES TO CHAPTER FOUR

1. The data which are employed here are drawn mainly from the *World Handbook II Daily Events Directory* (ICPSR) which records information on 136 polities for the period 1948–67. Using the country-month as the unit of analysis yields a total number of cases of 136 × 20 × 12 for each variable.
2. See D. Easton, *A Systems Analysis of Political Life* op. cit., pp. 193–5.
3. Authority *roles* are to be distinguished from incumbent political authorities: one can support the institution or the authority role of 'the Presidency' without supporting 'the President'.
4. Easton, *A Systems Analysis of Political Life*, op. cit., p. 210.
5. There are, of course, regional variations here: in the 'Atlantic' area, for example, changes in party system are perhaps the best indicator in this regard, whereas in the Third World military/civilian changes are probably more appropriate. The use of both indicators, however, covers either eventuality.
6. For a detailed discussion of these ambiguities, see D. Sanders and V. Herman, op. cit.
7. See C. Taylor and M. Hudson, op. cit., pp. 62–9.
8. As we implied earlier, while attempted coups do not invariably involve violence (though they usually do), even a bloodless coup must rely on the *threat* of violence. It makes sense, therefore, to count attempted coups as a violent challenge to either regime, government or community.
9. Taylor and Hudson, op. cit., pp. 110–15.
10. In 1948–9, 3800 people died as a result of political violence in Colombia; just under 1000 were killed in 1951–2. For a detailed discussion of 'La Violencia' see R. S. Weinert, op. cit., pp. 340–8.
11. J. Payne, 'Peru: The Politics of Structured Violence', *Journal of Politics*, vol. 27 (1965) pp. 362–74.
12. It could of course be argued that *coups* are, by their very nature, 'unpredictable'; if a *coup* is expected to occur, appropriate steps can be taken to prevent it. In this context by 'predictable' we strictly mean 'postdictable' (predictability is simply common parlance). We will provide a precise indication of what is meant by 'predictable/postdictable' later.
13. In Fig. 4.4 it should be noted that t_{14} lies exactly on the predicted regression line. Since it has no residual value, its 'instability score' is zero – but as we have stressed, comparison with the negative instability scores at t_7, t_9, t_{11}, ... indicates that the zero score at t_{14} still denotes a relatively high level of instability.
14. Moreover, since residuals from a least squares regression always yield a variable which has mean zero, the use of the least squares method enables the estimation of 'deviations' which are always measured in comparable units.
15. As we will see, however, residuals were in fact only taken at this stage for cases where $x_t \neq 0$.

16. The methodological principles underlying the use of these interaction terms are described in ch. 8.
17. It will be recalled from ch. 2 that this was the conclusion reached in the present writer's earlier study of Hibbs' work. A similar conclusion is also reached by Coulter: See P. Coulter, *Social Mobilisation and Political Development: A Macroquantitative Analysis of Global and Regional Models* (Lexington, Mass.: Lexington Books, 1975).

NOTES TO CHAPTER FIVE

1. Throughout this chapter we shall periodically use the following notation:

    RΔ = regime change instability,
    VC = violent challenge instability,
    GΔ = government change instability,
    PC = peaceful challenge instability.

2. The subsequent findings which we report refer only to linear forms of analysis: a number of non-linear models were tested, but all proved non-significant.
3. This approach is primarily associated with Huntington, although he certainly does not give it this name. See S. P. Huntington, *Political Order*, op. cit.
4. See R. Jackson and M. Stein, *Issues in Comparative Politics* (New York: St Martin's Press, 1971).
5. The rationale behind this assumption is that it is frequently the coup which effects the kind of changes (changes in norms, party system, military/non-military status) which in ch. 4 we characterised as denoting regime change.
6. Or, when cross-sectional data is being analysed, the non-recursive estimates of the reciprocal PC–VC linkage should indicate that the dominant direction of the relationship is PC $\rightarrow$ VC. The rationale behind this prediction is derived from Hibbs' conclusions as to the relative strengths of the reciprocal relationships between (1) sanctions and internal war and (2) sanctions and collective protest (see Hibbs, *Mass Political Violence*, op. cit., p. 182): a unit change in collective protest will produce a $0.48 \times 0.82 = 0.40$ change in internal war, whereas a unit change in internal war will only produce a $0.52 \times 0.18 = 0.09$ change in collective protest. See note 27, ch. 2.
7. See E. Kuh and J. Meyer, 'How Extraneous are Extraneous Estimates? *The Review of Economics and Statistics*, vol. 39 (1957) p. 381, cited in Hibbs, *Mass Political Violence*, op. cit., pp. 201–2.
8. There are two reasons why we do not pursue this line of enquiry here: (1) a sample of lagged correlation coefficients where lag = 10 years were estimated, and all of these esimates were non-significant; and (2) the comparison of event variables with a ten-year time lag is in a sense irrelevant anyway, because over ten years so many other

variables can undergo significant change, and it is extremely difficult to make the appropriate controls.

9. It will be recalled that our data cover the twenty-year period 1948–67 inclusive.

10. These relationships are:

(1) in the Atlantic region	PC → RΔ	
	VC → GΔ	
(2) in the Middle East	PC → GΔ	
(3) in the Far East	VC → RΔ	
(4) in Sub-Saharan Africa	VC → RΔ	
(5) in Latin America	VC → GΔ	

11. See Huntington, op. cit., chs 1 and 2.

12. While we do not have access to the necessary evidence to be able to identify and/or measure individual attitudes or beliefs in this regard, it seems not unreasonable to assume that there is a kind of 'hung for a sheep as for a lamb' logic underlying this tendency.

NOTES TO CHAPTER SIX

1. D. A. Rustow, *A World of Nations: Problems of Political Modernisation* (Washingtron, D.C.: Brookings Institution, 1967); G. Almond and G. Powell, *Comparative Politics: A Developmental Approach* (Boston, Mass: Little, Brown, 1966).

2. See Binder *et al., Crises and Sequences in Political Development* (Princeton, N.J.: Princeton University Press, 1971).

3. For definitions of these terms see ibid., pp. 68–75.

4. Data for all variables specified in this chapter were derived either from A. S. Banks, *Cross Polity Time Series Data,* op. cit. (base year 1965), or C. Taylor and M. Hudson, *World Handbook II,* op. cit. (base year 1965). The aggregated indices were obtained by taking the natural logarithm of each component indicator and adding the resultant scores together.

5. Average annual scores for the period 1961–5.

6. D. Apter, *Choice and the Politics of Allocation* (New Haven, Conn.: Yale University Press, 1971).

7. S. Huntington, *Political Order in Changing Societies* (New Haven, Conn.: Yale University Press, 1968) ch. 1. See also G. Ben-Dor, 'Institutionalisation and Political Development: A Conceptual and Theoretical Analysis', *Comparative Studies in Society and History,* vol. 17, no. 3 (1975) pp. 309–25.

8. L. W. Pye, *Aspects of Political Development* (Boston, Mass.: Little, Brown, 1966).

9. Banks, op. cit.

10. S. Huntington, 'Political Development and Political Decay', *World Politics,* vol. 17 (Apr. 1965) pp. 386–430. For an alternative statement of the linkage between development and instability, see A. Sofranko and R. Bealer, *Unbalanced Modernisation and Domestic Instability: A Comparative Analysis* (Beverley Hills: Sage Professional Papers in Comparative Politics, 1972).

11. See, for example, C. Furtado, *Economic Development of Latin America* (Cambridge: Cambridge University Press, 1970); J. Cockcroft, A. Frank and D. Johnson, *Dependence and Underdevelopment: Latin America's Political Economy* (New York: Anchor Books, 1972).

12. See, for example B. Stallings, *Economic Dependence in Africa and Latin America* (Beverley Hills, Calif: Sage Professional Papers in Comparative Politics, 1972); J. D. Esseks, 'Economic Dependency and Political Development in the New States of Africa', *Journal of Politics*, vol. 33 (Nov. 1971) pp. 1052–77.

13. See E. Shils, 'Centre and Periphery', in *The Logic of Personal Knowledge: Essays Presented to Michael Polanyi* (London: Routledge & Kegan Paul, 1961) pp. 117–30.

14. R. Kaufman, H. Cherkotsky and D. S. Geller, 'A Preliminary Test of the Theory of Dependency', *Comparative Politics*, vol. 7 (Apr. 1975) pp. 303–30.

15. See, for example, Bwy, op. cit.; Feierabend and Feierabend, op. cit.; Hibbs, *Mass Political Violence*, op. cit.

16. Dollard *et al.*, op. cit.; A. Buss, *The Psychology of Aggression* (New York: Wiley, 1973).

17. Hibbs, *Mass Political Violence*, op. cit., ch. 8. For a detailed analysis of this relationship in the Latin American context, see E. Duff and J. McCamant, *Violence and Repression in Latin America: A Quantitative and Historical Analysis* (New York: Free Press, 1976).

18. Taylor and Hudson, op. cit.

19. A. de Tocqueville, *Democracy in America* (New York: Vintage Books, 1954) p. 266.

20. See B. Russett, 'Inequality and Instability: The Relation of Land Tenure to Politics', *World Politics*, vol. XVI, no. 3 (Apr. 1964) pp. 442–54; M. Kling, op. cit. For a more generally applicable analysis, see L. Sigelman and M. Simpson, 'A Cross-national Test of the Linkage between Economic Inequality and Political Violence', *Journal of Conflict Resolution*, vol. 21, no. 1 (1979) pp. 105–28.

21. D. Rae and M. Taylor, *The Analysis of Political Cleavages* (New Haven, Conn.: Yale University Press, 1970); R. Rose and D. Urwin, 'Social Cohesion, Parties and Strains in Regimes', *Comparative Political Studies*, vol. 2 (1969) pp. 7–67; V. O. Key, *Politics, Parties and Pressure Groups* (New York: Thomas Cromwell, 1964).

22. See I. Budge and C. O'Leary, *Belfast: Approach to Crisis; A Study of Belfast Politics* (London: Macmillan, 1973). Also, Rose and Urwin, op. cit.

23. A. Zolberg, *Creating Political Order: The Party States of West Africa* (Chicago: Rand McNally, 1966). See also W. Barrows, 'Ethnic Diversity and Political Instability in Black Africa', *Comparative Political Studies*, vol. 9, no. 2 (1976) pp. 139–70.

24. See A. Kaplan, *The Conduct of Enquiry* (San Francisco: Chandler, 1964) pp. 298ff.

25. P. Cutright, 'National Political Development: Measurement and Analysis', *American Sociological Review*, vol. 28 (1963) pp. 253–64.

26. On the general problems of identification, see F. Fisher, *The Identification Problem in Econometrics* (New York: McGraw-Hill, 1966).

NOTES TO CHAPTER SEVEN

1. It should be noted that all the observed coefficients identified in Table 7.1 were in fact below $r = \pm 0.3$.
2. A possible reason for this empirical tendency may be that a typical feature of many economically underdeveloped countries is an authoritarian government which stays in office for a relatively long period of time, whereas in the more economically developed liberal democracies, governments tend to change rather more frequently.
3. The R^2 for this function was in fact $R^2 = 0.085$.
4. It is important to recognise the importance of the oil-rich Gulf states in this context: these score highly on both dependency (particularly export concentration) and stability.
5. See for example, Stallings, op. cit.; Esseks, op. cit.
6. This may be partly a consequence of the continued French influence in West Africa (exerted through the French Community) which aims at maintaining the economic and political stability of former French colonies.

NOTES TO CHAPTER EIGHT

1. The general equation which will be employed, of course, is

$$Y = \alpha + \beta_1 X_1 + \beta_2 X_2 + \beta_3 X_3 + \ldots + \beta_k X_k + \varepsilon.$$

2. The t statistic evidences the magnitude of the ratio of the estimated coefficient, $\hat{\beta}_k$, to its estimated variance or standard error. If the estimated coefficient is more than twice its own standard error (that is, if $t > 2$), then the null hypothesis that $\hat{\beta}_k = 0$ (the hypothesis that X_k has *no* effect upon Y) can be rejected. For a more detailed discussion of the use of t, see R. Wonnacott and T. Wonnacott, *Econometrics* (New York, Wiley, 1970).
3. Clearly, the figure of $r = 0.6$ is arbitrary. However, since collinearity in principle exists whenever two predictors are not orthogonal (that is say, completely uncorrelated), and since there is no agreement among statisticians as to the level at which intercorrelation between predictors becomes problematic, this figure is no less arbitrary than any other. The only exception to this criterion which was permitted was the $r - 0.8$ between the press freedom and democratic performance indices which both appear as significant predictors in the regime change instability best model. The decision to contravene the explicitly stated criterion in this instance followed a detailed examination of the relationship between regime change instability and

press freedom and democratic performance which suggested that the joint impact of press freedom and democratic performance upon regime change was sufficiently important to warrant their inclusion despite the existence of considerable collinearity between the two independent variables. For a detailed discussion of the possible effects of multi-collinearity on parameter estimates, see P. Schmidt and E. Muller, 'The Problem of Multi-collinearity in a Multi-stage Causal Alienation Model: A Comparison of Ordinary Least Squares, Maximum Likelihood and Ridge Estimators', *Quality and Quantity*, vol. 12 (1978) pp. 267–97.

4. Data on all three variables were obtained from Banks, op. cit. Communist Status refers to 1960.

5. Following the practice of Hibbs, this variable was included for control purposes. See Hibbs, *Mass Political Violence*, op. cit., ch. 9.

6. T. Gurr, 'A Causal Model of Civil Strife . . .', op. cit.

7. The aggregate effect of dependency upon governmental change instability for Europe/North America is $\beta = (0.32 - 0.24) = 0.08$.

8. $\beta = (0.32 - 0.34) = -0.02$.

9. On the concept of political performance and its relationship with stability, see R. McKinlay and A. Cohen, 'Performance and Instability in Military and Non-military Regime Systems', *American Political Science Review*, vol. 70, no. 3 (1976) pp. 850–64.

10. For the RΔ instability = f(democratic performance) relationship, $R^2 = 0.06$; for the RΔ instability = f(press freedom) relationship, $R^2 = 0.00$.

11. This interpretation of the data is of course reminiscent of some of the arguments put forward in the context of the theory of 'democratic differential consensus'. For a detailed discussion of the relevant literature, see I. Budge, *Agreement and the Stability of Democracy* (Chicago: Markham, 1970).

12. This argument is similar to the standard neo-Marxist explanation of the 1973 coup in Chile: the ruling elite, while they tolerated (the charade of) liberal democracy for fifty years, had to use their political muscle openly in a violent and bloody manner when the regime – the system of political rules – which preserved their economic dominance was fundamentally threatened by Allende's reformist zeal.

13. See, for example, R. Rose and D. Urwin, 'Social Cohesion, Parties and Strains in Regimes', *Comparative Political Studies*, vol. 2 (1969) 7–67.

NOTES TO CHAPTER NINE

1. The definitions of these latter three variables are derived from 'Blondel's Time Series Data', unpublished data collection, University of Essex. The remainder are derived from Taylor and Hudson, op. cit.

2. For a general discussion of the concept of cultural relativity, see E. Nagel, *Structure of Science* (London: Routledge & Kegan Paul, 1961) pp. 459–66.

3. See L. Althusser, *For Marx*, trans. B. Brewster (London: Allen Lane, Penguin Press, 1969).
4. C. Hempel, *Philosophy of Natural Science* (Englewood Cliffs, N.J.: Prentice-Hall, 1966) pp. 11–12 (my emphasis).
5. I use the term correlation here to imply *all* the various statistical operations which were described in chs 7 and 8.
6. The exceptions in this regard were (1) economic and political development *change* variables, which were measured over the period 1960–5; and (2) the 'acts of governmental coercion' variable, which also covered the period 1948–67. 1965 itself was selected because the data were most complete for that year at the time that the data analysis for this project was conducted.

NOTES TO APPENDIX TWO

1. The rationale behind the weighting procedure is that if we did not weight the index measuring changes in Blondel norms by a factor of 2, then a change along any one dimension of the Blondel regime norm space would produce a maximum score per country month of unity. (Without weighting, therefore, if a country changed along all three Blondel norms – means, goals and participation – its maximum score in that month would be 3.) The 'change in party system' and 'change in military/civilian status' variables, however, each have a maximum score per country month of 2. Multiplying the norms change score by 2, therefore, gives *equal* weight to each of the five indicators of regime change (Δ norms, Δ goals, Δ participation, Δ party system and Δ military/civilian status) which we identified, since each indicator now has a maximum possible score of 2.

Index

Africa, South of the Sahara, 161–2, 221, 223–4
aggregated data, 41–3, 91, 99–103, 119–20
Alker, H., 4, 227
Almond, G., 122, 124, 126, 226, 232, 236
Althusser, L., 202–3, 240
Apter, D., 122, 236
Arias, J., 16, 229
assassinations, 10, 62
Atlantic area, *see* Europe/North America

Bagehot, W., 225
Banks, A., 125, 227, 236
best model procedure, 169–172
Binder, L., 226, 236
Blondel, J., xv, 52–3, 67–70, 213–14, 233, 239
Booth, J., 229
Budge, I., 5, 16, 226, 237, 239
Buss, A., 134, 237
Bwy, D., 16, 225, 228

Castles, F., 50, 226, 232
changes and challenges, 58–63, 58
Chilcote, R., 16, 228
Cnudde, C., 15, 16, 226
Cockcroft, J., 15, 229
coercion, governmental, 12, 16–17, 20, 33–4, 133–7, 191–2
Cohen, A., 239
collective protest, 11, 19–20
   see also peaceful challenge instability
Colombia, 73–4
Communist regimes, 178, 184
concatenated theory, 141
Coulter, P., 235

coups d'état, 2, 6, 19, 62, 68, 74–6, 95–6
Crozier, B., 16, 229
Cutright, P., 226, 237
Czechoslovakia, 113

Dahl, R., 5, 226
Davies, J., 16, 228
deaths from domestic violence, 27, 68
definitional relationships, 27, 49
democratic development, 5–6, 8, 125
demonstrations, 10, 11, 68
dependency, 16–17, 128–33, 178, 180, 182, 191
deprivation, relative, 6, 16, 32–5
Deutsch, K., 4, 16, 35, 227
development, *see* political development and economic development
Dodd, L., 226
Dollard, J., 11, 133, 227, 237
domestic conflict behaviour, 10–11, 23–4, 197
Duff, E., 237

Easton, D., 5, 67–9
economic development, 6, 15–18, 121–3, 127, 142–5, 184, 189–91, 195
Eckstein, H., xiii, 2, 6–10, 226
Edelstein, J., 16, 228
education, 6, 32, 123–4
energy consumption, 124
Esseks, J., 237
ethno-linguistic fractionalisation, 16, 137–8, 182–4, 192–3
Europe/North America, 156–7, 218, 223

241

exports, 130, 178, 184

factor analytic approaches, 10–11,
    23–8, 62
Far East, 162–3, 222, 224
Feierabend, I. and R., xiii, 6,
    12–13, 44–7, 225
Feldman, A., 8, 227
Field, G., 16, 50, 226, 232
Fisher, F., 238
Flanigan, R., 15, 228
Fogelman, E., 15, 228
Fogelson, R., 228
Fossum, E., 16, 226
frustration, see social frustration
Furtado, C., 237

general strike, 53
Gluckman, M., 16, 229
Gordon, C., 228
government change instability
    definition and operationalisation
        of, 59–60, 62, 68, 70–71
    relation to other types of
        instability, ch. 5 passim
    best predictors of, 181–3
government repression, see
    coercion, governmental
Gurr, T., 6, 12–13, 30–5, 136,
    225, 227, 230

Harris, R., 233
Hempel, C., 202–3, 240
Herman, V., 16, 226
Hibbs, D., 6, 11, 19–21, 39–43,
    62, 95–7, 136, 204
hierarchical theory, 141
Hill, R., 228
Hoole, F., 11, 227
Horowitz, I., 16, 37, 229
Hudson, M., 227
Huntington, S., 12, 16, 115, 127,
    190, 209, 225, 228
Hurwitz, L., 16, 226

identification, 146
imperialism, 129
income inequality, 137–8, 193–4

indicators
    in other studies, 32–7
    in this study, 142, 68
industrialisation, 6, 16, 123–4
institutionalisation, 13, 16, 20, 34,
    114–15, 122, 200
internal war, 8–9, 26, 95
    see also violent challenge
    instability

Jackson, R., 235
Janos, A., 7, 226
Janowitz, M., 17, 225

Kaplan, A., 141, 237
Kaufman, R., 237
Key, V., 139, 237
Kling, M., 16, 229

land inequality, 16, 137–8, 193–4
Latin America, 130–3, 159–61,
    178, 180, 191–3
Lerner, D., 15, 16, 226
Lijphart, A., 5, 226, 233
Lipset, S., 3–8, 16, 44–7, 50, 226
literacy 16, 123
Lupsha, P., 228

Madian, A., 14, 228
Markus, G., 29, 230
Marsh, A., 230
Marxist approaches and
    interpretations, 15, 128–33,
    192–3, 202, 239
Mazrui, A., 233
McCamant, J., 237
McConahay, J., 14, 228
McCrone, D., 15, 16, 226
McKinley, R., 239
McPhail, C., 228
Meehan, E., 233
Merritt, R., 4, 227
Middle East/North Africa, 158,
    219, 223
Miller, E., 229
Morrisson, D., 11, 227
Multicollinearity, 170–1, 238–9

Nagel, E., 239

Nesvold, B., 228
Neubauer, D., 226
'normal' patterns, 77–89
Northern Ireland, 54
non-recursive models, 39–43,
    106–8
Nye, J., 16, 228

Oberschall, A., 9, 29
O'Kane, R., 17, 229
O'Leary, C., 237
Olsen, M., 16, 18, 229

Paige, J., 6, 13, 228
Passos, A., 15, 16, 228
Payne, J., 74, 234
peaceful challenge instability
    definition and operationalisation,
        61–3, 68, 70–1
    relation to other types of
        instability, ch. 5 passim
    best predictors of, 179–80
political community, 60–2
political development, 5–8, 121–8,
    142–5, 184, 188–9
political instability
    definition of, 6
    deviations from normality as,
        77–89
    discontinuity approach to, 51–3
    frequency approach to, 54–5
    hypotheses concerning influences
        upon, 140–1
    interrelations among types of, 98
    journalistic approach to, 55–6
    'syndrome', 95
    types of, 67–71
polyarchy, 8, 88–9, 125
population, 178–80, 239
Popper, K., xvi, 230
Portugal, 51
Powell, G., 121, 236
praetorianism, 95
press freedom, 177, 184–6
Przeworski, A., xv, 225
Putman, R., 17, 229
Pye, L., 122, 226, 236

Rae, D., 139, 237

regime change instability
    definition and operationalisation
        of, 60–2, 67–70
    relation to other types of
        instability, ch. 5 passim
    best predictors of, 183–8
regime norms, 60, 68–70, 214
religious fractionalisation, 139,
    192–3
Robinson, W., 31, 134, 321
Rokken, S., 4, 227
Rose, R., 139, 237, 239
Rummel, R., 6, 10, 225
Russett, B., 16, 227, 237
Rustow, D., 121, 236

Schadee, H., 6, 28, 230
Schneider, A. and P., 37, 225
Schwartz, D., 228
Sears, D., 14, 228
Shils, E., 129, 237
Sigelman, L., 137
similar conditions assumption,
    143–6
Simpson, H., 237
Smetlser, N., 228
Snyder, D., 6, 16, 225
social frustration, societal
    frustration, 12–13, 32–5
social mobilisation, 36
Sofranko, A., 236
Stallings, B., 237
static v. dynamic interpretations,
    44–7
Stevenson, H., 11, 227
structured cleavage, see
    ethnolinguistic and religious
    fractionalisation
Stycos, J., 16, 229
Syria, 75
system specific patterns, 71–7

Tanter, R., 10, 29, 226, 227, 229
Taylor, C., 227
Taylor, M., 16, 139, 226, 237
Terrell, L., 225
Teune, M., xv, 225
Textor, A., 227
Tilly, C., 6, 16, 225

urbanisation, 6, 16, 45–7, 123–4, 178–80
Urwin, D., 139, 237, 239

Van Doorn, J., 226
Verba, S., 226
violent challenge instability
  definition and operationalisation of, 61–3, 68, 70–1
  relation to other types of instability, ch. 5 *passim*
  best predictions of, 180–1

Weinert, R., 15, 16, 229
Whitt, H., 228
Williamson, R., 228
Wonnacott, R. and T., 238
World Handbook II, 70, 234

Zimmerman, E., 225, 230
Zolberg, A., 139, 237